Our Nazis

Our Nazis

Representations of Fascism in Contemporary Literature and Film

Petra Rau

EDINBURGH
University Press

© Petra Rau, 2013

Edinburgh University Press Ltd
22 George Square, Edinburgh EH8 9LF

www.euppublishing.com

Typeset in 10.5/13 pt Sabon
by Servis Filmsetting Ltd, Stockport, Cheshire, and
printed and bound in the United States of America

A CIP record for this book is available from the British Library

ISBN 978 0 7486 6864 9 (hardback)
ISBN 978 0 7486 6865 6 (webready PDF)
ISBN 978 0 7486 6866 3 (epub)

The right of Petra Rau
to be identified as author of this work
has been asserted in accordance with
the Copyright, Designs and Patents Act 1988.

Contents

Acknowledgements

This book has been in slumber for a long time and took shape under the encouragement of Gill Plain and Kate McLoughlin. I am very grateful for their support, advice and belief in the project. The research network War and Representation, which they also organise, has been an excellent platform to try out ideas.

Over the years many colleagues have contributed actively or unwittingly to this project. They have revealed to me secret caches of war films hidden from unsuspecting partners in attic rooms; embarked on impromptu undercover missions to retrieve DVDs from bargain baskets in supermarkets they don't normally frequent; whispered to me book titles that I shouldn't be seen reading on public transport. The number of website addresses and YouTube videos I was sent by well-meaning individuals cannot be counted. To this silent interest group that has sworn me to confidentiality, I say a big 'thank you': your secrets are in the vault. Notwithstanding these collective efforts, any omission of significant material is entirely my own fault.

I am also very grateful to those colleagues and friends I can name because they have nothing to do (they think!) with dodgy DVDs or books advocating dubious politics but have read drafts, recommended scholarly material or dragged me to dark places: Christine Berberich, Danny Cohen, Bran Nicol, Deborah Shaw, Victoria Stewart and Glyn White.

I would like to thank the Centre for Studies in Literature at the University of Portsmouth for generous financial support for this project, and all friends and former colleagues there for their patience and encouragement. A much shorter version of Chapter 2 was previously published in my edited collection *Conflict, Nationhood and Corporeality: Bodies-at-War* (Palgrave, 2010).

As always, I must thank Cath, Pip and Otto for enduring with me countless hours of enforced labour under 'fascism'. The next book, I promise, will be very sanguine and hopefully not involve any swastikas. I dedicate *Our Nazis* to my Aunt Uschi, with gratitude for our Silesian adventure: I have a hunch this is where it all started.

Sources of Illustrations

Figures 4.1 and 4.2 from *The Young Lions* (1958), dir. Edward Dmytryk (DVD: Warner Bros, 2004)

Figure 4.3 from *I Confess* (1953), dir. Alfred Hitchcock (DVD: Twentieth Century Fox, 2005)

Figure 4.4 Tom Batchell, illustration for *The New Yorker*, 5 January 2009, used by permission of the artist

Figures 4.5 and 4.6 from *Valkyrie* (2008), dir. Bryan Singer (DVD: Twentieth Century Fox, 2009)

Figures 5.1 and 5.7 to 5.11 from *Inglourious Basterds* (2009), dir. Quentin Tarantino (DVD: Universal Studios, 2009)

Figures 5.2 and 5.3 from *Schtonk!* (1993), dir. Helmut Dietl (DVD: Eurovideo, n.d.)

Figures 5.4 and 5.6 from *The Producers* (1968), dir. Mel Brooks (DVD: Momentum Pictures, 2004)

Figure 5.5 Members of the Hitler Youth parade in the formation of a swastika in honour of the Unknown Soldier, Germany, 27 August 1933, used by permission of The Associated Press

Series Editors' Preface

This series of monographs is designed to showcase innovative new scholarship in the literary and filmic representation of war. The series embraces Anglophone literature and film of all genres, with studies adopting a range of critical approaches including transhistorical and inter-cultural analysis. 'War' in this context is understood to mean armed conflict of the industrialised age (that is, from the late eighteenth century onwards), including not only conventional war between sovereign states but also revolution, insurrection, civil war, guerrilla warfare, cold war and genocide (including the Holocaust). The series is concerned with the multiple, often conflicting, significations that surround the act and event of armed combat, and volumes will also consider the causes, consequences and aftermath of wars; pro- and anti-war literature and film; memorialisation, trauma and testimony. The premise of the series is that new critical perspectives need to be developed in order better to understand war representation. Rather than simply analysing war texts, or even situating those texts in their contemporary cultural contexts, *Edinburgh Critical Studies in War and Culture* will identify the conceptual categories and forms by which war has been mediated in literature and film, and illuminate the cultural influences that produce them. Wars shape bodies, minds and literary forms; they mediate the possibilities of expression and create discourses of repression; they construct ambivalent subjectivities such as the enemy and the veteran; they invade and distort popular genres from crime fiction to fantasy; they leave tangible scars on the landscape and generate the production of memorials both concrete and imagined. This series explores the role of literature and film in mediating such events, and in articulating the contradictions of 'war' and 'culture'.

Kate McLoughlin and Gill Plain

Introduction: 'Having Your Nazi Cake and Eating it'

> To name a sensibility, to draw its contours and to recount its history, requires a deep sympathy, modified by revulsion. (Sontag [1964] 1994: 276)

> I remember seeing one of those funny little dioramas by fetishist modelmakers, with a little humpback bridge, with a little stream of fresh water running through and a little boy fishing, and over the bridge is a little unit of Panzers and soldiers ... the interesting thing is when you look at these dioramas they're always SS, they're always the worst of the worst, they're always the hyper-Nazis – they're never the enlisted, well-intentioned German who couldn't help himself – it's always the ideological fascist, the ones who are after genes, they're annihilating genes rather than people – but there's one little thing that says 'life goes on'. So the kind of displacement in this little diorama is this little boy fishing, having your Nazi cake and eating it. But in actual fact, the Nazi-ness of the work is also a red herring. (Jake Chapman, in Harris 2010: 181)

Models are always more and less than the reality they ostensibly replicate. They are a fantasy and an interpretation as well as an approximation *en miniature*. What precisely constitutes 'Nazi-ness' in a model, a film, a piece of fiction? The comments of artist Jake Chapman above indicate that reproduction is not merely an attempt at verisimilitude but already contains some excess in the very effort to replicate. In the peculiar diorama of war described above, the fetishism lies not in the emphasis on 'hyper-Nazis' or the precise model of the Panzer but in the loving detail of the pastoral scene that augments the contrast between innocence and evil. For Chapman, 'Nazi-ness' here is not the German affiliation of the model soldiers; that's the 'red herring'. It is *the act of choosing* to represent Nazi soldiers and to juxtapose them with a bucolic scene. It is the phantasmatic core that underlies this scenario, in which the modelmaker immerses himself in the details of militaria collectors' handbooks to 'get it right'. The bucolic detail (an avatar of the days of model railways chugging across hills and through tunnels) functions as a disavowal (or 'displacement') of the desire fully to inhabit the fascist universe. To indulge in this fantasy but to present it as a narrative of good and evil is precisely what constitutes 'having your Nazi cake and eating it'. This 'Nazi-ness' is enlivened by the search for an essence of Nazism, for the need to capture the specific fascist 'sensibility' while at the same time professing an utter revulsion at its politics. What is cloaked in the *mise-en-scène*, however, is revealed in the cultural ubiquity of representations of fascism: a deep, inadmissible sympathy; at the very least an unstoppable curiosity about fascism.

Modelmaking and its updated version PC-gaming are only one medium among a whole cluster of highly lucrative contemporary cultural manifestations that re-engage with fascism and its many facets: its birth and rise during the Weimar Republic; its military expansion and genocidal racial policies; its prominent leaders, opponents and victims; its subterranean life under Cold War conditions or in fugitive exile; the psychopathology of the Führer and the moral compass of the 'ordinary' German. Even its fate in an alternate universe, its grotesque aspects and – self-reflexively – the demands we bring to its representation have been the subject of contemporary films, novels and art exhibitions. This cultural production is certainly part of the recent return to the Second World War in historical fiction and film, but it does not always share the sceptical, meta-historiographical agendas and ideological instabilities that inform many of these re-imaginings (Rau 2009b). Like much of the literature of the 1940s, contemporary writing about the war deliberately sets itself against wartime propaganda and the myths of popular memory. Recent film and fiction about fascism is equally intertextual and grafts itself onto earlier representations. The politics of this representational history deserve closer attention than a mere customary nod to Susan Sontag's essay because the context has changed.

The poetics of fictional fascism range from the traditional historical narrative that imitates the style of the past to the tongue-in-cheek postmodern farce; from research-laden 'faction' to texts that forfeit any claims to authenticity. They comprise literary fiction alongside popular thrillers with serial heroes, alternate history and graphic novels. Arthouse film has been as complicit with this phenomenon as the Hollywood blockbuster. The internet now has sites dedicated to 'kitlers' (unfortunate cats that look like Hitler) while YouTube features videos in which LEGO aficionados recreate party rallies or the 'Final Solution' in plastic blocks to the soundtrack of Lady Gaga's *Bad Romance*.[1] And anyone in need of replica Nazi uniforms for a fancy dress party or an outing of the local WW2 re-enactment society can easily obtain a set from eBay. How are we to read this endless recycling of fascist iconography in various forms and media? Is it postmodern playfulness and bricolage that mocks the portentousness of the fascist habitus? Is it simply poor taste? Have we reduced violent history to an immediately recognisable and lucrative brand in late capitalist society? Has our much-professed revulsion at Nazism been gradually modified by a thoroughly disavowed sympathy, or is it really the other way around? Is this phenomenon a telling symptom of a changing historical consciousness in part of the Western world?

This book discusses the place and meaning fascism holds in the contemporary cultural imaginary of the West, specifically in Britain and the USA. That is to say, this is a book about 'the Nazis' as a representational trope, a rhetoric about totalitarianism and a specific iconography – in short, a discourse that often purports to describe (or 'realise') what it actually constructs, predominantly through film and literature. In the words of Jake Chapman, it is about cultural constructions of 'Naziness' and the processes that make these constructions red herrings; the 'Nazi cake' is just as interesting as the ambivalence necessary for its consumption. Therefore, 'the Nazis' tell us less about historical fascism than about the cultures that have imagined them in film, art and literature, hence the inverted commas. In *Imagining Hitler*, Alvin Rosenfeld focused his analysis mainly on American fiction but stated confidently that the phenomenon of the Hitler mystique was actually one common to the entire Western imagination (1985: xvi). I do not think this is true: one does not have to *project* what is still part of one's historical family narrative in many European (and South American) countries. The production of, and the market for, 'fascism' still lies firmly in those countries that never experienced fascist governance. Michael Butter, who continued and refined Rosenfeld's work in *The Epitome of Evil* (2009), demonstrated how specific the use of the Hitler trope was to the cultural and political American context throughout the decades. In Britain and the USA, fascism used to offer a phenomenology of absolute alterity: the Nazis were simply other, a complete counterconstruct to the values of liberal democracy. Merely citing *them* seemed to remind us of who *we* were, or who we wanted to be. As Michel Foucault argued, on the most banal level calling someone or something 'fascist' was often a facile censure and at the same time indicative of 'a general complicity in a refusal to analyse what fascism really was'. Such dismissal reduced fascism to a 'floating signifier' with which any form of power and any desire for it could be summarily denounced (Foucault 1980: 219). In the popular discourse, historical specificities often fall by the wayside, and then the term fascism – and often 'fascism' – refers to any local versions of right-wing authoritarian, totalitarian, ultra-nationalist and corporate rule, Spanish Falangism, Romanian Black Guards and the Hungarian Crossed Arrow, Brazilian Integralism but most importantly German National Socialism. 'Fascism' assumes a common denominator but prefers Nazism as its most effective iconography. Nazism has simply become the synecdoche for fascism. As we shall see, engaging 'fascism' is not the same as engaging *with* fascism; more often than not, its citational practice prevents a better understanding of the nature, mechanism and psychology of historical Nazism, but its self-conscious use can also highlight the desires we bring to 'fascism'.

What interests me about this phenomenology of fascism in the Anglo-American imagination is its specific cultural function beneath the persistent rhetoric of historical inquiry, its varying tropes and genres, and its periodic flaring up at specific cultural moments. One such crucial nodal point of engaging fascism is the end of the Cold War. While the most recent manifestations of 'fascism' have to be seen in the cultural and political context of the post-communist era, they are not necessarily completely subsumed by the concerns of the present. Yet they often refashion fascism, and this revaluation tells us a great deal about the changing nature of the historical and cultural imaginary in Britain and the USA. In so far as the films, novels and exhibitions I discuss here engage with fascist history (as opposed to merely acting as a backdrop for romance or costume drama), they retroactively manufacture the past according to a particularly British or American vision that has instrumentalised if not altogether appropriated the German past and even depends on it for the shaping of contemporary identities.

The past is a foreign country: from 'the Nazis' to 'our Nazis'

More than sixty-eight years after their military defeat, the Nazis as a political formation with specific racial, cultural and military policies continue to preoccupy scores of historians who have documented, analysed and interpreted every aspect of life in and war with the Third Reich. The trade magazine *The Bookseller* recently announced that the number of books annually published on the Nazis in the UK alone had more than doubled in the last ten years, from 380 in 2000 to 850 in 2010 (cited in Anderson 2011). In fact, anyone consulting the history section in a British bookstore or local library, or the average weekly television schedule, might be forgiven for making the assumption that somehow the twelve cataclysmic years of German twentieth-century history have become a quintessential part of *British* history. Cable TV stations such as *The History Channel* would go out of business if they had to take seriously the notion that 'history' could not simply be reduced to endless reruns of *The World at War* or *The Nazis: A Warning from History*. In contrast, the situation is much more complex in Germany or in formerly Nazi-occupied countries, because there the Nazis are not a foreign or ideological other even when they are merely characters in a novel, grotesque villains on the screen or names in a history book. They are part of one's own national narrative and family album, and therefore subject to different representational rules, cultural and political contexts as well as different trans-generational phenomena (see Fuchs 2008; Riera and Schaffer 2008; Lebow, Kansteiner and Fogu 2006; Paris 2000). (In fact, speaking of fascism in the third person as 'the Nazis' is rather suspect in Germany, despite the increasing remoteness of the Third Reich, because it might signal a desire for disengagement with or exculpation from difficult history.) As we shall see, there is a complex relationship between 'fascism' and the cultural presence of the Second World War in the popular memory of Britain and the USA, and the way in which that presence is made to serve political purposes and underpins national narratives of heritage and identity.

British writers and directors take up more space in this discussion than their American counterparts, not least because the British case is more straightforward. Wartime literature was already much more concerned with the destabilising effects of violent conflict on notions of social, sexual and national identity, as we can see in the fiction of, for instance, Elizabeth Bowen, Stevie Smith or Henry Green. Its discord with propaganda is conspicuous. But even propaganda made a much more concerted effort to construct national cohesion than remind the public of the nature of the enemy, not least because demonisation strategies had lost all credibility after the First World War (Piette 1995: 142–98; Tate 1998: 46). Patrick Deer speaks of a 'battle' among 1940s writers over memory and national culture (2009: 192–235). In contemporary popular memory, however, the Second World War is a glorious moment before the disintegration of the Empire and the decline of Britain's international standing as a 'great power'. Its commemoration offers the last occasion for monumentalist narratives of national history as criticised by Nietzsche in his essay on 'On the Uses and Disadvantages of History for Life' ([1874] 1997: 68). The war proved to be tremendously useful to Margaret Thatcher in the 1980s. Her grand version of national history was an object lesson in the political expediency of a rhetoric of nostalgia based on selectivity and decontextualisation that imprinted itself on the cultural landscape of the entire decade, from Paul Scott's Raj Quartet to the chiffon-and-sepia effects of Merchant Ivory adaptations. Thatcher's repeated recourse to Churchill during the Falklands war aggrandised this conflict to a necessary war that defended British territory as if Britain still had an empire to safeguard. Her belligerent response to the Argentine invasion of the Malvinas islands was structured around the spectre of an earlier violation of national territory, which had already roused her famous predecessor during the Battle of Britain to the well-known hyperbole of the Finest Hour speech: what was at stake in this fight against the forces of darkness was 'the survival of Christian civilisation: upon it depends our own British life and the long continuity of our institutions and our empire'.[2] 'The war', as it is often called in the United Kingdom, continues to be a universal reference point for mythical national cohesion and collective effort. Its slogans are reiterated by politicians and the tabloids in moments of national crisis, from the July bombings in 2007 ('London can take it!') to the credit crunch ('Make do and mend'). As the historians Angus Calder and Sonya O. Rose have shown, using 'the war' as the basis for defining national character is a practice more indebted to official wartime propaganda than to an accurate and differentiated understanding of wartime history (Calder [1969] 2001 and 1992; Rose 2003). Popular memory of the world war amounts to an industry, its commemoration is virtually mandatory for all public figures, and its mythology seems impervious to revision.

The case is different for the USA, not least because the conflict in the Pacific was always considered more crucial, lengthy and proximate than the conflict in Europe. As a multi-ethnic country, the USA faced the problem of fighting enemies whose difference was not so easily defined without reclassifying American citizenship itself. In practice this meant 're-location' or internment of those now deemed enemy aliens rather than immigrants from Japan, Italy and Germany.[3] The threat from Japanese imperialism gave the US war effort a decidedly racial inflection: it was easier to construct 'the Nips' and 'the Japs' as a conspicuous other than 'the Krauts', particularly since many white Americans had European heritage. Only with the rise of Holocaust awareness in the wake of the Eichmann trial in 1961 and, in a second wave, with the Americanisation of the Holocaust and its institutionalised commemoration since the 1980s did fascism find a place in the wider historical imaginary.[4] The TV melodrama *Holocaust* (1978) was as seminal a moment in visualising violent history for a new generation and similar in impact as the earlier series *Roots* about slavery. Between those waves of awareness in the 1960s and 1980s, the protracted and controversial Vietnam War replaced the Second World War in American consciousness. This conflict could not be mythologised as a good or a just war. Yet 'fascism' served as a reminder of American values, and according to Michael Butter (2009), has particularly used Hitler as a trope to articulate political anxieties from the left and from the right. In the light of an increasingly violent foreign and domestic political culture, Nazism seemed not only a known form of evil, it was already transmuting into a metaphor for corruption, racism, conspiracy and the dark side of political power. Yet there were also signs of a lighter touch, of a sense of 'fascism' as entertaining cliché: the tremendously popular TV series *Wonder Woman* (1975) started its first season with the heroic intervention on the side of the Allies of a mythical ageless Amazonian culture in the Second World War. In contrast to European arthouse productions of 'fascism', Hollywood cinema was then still preoccupied with the outrage of Nazi crimes and perpetrators gone unpunished. The first version of Nazis-on-the-loose came with Frederick Forsyth's thriller *The Odessa File* (1972), and successfully trialled the investigative journalist as the historian-cum-detective. William Goldman's bestselling novel *Marathon Man* (1974), about the submerged presence of Nazi war criminals in the USA and in the Americas, helped foment outrage over the difficulties Nazi hunters like Simon Wiesenthal and Beate Klarsfeld faced in persuading governments to extradite known Nazis in hiding (Walters 2010; Goñi 2003). Ira Levin's alternate history *The Boys from Brazil* (1976) and George Steiner's *The Portage to San Cristobal of A.H.* (1979) fancied Mengele and Hitler alive in a South American exile. Many of these plots were adapted into successful films. However, the return to the Second World War in recent years, in political rhetoric and cultural production, speaks eloquently of the desire to leave the moral complexities of the Vietnam War behind and shape the perception of America's wars in the Middle East on the template of a previous conflict. The political rhetoric of the Bush administration encouraged us to think of Saddam Hussein as a new Hitler, his party as a version of the NSdAP (*Nationalsozialistische deutsche Arbeiterpartei*, or National-Socialist German Workers' Party), and the war in Iraq as a liberation from a dictator.[5]

If the unmanageable number of biographies, academic analyses and documentary programmes are ample evidence of the extent to which the Third Reich has colonised the historical imagination, they also perhaps demonstrate its failure to satisfactorily *explain* or contain its subject matter for a general audience. Rather, the ever more descriptive and cumulative inventory of Nazism in historiography has long begun to rival Nazism's own bureaucratic obsession with information gathering which in turn allowed such detailed study in the first place. If this sounds like a harsh critique of historians and their craft, I should perhaps state here categorically my respect for the rigours of the discipline. Not only do historians offer us a complex, balanced and highly differentiated narrative of the war and fascism, they have also pointed to the alarming approximations between totalitarian regimes and democratic cultures under wartime conditions; the entrenched racism that underpins the American war in the Pacific; the reprehensible conduct of armies on either side of the conflict; or the reassessment of military strategies such as area bombing or expulsion of civilians as war crimes.[6] Yet such efforts at an ever more comprehensive mapping of the conflict seem to have made little impact on its public memory or on popular historical consciousness. I do not think that the way in which historiographical narratives have 'emplotted' Nazism (to use a term coined by Hayden White) answers to the continued desire to be fascinated by 'fascism'. In its impact on popular memory, the cultural production of 'fascism' is fundamentally different from the historiography of fascism. Perhaps most importantly, historiographical narratives do not allow us to *inhabit* that era and its people in the same fashion as cinematic or fictional plots do. This is the crucial motivation, in Anglo-American culture, for the cultural fantasy that is 'fascism'. Precisely because American and mainland British culture have no experience of fascism or any other form of totalitarianism or dictatorship that could be retrieved through family history, testimony or recollection, the only way to access it is by engaging another country's history. In the case of 'fascism', the past is truly a foreign country even if it is habitually evoked to fashion one's own national narrative *ex negativo*. 'Fascism' is as exotic and exoticised as the Orient or Africa: barbarous, strange, alien; and equally eroticised and glamorised in its otherness. The result of this process is an appropriation that furnishes a cultural fantasy: paradoxically, 'the Nazis' have gradually become 'our Nazis'. How this transition functions in contemporary culture; how it has developed historically in film and literature; how artists and photographers have responded to it with alarm and critique – that is the trajectory of this book.

'Fascism', then, fills an experiential gap in Anglo-American history and culture. For this reason, historical fascism and foreign dictatorships in general are useful appropriations for a British national curriculum, argues the renowned historian Richard J. Evans:

> It appeals to teenagers for the same reasons that it appeals to adults: the collapse of German democracy in the early 1930s, the misery of the Depression, the rise of Hitler, the racism, sexism and criminality of the Nazi regime, the Holocaust, the drive to war – all of this raises critical questions of politics, morality and human behaviour in a dramatic form that has no parallel in British history. Stalin, Mao and other dictators pose similar challenges to the adolescent mind. The nearest thing British history has to offer in comparison is Henry VIII ('England's Stalin', as the Tudor historian W.G. Hoskins once

called him), but otherwise to teenagers it all seems relatively dull. (Evans 2001: n.p.)

To be fair, this paragraph is part of an essay fiercely critical of a patriotic revision of the history curriculum demanded by the Conservative Secretary for Education Michael Gove. In it, Evans warns of a return to insular monumentalist historiography, of the confusion between history and memory, and advocates the teaching of world history, not least to acknowledge a multicultural diversity in the British classroom. In *Cosmopolitan Islanders: British Historians and the European Continent* (2009), Evans analysed the complex reasons and political motivations for the professional scrutiny of European history (an interest he feels is waning largely due to diminishing foreign language skills and overregulated academic assessment structures). Yet it is notable how many of the renowned historians cited by Evans echo the sentiments quoted above and note the contrast between the drama of fascism and the dullness of national history. One wonders how 400 years of empire could possibly have produced such tedium. Small wonder then, that Evans feels justified in using the same exoticising strategy for retaining the remit of the national history curriculum: fascism (like 'fascism') promises edutainment.

'Fascism', however, is a profoundly ambivalent phenomenon. Like a classic hysterical symptom, it fulfils two contradictory desires and negotiates conflicting identities. On the one hand, 'fascism' refers to a foreign evil, an ideological otherness onto which those desires incompatible with democratic values can easily be projected. Particularly in postwar film, that foreignness had to be literalised. Many German and Austrian actors found ample employment in British and American war movies. Alongside the ubiquitous uniforms, their German accents and habitus were supposed to authenticate 'Nazism' and often lay the foundation for an international career as a cinematic baddie (typically as a Bond villain), as was the case with Gert Fröbe, Curt Jürgens, Klaus Maria Brandauer, or Hans Jürgen Prochnow. Contemporary writers have also made an effort to render German accents, transliterate Berlin slang, make frequent use of German street names, proper German names and Nazi military ranks, or specific formulas that remind the reader repeatedly that these people really are Germans, *mein Herr*.[7] While the narrative has to remain accessible for the English-language reader, its otherness must still be signified. Hence the curious composite names of protagonists like Philip Kerr's Bernie Gunther, Robert Harris's Xavier March or Jonathan Littell's Maximilien Aue, who in German would be Bernd, Xaver or Max, all of them from south of the Danube. The signification of alterity reassures the reader of their difference from the characters.

On the other hand, 'the Nazis' perhaps become integral to the self precisely in those moments when culture casts them as other. The insistence on the alterity of fascism, on its exotic nature, often merely cloaks the projection of unconscious desires onto an other, as we shall see, while it simultaneously allows the audience or the reader to dramatise and inhabit the fascist longings they habitually disown. On the set of Bryan Singer's *Valkyrie*, Kenneth Branagh enthused that it was really the uniform that transformed the actor rather than the actor who fleshed out the costume. This disavowal points to the complex and difficult relationship Anglo-American culture has to the pursuit of power. It has to be seen to be restrained and tempered by democratic virtues or to be the unavoidably paradoxical means towards establishing or defending democratic values. It can never be acknowledged as a desire in and of itself and therefore leads a submerged existence.

It is notable that certain narrative genres lend themselves to projections of a fascist landscape, particularly hardboiled crime and alternate history since these fictional worlds are already morally and factually compromised. They have in effect replaced the war film or war novel as the prime genre of 'fascism'. If signifiers of fascism's foreignness achieve distance, the first-person perspective has the opposite effect: identification. It transports the reader directly into a fascist timescape, be it the last days of the Weimar Republic, the twelve years of the Third Reich and the various theatres of war, or the aftermath of Nazism: 'I am a camera, with its shutter open, watching, not thinking.' Christopher Isherwood's famous opening line from his novel *Good-bye to Berlin* (1939) naively proclaimed the objectivity of the English observer of Germany's descent into Nazism. Thrillers and hardboiled fiction, if they do not adopt the first-person singular narrative voice of the German protagonist, still often cling to his limited point of view – that of an 'ordinary' Chandleresque detective, deeply implicated in the capital crimes he is trying to investigate and tainted by the pervasive criminality of the regime's impact on social structures. If the national identity of the detective is one step too far, a German lover is just as useful a device to entangle the protagonist in the fascist or post-fascist mess, be it in the many postwar pulp novels set in defeated Germany such as Colin MacInnes's *To the Victor the Spoils* (1950), Mario Puzo's *The Dark Arena* (1955), or James McGovern's *Fräulein* (1957). We find the same strategy in contemporary thrillers, such as Alfred Kanon's *The Good German* (2001) or David Downing's Berlin Station series (2001–present). The German protagonist with his many shades of grey is one of the most successful narrative functions of 'fascism', as the commercial success of Philip Kerr's seven volume Bernie Gunther series demonstrates. While he (never she) allows for a more differentiated examination of how totalitarianism corrupts moral integrity, this figure also facilitates a certain touristic attitude to Nazism that blurs the boundaries between 'fascism' and fascism. Both monstrously other and alarmingly ordinary, simultaneously 'them' and 'us', 'our Nazis' enable the vacillation between revulsion and projection, identification and disavowal, instruction and entertainment.

The artistic realisation of such fascist impersonations seems to be part of an actor's portfolio of villainy, if not a long-harboured ambition. Pjotr Uklański's photo frieze *Untitled (The Nazis)* (1998) drew on posters and film stills from innumerable Hollywood productions that featured a stellar cast of screen Nazis. Who could forget Laurence Olivier's terrifying performance as the fugitive camp doctor Christian Szell in John Schlesinger's adaptation of Goldman's *Marathon Man* (1976)? His dispassionate portrayal of sadism earned him an Academy Award. More recently, screen Nazis have been allowed a level of humanity: Liam Neeson (as Oskar Schindler in Steven Spielberg's 1993 adaptation of Thomas Keneally's novel *Schindler's Ark*) and Kate Winslett (as Hanna Schmitz in Stephen Daldry's 2010 adaptation of Bernhard Schlink's novel *The Reader*). Yet film critics such as Manohla Dargis (2008a) and Ron Rosenbaum (2009) swiftly criticised scriptwriters and directors for steering the audience's empathy towards these fascist characters: they were not monstrous enough but curiously human and irrational. Time and again, as we shall see, it is the ordinariness of the perpetrators that discomfits critics who prefer a clearer verdict on individual behaviour under totalitarianism.

As I shall demonstrate, such impersonations and appropriations almost always evoke controversy because the desires they satisfy – living fascism – cannot be openly acknowledged. One of the problematics of appropriating 'fascism' in its many forms lies certainly in the fact that its ostensible familiarity contributes to the palling of its historical horror. By engaging 'fascism' as a trope or a set of increasingly clichéd representations one does not necessarily analyse or even illustrate fascism as a historical phenomenon. Literary scholars have argued that its tropes can nonetheless provide a platform for dramatising contemporary anxieties. According to Gavriel Rosenfeld's *The World that Hitler Never Made* (2005b), alternate histories such as the Hitler-wins scenario respond to the threat of European integration and renewed German self-confidence. Michael Butter's *The Epitome of Evil* traces the nodal points in American culture for which fictionalisations of Hitler acted as a vehicle for working through historical crises of imperialist self-confidence and doubts about its democratic mission, as in the Vietnam War and the war on terror. Both make very convincing cases and I am indebted to their methodologies. Several colleagues from overseas have told me how 'useful' (literally!) their students find Nazism in 'working through' historic problems of racism such as slavery or white settler violence. But perhaps one must also ask (awkward though this is for a German) why such indirect manoeuvring should be necessary in the first place? Why does cultural criticism of one's own difficult history have to be exoticised or refracted through 'fascism'? When is such a strategy, to use Foucault's terms, an empty denunciation, or a misprision? When does 'fascism' amount to no more than a touristic attitude with which someone else's nightmare can be vicariously experienced without carrying the burden of historical responsibility?

The Germans have, in recent years, demonstrated a transgenerational willingness to look at the Nazi past in autobiography, family biography, fiction, film and memorialisation. The results are uneven but have given rise to a lively critical debate in Germany and elsewhere.[8] This is not always an attempt at the much cited *Vergangenheitsbewältigung* (coming to terms with the past); rather, an acknowledgement of a past that cannot be mastered but needs to be discussed in its complexity as a national *and* a familial history.[9] If both come laden with shame and guilt, this translates into the burden of historical responsibility for the postwar generations. For many among the third generation, the history of Nazism and the Holocaust is integral to an understanding of democratic postwar German citizenship, indicated by the resounding success of the controversial Wehrmacht exhibition in 1996/7 that demonstrated to an audience of hundreds of thousands the implication of the ordinary Wehrmacht soldier in crimes on the Eastern Front. If these photographs incriminated ordinary men and answered unasked questions about family members, Gerhard Richter's *Uncle Rudi* (1965) – the painting that graces the cover of this book – did something more complicated. Richter repainted a documentary image, a photograph of his uncle Rudi posing before a wall and a block of flats and smiling blithely into the camera. He wears the Wehrmacht coat, his cap at an almost rakish angle, and appears to hold some object in either gloved hand. It's hard to see what these objects are but they might be a half-eaten sandwich or an apple core, or something entirely different. The curiously naive facial expression in conjunction with the connotations of this uniform captures the ordinariness of this single man amongst the millions of other ordinary men, similarly posing before similar walls and similar flats in similar coats for similar families. Yet Richter is not content with photographic realism. After repainting the photographic image he blurs it with brush and squeegee strokes. If the initial repainting copies what the photograph depicts, the subsequent blurring questions both the denotation and the interpretive potential of the photographic image: *what* do we *see*, and *how* do we make sense of it? Referencing both the genre of 'history painting' and the documentary medium of photography this technique also questions the heroism habitually associated with the former and the veracity ascribed to the latter. What does this painting 'do' to the family photograph? How does the elevation of the family album to an art object change the image's meaning? Richter donated the painting to the Czech Museum of Fine Arts, in memory of German war crimes at Lidice, but as one of the famous paintings by one of the most highly esteemed contemporary artists it is regularly part of major exhibitions and retrospectives (such as *Gerhard Richter: Panorama* at London's Tate Modern in 2011). If sold, it would command astronomical sums. Yet: what would my students and colleagues think if I hung a reproduction (easily ordered from gerhardrichter.com) on a wall of my office? Would it turn *Uncle Rudi* into my uncle Rudi? Would the object revert to an (ostensible) family photograph or even suggest fascist sympathies particularly for those who do not recognise it as 'a famous Richter'? In other words, does the image's status as an art object insure against such a denotative interpretation and act like the squeegee on the photo-painting? Uncle Rudi may or may not have been a Nazi, but *Uncle Rudi* as an artefact about fascism has become one of 'our' Nazis on the international art scene, part of, and ironic commentary on, an iconography that is both overdetermined and strangely devoid of meaning.

As Omer Bartov (2000: 51) has emphasised, German re-engagement with fascism should not detract from the fact that, for the wider public, the confrontation (as opposed to the engagement) with the human realities of mass murder has often happened as a result of outside intervention, from the Allies' insistence that local communities near camps look at the horrors perpetrated there to the import of foreign films and books: the miniseries *Holocaust*, *Schindler's List*, *The Pianist*, *Hitler's Willing Executioners*, *The Kindly Ones* are all non-German products that resonated widely in Germany. Unlike the German historiographical discourse – largely bloodless and cerebral – these treatments targeted the public's affective response through the representation of blood and gore. Language and identity play an important role in the discussion about who can and does have a voice. Sue Vice has also emphasised that the more controversial fictional texts dealing with the Holocaust tend to come from Anglophone writers – controversial because they

are less likely to be written by survivors (2000: 2). Similarly, perpetrator fiction remains a taboo in German literature (not least because the
legal situation concerning the representation of fascist ideology and
iconography, even in artistic form, is very different in Germany, with
the result that many German publishers shy away from publishing non-
historiographical material). When the German-Jewish survivor Edgar
Hilsenrath sought to publish his satire *Der Nazi und der Friseur* in 1969
he received rejections from more than sixty German publishing houses.
Only after *The Nazi and the Barber* (1971) had sold over a million
copies in English, in French and in Italian did a small publishing house
accept the German manuscript in 1977 (McGlothlin 2007: 234–5).
Hilsenrath's black comedy features SS camp guard and mass murderer
Max Schulz who survives the war by taking on the identity of his dead
Jewish neighbour Itzig Finkelstein. Having emigrated to Tel Aviv, he
lives out his life as a 'Holocaust survivor'. The book's controversy
revolved around this two-fold masquerade of a perpetrator pretending
to be a Jew, and a Jewish survivor writing from the perspective of a mass
murderer. The irony of this preposterous situation (as well as the book's
peculiar publishing history) is perhaps characteristic of how strongly the
stakeholder debate was policed at the time: Germans could write about
perpetration historiographically (in the abstract) and Jews could write
about the Shoah through testimony (personalised), and never the twain
should meet. Hilsenrath's grotesque satire intervened in the Holocaust
discourse not only by radically unsettling the categories of perpetrator
and victim, 'German' and 'Jew' (as if these were mutually exclusive),
but also by suggesting that the increasingly sanctified conception of the
Holocaust arrested the discourse rather than sustained it.

In this context, one might perhaps also interpret Germany's renewed
cultural production about war and fascism as a re-appropriation: the
desire to tell one's own story (or that of the parents or grandparents)
rather than have it fictionalised, exoticised and instrumentalised by
others. Even Günter Grass, a writer by no means shy of examining
pasts national or personal, sounded impatient in an interview with the
Guardian: 'No country has the right to point only at the Germans.
Everybody has to empty their own latrine' (cited in Jaggi 2010: 13).
Violent history as scatological refuse is perhaps not the most salubrious
of metaphors, but Grass makes a strong point here about 'fascism' (and
fascism) being culturally overdetermined in the global memorial landscape at the cost of self-scrutiny. To what extent does the exoticising
engagement of 'fascism' detract from one's own historical burdens? In
the touristic appropriation of fascism, history is reduced to the 'already
known' territory of the Central European cataclysm, and if the Germans

balk at this, they are habitually accused of wishing to relativise their place in the hierarchy of historical horror.

The presence of 'fascism': safe history

Why should the British in particular have the need to resort to the comforts of such 'safe' history after the Cold War? The resurgence of historical fiction and film extends beyond 'fascism' and includes the Renaissance, the Victorian age, the First World War and the 1940s. Yet 'fascism' is the only temporally and geographically truly exotic period because it has no equivalent in modern British political history. On the other hand, the 1930s and '40s are still just within living memory, and our liminal position between the age of testimony and the era of re-imagining lends the engagement of fascism a certain urgency. As long as the witnesses of war and Holocaust are alive that past is not yet fully gone. This transitional moment has ramifications for the poetic liberties filmmakers and writers dare take with history and its witnesses to create dramatic effects. Bryan Singer, for instance, consulted extensively with the Stauffenberg family about his rendition of the plot to kill Hitler. Cinematic or literary representations of the Holocaust rarely happen without conferring with survivors and their families, museums or historians.[10]

The 1990s offer us a completely different European political landscape to the one of previous decades. The frequency with which political borders were being redrawn on the continent throughout the twentieth century is in itself a phenomenon radically alien to the British and recent American historical experience. The position of Britain and America vis-à-vis the new Europe – and a newly reunified Germany – changed dramatically. The USA emerged from bipolar global politics to find itself an unrivalled superpower whose hegemony would extend into Eastern Europe. Britain's reaction to prospective German re-unification and its continued economic dominance in the European Union, however, was extremely anxious. In the manner in which military and cultural history is transferred onto playing fields, that anxiety seemed compounded by England's defeat against the German team in the semi-final of the football World Cup in July 1990.[11] The late Nicholas Ridley, then Trade and Industry Secretary in the Thatcher Government, had to resign two days after he had declared, in an interview with the *Spectator*, that the Germans were a power-hungry nation and keen to dominate in the new Europe (Lawson 1990: 8–10). Three days later the *Independent on Sunday* published the Chequers memorandum, the minutes of a topical seminar convened by the Prime Minister in March 1990 to discuss the Germans and Germany (Anonymous 1990: 19). The Ridley-Chequers affair became a journalistic event and significantly contributed to one of the most severe crises of the Thatcher government before a change in leadership in the following year (Moyle 1994: 107–22). The political cartoons alone were ample evidence of how unrestrainedly the venting of prejudice tapped into an ossified version of history defined by essentialist notions of national character (Moyle 1997: 422–3). Robert Harris's alternate history *Fatherland* (1992) and Philip Kerr's *March Violets* (1991) are direct literary responses to the perceived threat of renewed German self-confidence.[12] Both became bestsellers: 'fascism' delivered a familiar enemy and a known past; Nazi Germany was altogether easier to deal with (because it had already been vanquished almost five decades ago) than a democratic Germany and its strong position in Western Europe. 'Fascism' was history made safe in the face of the contingencies of the day. German unification had a very unsettling effect on Britain and France, not least because it suggested that for the Germans the war might now finally be over and its most conspicuous geopolitical wound healed, while there could not be any recompense for the loss of empire or imperialist influence the war had cost the Allies (Markovits and Reich 1997: 120–34). European integration and the prospect of monetary union further threatened British independence.

The fall of communism released Eastern European states from the grip of the Soviet Union into national independence; in time this also prompted new commemorations (this time, of the victims of communism) but also a critical examination of the postwar politics of memory and wartime history (Lebow, Kansteiner and Fogu 2006). The Germans emerged from the historians' debate of the 1980s (about whether the Nazi past should be integrated into a larger narrative of twentieth-century German history or retain its special place) and examined their place in the new political landscape of Europe and their new unified national identity (Augstein 1987; Evans 1989). It is no coincidence that Berlin as the new-old capital saw building projects that attempted to combine national history and historical responsibility: the Jewish Museum, the restored Reichstag building and the adjacent Holocaust memorial – all of these projects were subject to both international scrutiny and national debate. By the 1990s Holocaust commemoration had certainly been Americanised with the inauguration of the Holocaust Museum in Washington DC, the Spielberg video project and Spielberg's tremendously influential 1993 adaptation of Thomas Kenneally's *Schindler's Ark* (1984). Since 2005 this commemorative remit has been extended in the West with various Holocaust Remembrance days, permanent Holocaust exhibitions, and memorials throughout the European Union, Israel and the United States. While the memory of suffering has certainly been institutionalised in the USA and Europe through a culture of empathy, there is less of a motivation to grasp fascism as an intellectual and emotional phenomenon. This remains a German 'problem' while both persecution and liberation have been integrated into national narratives in Israel and the USA. Engaging 'our Nazis' does not extend to a concomitant examination of 'our' fascist tendencies. The perpetrator *perspective* remains taboo – although it has risen to unprecedented prominence in contemporary crime writing, notably in serial killer fiction. The problem that so much of the visual and written documentation of the Holocaust makes the historian see it with the perpetrators' eyes caused Saul Friedländer considerable 'unease' (1993b: 111). In his magisterial *Nazi Germany and the Jews* he therefore incorporated the victims' voices alongside the point of view of bystanders and perpetrators. Even when historians tackle the psychology of perpetrators they can cause controversy through their explicatory paradigms, either reassuring the contemporary audience of their essential difference from the exotic, demonised perpetrators (Daniel Jonah Goldhagen's *Hitler's Willing Executioners*) or disconcerting them by outlining the relative ease with which the average person can be turned into a mass murderer (Christopher Browning's *Ordinary Men*). I will revisit the perpetrator debate in Chapter 3, when I tackle Jonathan Littell's monumental novel *Les Bienveillantes* (*The Kindly Ones*, 2006), told from the point of view of the SS officer Maximilien Aue. The controversy this novel provoked also needs to be contextualised in contemporary culture's paradoxical attitudes to violence and its consumption as entertainment.

As we shall see in Chapter 2, the moral imperative to understand the Shoah as unique, ranking top in the hierarchy of evil, has done little to curb the fascination with fascism, let alone foster an understanding of the psychological hold fascism exercised. Indeed, the discursive construction of transnational Holocaust memory seems to have little political power to implement its ethical demands: in fact, the commemorative drive in the 1990s and the new millennium stands in stark contrast to the genocides in Rwanda, the former Yugoslavia and Darfur, and the Turkish government's ongoing reluctance to acknowledge the Armenian massacre of 1917 as genocide. One of the paradoxical aspects of 'fascism' as a symptom of safe or remote history is that it precludes a comparative approach, any broader spectrum of ideological and institutionalised violence, and any critical self-scrutiny, while its explicit purpose as a trope or a metaphor is precisely to draw comparisons between contemporary culture and historical fascism. The work of Jake and Dinos Chapman is particularly interesting here, not least because it uses fascism as an almost universal reference point in installations such as *Hell* (1999–2000), *Fucking Hell* (2008) and *Jake or Dinos Chapman* (2011). The understanding of fascism in these artworks is so loose, broad and vague (as well as repetitive) that it is hard to see it as truly radical or indeed meaningful. Like Tarantino the Chapman Brothers offer comments on the uses of 'fascism' within our cultural imaginary rather than offer an engagement with fascism; the latter, I would argue, is something that 'fascism' actually obstructs if it has not prevented it altogether. As a result their work perhaps best illustrates the gulf between the liberal uses of 'fascism' and the moral guidelines for representing the Holocaust. The ubiquitous insistence on the commemoration of war and Holocaust (and the concomitant denunciation of forgetting as unethical) has a number of reasons. It is certainly a ritualised recognition of the struggles and sacrifices of those who fought for freedom and those who suffered persecution. Yet one must equally recognise that both memory and forgetting serve political expediencies in all political systems whether totalitarian or democratic (Todorov 2003).

If the fall of the Berlin Wall rearranged the political landscape, so did the terrorist attacks on the World Trade Centre on 11 September 2001. The 'war on terror' that the Bush administration declared on the enemies of the American way of life renewed the special relationship between Britain and the USA in the controversial wars in the Middle East, the invasions of Afghanistan in 2001 and Iraq in 2003. Even if terrorism and terrorists were rather opaque enemies they could be racially defined, declared religiously motivated extremists, and exoticised. Notions such as 'patriotism' and 'un-American activities' – terms that echoed the anti-communist witch hunts of the 1950s – suddenly gained new currency. The cultural response to this nationalist rhetoric has been quite diverse. David Charnay's alternate history novel *Operation Lucifer* (2002) sought to forge a link between the politics of Osama Bin Laden and a surviving Hitler to validate American anti-terrorist measures such as Guantanamo Bay.[13] On the other hand, Mohsin Hamid's Man-Booker nominated novel *The Reluctant Fundamentalist* (2007) examined whether the disenchantment with late capitalist consumer culture and secularised Western democracy, the search for transcendence and for ethnic roots, should be equated with Islamist fundamentalism.[14]

Countless thrillers have since put their gormless protagonists in the way of relentless intelligence agencies that mistake them for or frame them as terrorists; such plots highlight the way in which the paranoia of a security-obsessed surveillance society erodes the civil liberties it purports to protect. Even as plans for the withdrawal of forces are under way and military capacities are harshly curtailed as a result of the credit crunch, the controversies surrounding the wars in the Middle East remain manifold: the incompetencies in the Iraq occupation; the human rights abuses of detainees in Abu Ghraib and Camp Breadbasket; the practice of 'extraordinary rendition' and torture; the existence of Guantanamo Bay for terrorist suspects; the overall sidelining of the United Nations in the unilateral decision of the Allies to go to war and the manufactured threat of WMDs – those who saw the wars as blatant Western imperialism pointed to the discrepancies between the West's rhetoric of democratic values and the practice of foreign policy in the interest of oil-dependent nations. In this context, comparing the Bush administration to the German fascist regime in the 1930s and '40s ('Cheney-Goebbels' was a particular favourite) became shorthand for dismissing intelligence about foreign threats as deliberately misleading or mendacious. The real concern behind such hyperbole was clearly the lack of critical scrutiny in the wider public which, in a climate of fear, preferred xenophobic propaganda to tolerant multiculturalism, let alone critical scrutiny of one's own 'way of life'. Such denunciations revealed anxieties over the fragility of democracy. As the Bush administration constructed Saddam's government as 'fascist' and supported views of Osama Bin Laden as a Hitleresque terrorist, and as the leftist opposition in turn denounced Bush's policies as 'fascist', this label turned into a truly Foucauldian floating signifier. The same glib usage surfaced again in the current Euro crisis: posters protesting the harsh austerity measures imposed on Greece by the European Central Bank (to which Germany is a major contributor) regularly show Chancellor Angela Merkel in Nazi uniform. At least bloggers now curtail such rhetoric via invoking 'Godwin's Law', after the internet legal expert Mike Godwin who posited in the 1990s that the likelihood of any participant in an internet discussion comparing anyone to Hitler or Nazis increased proportionately with the length of the debate and, by the same token, signalled that the discussion had exhausted its logic or any meaningful arguments (Godwin n.d.).

Against such confusion about new and old fascism(s), Nazism seemed to hold some comforts: at least then it had been clear who the bad guys were. However, the post-9/11 films that dramatise fascism – Bryan Singer's *Valkyrie* and Quentin Tarantino's *Inglourious Basterds* (2009) – had entirely different receptions although all featured renowned actors. For a long time film superseded literature in the cultural inventory of responses to the Second World War, and its paradigms for fascism are given considerable space in this book. *Valkyrie* was a star-studded action film in period costume; a conventional war film unusual for Hollywood only in its all-German setting. Ostensibly it rescued from oblivion the failed Stauffenberg plot to assassinate Hitler in 1944, although it had already been the subject of three novels, three TV documentaries and four feature films. Chapter 4 deals with the most recent dramatisation of this plot and reads it alongside Justin Cartwright's novel *The Song Before It Is Sung* (2007). Both construct another important trope of both war films and 'fascism' – the Good German, a figure with a high-profile cinematic history but an inevitable terminal ending. In contrast Quentin Tarantino's *Inglourious Basterds* (2009) delivers a successful assassination of Hitler, by a Jewish guerrilla crew to boot. It offers a revenge fantasy packaged as alternate history, and for this reason it was successful at the box office but controversial for the critics. The discussion of the film and the cinematic archive it draws on and mocks furnishes the final chapter. Tarantino's play with genres and with the conventions of violent cinema in general (and 'fascism' in particular) seemed to remind us that we tend to mistake 'fascism' for fascism. Does his ambivalent use of conventions genuinely engage with the complex relationship between history, memory and cinema, or is it merely a particularly calorific instance of 'having your Nazi cake and eating it'?

'Fascinating Fascism' revisited

The re-emergence of Leni Riefenstahl, among other signs of a 'fascist' revival, first disturbed the cultural critic Susan Sontag, whose essay 'Fascinating Fascism' (1975) remains a cornerstone of the debate. In it Sontag identified the contemporary proliferation of fascist aesthetics in art, film and popular culture: Leni Riefenstahl's book on the Nuba; militaria collectors' handbooks such as Jack Pia's *SS Regalia* (1974); a cluster of European arthouse films suggesting links between sexual desire and fascism; and the fetishistic paraphernalia of sex shops and in gay subculture. Sontag identified this phenomenon as indicative of a shift in taste:

> It is not that Riefenstahl's Nazi past has suddenly become acceptable. It is simply that, with the turn of the cultural wheel, it no longer matters. Instead of dispensing a freeze-dried version of history from above, a liberal society settles such questions by waiting for cycles of taste to distil out the controversy. (Sontag [1975] 1996: 84)

That deft phrase 'the turn of the cultural wheel' marks Sontag's discomfort with Western culture's short-term memory, its partial forgetting (in both senses of the word) of traumatic history encouraged by the political expediencies of Cold War politics. Even if Western democracies did not officially regulate the uses of the past in the same manner as the communist regimes of the Soviet Union or China, the mere passing of time seemed to produce the effect of decontaminating the Third Reich and relegating it to arthouse cinema or subcultural tastes in leather. When Sontag first responded to 'fascism', Holocaust memory had not yet been institutionalised. Yet fascism's threat was already archival, and precisely because it was considered contained, remote and historical, its aesthetics could be naively divorced from its genocidal ideology by a mass audience who no longer had a 'historical perspective' in its treatment of fascist art and ideology, and therefore failed to spot 'the fascist longings in our midst' (Sontag [1975] 1996: 97). Sontag had identified the first stage of appropriation: because fascism had become temporally other (historically remote), it could be re-used as 'fascism' – in fetishistic leather gear, in the proud display of collectors' items, in the appreciation of Riefenstahl's artistic 'eye'; violent history was reduced to mere citation.

What reverberates in Sontag's note of alarm about the lack of historical consciousness that reduces the signification of fascism to 'fascism' (or 'formalist appreciation' as she called it) is her modernist elitism, which expresses itself as a goodly dose of disparaging scepticism about the ability of mass culture to be politically self-aware:

> Art that seemed eminently worth defending ten years ago, as a minority or adversary taste, no longer seems defensible today, because the ethical and cultural issues it raises have become serious, even dangerous, in a way they were not then. The hard truth is that what may seem acceptable in elite culture may not be acceptable in mass culture, that tastes which pose only innocuous ethical issues as the property of a minority become corrupting when they become more established. Taste is context, and the context has changed. ([1975] 1996: 97–8)

There is a sense here that fascism, even 'fascism', still has the power to enthral, particularly when it reaches the masses through wide dissemination or through popular culture. Given the corrupting success of mass propaganda during the Third Reich, such fears are perhaps not entirely misplaced. Alvin Rosenfeld reached a similar verdict over popular culture's ability to engage with fascism in his study *Imagining Hitler*: 'the contemporary imagination . . . with respect to the whole Nazi past, seems drawn between a willed forgetfulness and a kind of mythologizing memory' (1985: xx). Perhaps the impasse between myth and oblivion could have the same effect as 'freeze-dried' history? Art, Rosenfeld argued, should not simply divest itself of the moral responsibility for its cultural impact: 'The role of art in the erosion, as well as the establishment, of historical memory is fundamental, for most people do not have a primary relationship to "the facts" and learn about them second-hand, through the mediations of word and image' (1985: 105). Both Sontag and Rosenfeld were concerned that 'fascism' would shape people's idea of fascism. The original mass appeal of fascism had depended on what Walter Benjamin called the 'aestheticisation of politics', it was constructed around phantasmatic kernels such as the Führer myth, and it required the constant specularisation of its success in choreographed, ritualised mass events. To no small extent, then, did fascism already produce its own 'fascism'.

In contrast, Sontag's appreciation of Hans-Jürgen Syberberg's *Hitler, Ein Film aus Deutschland* (1977) hinged on its deliberate avoidance of any form that might be accessible to 'mass culture'. Seven hours long, a highly allusive collage of genres with citations from Wagner to Brecht, from UFA classics to puppet theatre, this was not a film that one could 'watch' (or screen, for that matter) in any straightforward way. It required historical consciousness, elite culture and elite taste, as well as a sense of kitsch, to appreciate Syberberg's monumental undertaking. Yet the same could be said for Riefenstahl's *Triumph of the Will* (1935), and the gargantuan party rally it depicted. Both filmmakers aspire to epic proportions – Syberberg to perforate myth, Riefenstahl to create it and represent transcendence. Both fail, because every epic needs a dynamic structure to engage the listener or spectator while neither has much of a narrative arc that engages the audience. Despite their artistic merits both films are excruciatingly dull, and are often merely cited through stills or wide-angle panorama shots, which reduces both directors to choreographers of claustrophobic or enormous spaces.

Syberberg's ostensible aim was to confront Nazism, or more precisely, to examine Hitler through 'our relation to Hitler (the theme is "our Hitler" and "Hitler-in us")' according to Sontag ([1980] 1996: 139). In the USA, the film was also released and the videotape distributed under the title *Our Hitler*. Since this was a German filmmaker one could easily interpret the first-person plural as expressing the director's agenda as a moral imperative for his nation's problematic relationship to the past: it was time to scrutinise precisely what in German culture and history and in the German psyche Hitler had embodied that had enabled his rise to power and his genocidal regime.[15] Sontag, however, extended the first-person plural dramatically, as she would do again in her indignant essay on the trophy photographs of prisoner abuse in Abu Ghraib ('the photographs *are* us'), to emphasise that political responsibility requires historical consciousness (Sontag 2007: 131). In the essay on Syberberg, as in 'Fascinating Fascism', the focus is on the form, the effect and the ethics of confronting and representing fascism in Western culture more broadly.

Cultural critics in the 1970s and 1980s felt that 'fascism' uncritically or naively replicated (rather than scrutinised) fascism's attraction. 'What is uncanny about the new fascination with Hitler is its resemblance – often recognizable in impulse, idiom, tone, and direction – to the fascination of the 1930s and 1940s', argued Rosenfeld (1985: xviii). Saul Friedländer reached similar conclusions in his essay *Reflections of Nazism*. He located his uneasiness about the new discourse on Nazism in the dissonance between the authors' and filmmakers' declared condemnation of Nazism, the will to understand fascism and the aesthetic effect produced by the cinematic or literary narrative. For him, the manner of representation could never reduce the erotic fascination of power that had existed under Nazism. Rather, it re-evoked Nazism alongside the values its iconography embodied (Friedländer 1993a: 20; 77). For this reason, any representation of Nazism was tainted. The crucial question was, however, had fascism's psychological hold been erotic or had 'fascism' eroticised it?

'Fascism' and the male theatre of desire

In 'Fascinating Fascism' Sontag foregrounds the emotional response to (or psychological hold of) fascism as well as postwar culture's naive attitude towards this effect, which ranges from being 'curiously absentminded' to downright hypocritical and dishonest. Note such phrasings as 'the fascist longings in our midst'; 'the manipulation of emotion' through which Riefenstahl's films provide 'exhilaration'; or the 'destructive feelings' (Sontag [1975] 1996: 97, 95) which her films and 'fascism' in general propagate. Historical Nazism offered an eroticised engagement with death as a glamorised ritual or a glorified sacrifice that neither liberal democracy nor leftist ideologies could provide. For both Sontag and Friedländer, the erotic and the thanatic appeal of 'fascism' were rooted in the manner in which Nazism had staged its ideology. The emotional effect of fascism lay in its theatricality, in the dramatisation of desire that played itself out through 'an erotic surface' at mass events (Sontag [1975] 1996: 102), in which a masculine leader controlled and satisfied the 'feminine' crowd. From such a surface originated the later citation of Nazism Sontag saw in sadomasochistic practices, or in the fetishistic treatment of Nazi regalia in collectors' handbooks: 'Today it may be the Nazi past that people invoke, in the theatricalisation of sexuality, because it is those images (rather than memories) from which they hope a reserve of sexual energy can be tapped' ([1975] 1996: 104). The distinction between images and memories is pertinent since the difference between a way of seeing and actual experience marks a generational gap, and describes the transition from fascism to 'fascism'. The latter, for Sontag, turned into an erotic rebellion, a seeking of extraordinary thrills that rejected the banality of suburban vanilla sex and the oppressive liberalism of a consumer society. Bondage was the new black: the manifestation of a desire for both complete submission to, and the exercise of, boundless power.[16]

Sontag's approach to 'fascism' as servicing a libidinal economy seemed validated by the translation, in 1986, of an earlier German study that interpreted the ideology of fascism as enabling a particular psychosexual dynamic – Klaus Theweleit's two-volume encyclopaedic compendium *Male Fantasies* (1977/78). Theweleit saw fascism as a violent response to a crisis of masculinity after the First World War, a fending off of feminised culture and politics, of democratic 'chaos'. *Freikorps* militancy and fascist politics literally became a form of acting out male fantasies. Fascism, according to his theory, divided men into a boundless, 'flowing' feminine interiority which was controlled, kept at bay and repressed by a masculine exterior boundary that acted as an armour. Choreographed mass events (oaths, pageants, party rallies, initiation and funereal rituals) offered men the possibility of reconciling this divide in themselves. The ritual functioned as a remasculinising reunion or coitus, hence the ecstasy and the exhilaration. In these rituals men could both enact the repressed (become part of a feminine flowing mass) and embody repression through being confined in stringent formations (Theweleit 1977: 550–5). The fascist therefore constantly enacted his own sadomasochistic theatre of repression-and-release, submission and liberation, in the service of the nation. 'Sex: German' is the passport entry that would have delighted every fascist, quips Theweleit ([1978] 1985: 98). If we bear in mind that most of the books and films analysed here are indeed the products of the male imagination about German fascism and appear to be read and watched by a predominantly male audience, this makes for a tempting theory. Jonathan Littell explicitly engaged with Theweleit's ideas in both his novel *The Kindly Ones* and in his essay *Le Sec et l'humide* (2008), which is why psychoanalytically inflected explicatory models for fascism will be revisited in Chapter 3.

However, historical fascism was not a movement that bypassed women, nor is 'fascism' only consumed by men. In *Sexuality and German Fascism* (2004), Dagmar Herzog has argued that although gender roles appeared to be relatively fixed, the sexual mores under

Nazism were complex and contradictory and did by no means restrict women to the extent we imagine today. What is perhaps important here is the extent to which 'fascism' either completely ignores this complexity or exploits it. The hardboiled thriller in particular suggests a relegation of women to the position of the sexual and the racial subaltern. Does 'fascism' allow for the articulation of pornographic and misogynistic fantasies under the mantle of presenting reactionary politics with historical verisimilitude? The problematics of gendering 'fascism' (or analysing its putatively greater appeal to men) will be addressed in several chapters, specifically in the discussion of gender in hardboiled thrillers and in perpetrator fantasies.

European arthouse cinema in the 1970s and 1980s certainly offered representations of fascism whose plots enacted the protagonists' libidinal investment in politicised power differentials. Sexual desire and fascist seduction are common metaphors in Luigi Visconti's *The Damned* (1969), Liliana Cavani's *The Night Porter* (1974), Louis Malle's *Lacombe Lucien* (1974), Pier Paolo Pasolini's *Salò* (1975) Ingmar Bergman's *The Serpent's Egg* (1977) and Rainer Werner Fassbinder's *Lili Marleen* (1981). What characterises all of these arthouse films is that they acknowledge, even foreground, the allure fascism exerts for its followers, over its victims, and even, by implication, for the audience. In *The Damned*, mother and homosexual fascist son conduct an incestuous relationship. Pasolini's barely watchable *Salò* sees Italian fascism through Sadean aesthetics. The performances of the titular song 'Lili Marleen' in Fassbinder's melodrama are staged as a gendered allegory of national seduction, while the girl France in *Lacombe Lucien* consents to a sexual relationship with the eponymous fascist collaborator. Most problematically, in Cavani's *The Night Porter* a Jewish survivor is strangely compelled to take up her sadomasochistic relationship with a former concentration camp officer. Sex in these films, notably transgressive sex, is not only shorthand for a perverted ideology (an aberration in social, cultural and political life) but the key metaphor to explain its attraction.

Inevitably, these films were criticised for the eroticisation of Nazism – of making fascism look glamorous and sexy. This reception perhaps also indicated how close to the bone their points were, however crudely made. All of these productions were highly theatrical in style, and in places even ironically melodramatic, with references to Weimar cabaret (Visconti, Cavani, Bergman), Third Reich celebrity entertainers and the famous 'Wunschkonzert' broadcast (Fassbinder), and the effect of dressing up and 'looking the part' of the fascist (Malle, Cavani). Each of them suggested their own aetiology of fascism, as a vehicle or container for repressed desires. The gender politics of *all* these films are by no means coherent or fixed: women are often victims of fascist and sexual abuse, but they are equally abusers or agents of seduction for whom Nazism constitutes a platform for the acquisition of power (Byg 1997: 176–89). Fascism in itself is not erotic (other than in the overtly fetishistic donning of uniforms) but lends power; associating with fascism, then, offers a form of empowerment that also bestows erotic allure. This is the link between, for instance, Marlene Dietrich in Billy Wilder's *A Foreign Affair* (1948) and Hannah Schygulla in Fassbinder's *Lili Marleen*. In Wilder's comedy, Dietrich's character, a nightclub singer in an Allied bar in occupied Berlin, embodies a compromised German nation. Newly dependent on US handouts and the army rations traded on the black market, Dietrich and Germany's political future are for sale. Scrutinised and assessed as to her ideological contamination via the proverbial *Persilschein* (literally a laundry ticket, the denazification certificate that absolved the bearer of any party affiliation), and haunted by a loathed husband now gone underground as a Nazi war criminal, Dietrich is pursued by a past that literally will not go away despite the new affair with American democracy. In Fassbinder's *Lili Marleen*, Schygulla rises to fame thanks to the wartime popularity of the title song on the nightly *Wunschkonzert* broadcast to the troops. Her success comes at the price of personal integrity and friendship. Fassbinder's ironic Riefenstahl-esque cinematography positions the singer time and again before a giant swastika on gargantuan stages, empty but enthralled to her fame, till she collapses, drug-addled and deeply implicated in the corruption of the regime's culture industry. Both female leads embody the fascist nation and the seduction of ideology (no turn of the cultural wheel here, it seems). The *mise-en-scène* of these characters' performances dramatises the conflation of a whole range of signifiers: woman, nation, fascism.

For Sontag, fascist aesthetics provided a script for a sadomasochistic 'master scenario', a 'magnificent experience' that ordinary civil society could not deliver: in their 'preoccupation with situations of control, sub-missive behaviour, extravagant effort, and the endurance of pain . . . they endorse two seemingly opposite states, egomania and servitude' ([1975] 1996: 103). The sexual appeal of fascist aesthetics stemmed less from an inherent eroticism (indeed fascism sought to channel sexual energy into sacrifice and service for a community) than from its romantic ideal of the absolute triumph of power. The turn-on lies in what fascism enables one to do, the abdication of responsibility and the release of repression.

The eroticisation of 'fascism' is now firmly established in the cultural imaginary, not least as a metonymy for its sinister corruption, from Peter O'Toole's leering psychopath in Anatol Litvak's *The Night of the*

Generals and Helmut Berger's Visconti reprise in Tinto Brass's *Salon Kitty* (1976) to the Gestapo officer in the British TV series *'Allo 'Allo* (1982–92) and the basement Nazi in *Psychoville* (2011). A much cruder version of sexualised 'fascism' surfaced in 1970s pornography, such as Sergio Garrone's *SS Experiment Love Camp* (1976) or Don Edmonds's *Ilsa, She-Wolf of the SS* (1975). Here the fascist *is* a sadist pervert whose inviolable body is contrasted with the torturable bodies of his or her victims. The setting, the uniforms and the 'historicity' of the scenario have the function of legitimising the representation of sexual violence and reassuring the passively watching audience of the perverse otherness of the perpetrator.[17] There are a number of highly sexual scenes in the literary texts under discussion, from Philip Kerr's violated racial subalterns in his Bernie Gunther novels to the masturbatory and incestuous episodes in Littell's *The Kindly Ones*. What is the explicatory potential of such scenes – do they merely underline the obscenity of fascist evil or are they obscene in themselves?

I argued earlier that 'fascism' as a cultural fantasy encompasses a narrative with shifting roles, or scenarios in which contradictory desires can be acted out or given equal weight. They allow for a simultaneous enactment and disavowal of transgressive desires; an appropriation as well as a distancing. In 'A Child is Being Beaten' (1919), Freud analysed the grammar of sadomasochistic fantasy in which the child unconsciously transferred her position from that of being the one who *is* beaten by her father to being the one who is *watching* another child being beaten by a figure of authority. Thus the object of authoritarian violence becomes its spectator. The syntax of this fantasy encapsulates for me the relationship to historical fascism in the dramas of 'fascism'. Identification with either the perpetrator or the victim position is morally prohibited and therefore disavowed, so the spectator or bystander role is habitually assumed not least because it tallies with the historical situation of the British and American experience. In Chapter 2, on Ian McEwan's *Black Dogs* and Robert Harris's *Fatherland*, I examine the ethics of such fictionalised witnessing: how does the spectator rationalise fascination or justify arousal? Does it not amount to a kind of 'dark tourism' that reserves the optional excursion into the melancholic pleasure of suffering or the freedom from any moral restriction in perpetration? Is today's 'fascism' actually the result of the demands of empathetic history or, in contrast, a symptom of Holocaust fatigue?

'Fascism' in the age of empathetic history

In *Twilight Memories* (1995), Andreas Huyssen has argued that our current preoccupation with commemoration and our desire to 'connect' with history is a symptom of anxiety about the accelerating pace of high-tech modernity. A musealised past and its interactively presented artefacts are treated like totems warding off the dematerialisation of the world through cyberspace, internet and mobile technology. This past, however, is not merely archived but presented and 'emplotted' for the visitor. Museums assist in the *construction* of historical consciousness rather than assume its pre-existence via a reasonable education and intellectual curiosity. Commemorative institutions are also facilitators of hegemonic national history. For instance, the permanent exhibits in the Imperial War Museum in London and the Holocaust Memorial Museum in Washington DC offer versions of the past that emotionally engage the visitor in ways considered morally appropriate or safe (Noakes 1997: 89–105; Cole 1999: 164; 157). Particularly when a museum presents someone else's history, an *affective* relationship to the subject-in-history is now considered the most educational and effective way of connecting with the past, particularly with traumatic history; yet the quality of this affect, and how to steer it and regulate it, is also some cause for concern.

Alison Landsberg has argued that the various media that now facilitate our engagement with the past (primarily films and exhibitions) constitute 'prosthetic memories' (2004: 2). These have the unique ability to generate empathy:

> This new form of memory . . . emerges at the interface between a person and a historical narrative about the past, at an experiential site such as a movie theatre or a museum. In this moment of contact, an experience occurs through which the person sutures himself or herself onto a larger history . . . the person does not simply apprehend a historical narrative but takes on a more personal, deeply felt memory of a past event through which he or she did not live. The resulting prosthetic memory has the ability to shape that person's subjectivity or politics. (2004: 19; 24)

While empathy is not the same as identification or sympathy, it manoeuvres the audience into a position from where they believe they can emotionally access ('deeply feel') the past. Landsberg is careful to emphasise that this is not a straightforward appropriation, merely a 'suturing', a stitching oneself into a larger history through which an individual comes to understand him- or herself as a subject-in-history. For Landsberg, this experience of contact or suturing does not alter the notion of the past as different or distant, but changes the individual's relationship to that 'deeply felt' past. Nor does such an experience simply expose the audience to hegemonic narratives. She credits them with the ability to fashion a more creative or critical response to what they see. For Rachel N. Baum there is merit in such 'pedagogical emotions', particularly when they lead to contemporary 'action', that is the revision of prejudicial behaviour towards tolerance as well as replacing indifference with defence of human rights (1996: 44–57; also Gallant and Hartman 2001). Perhaps this emphasis on empathy and other 'pedagogical emotions' is an inevitable byproduct of the discursive rules surrounding the Shoah. These prescribe respectful empathy shy of unseemly identification with the victims of persecution and genocide. The philosopher Gillian Rose, among other critics of 'Holocaust piety', has suggested that such dogma is not conducive to keeping the memory of the Shoah alive:

> To argue for silence, prayer, the banishment equally of poetry and knowledge, in short, the witness of 'ineffability', that is non-representability, is *to mystify something we dare not understand*, because we fear that it may be all too understandable, all too continuous with what we are – human all too human. (1996: 43)

I don't think this is a rejection of ethical considerations to do with representations of suffering, nor a relativising of the Holocaust into a continuum of violent history and genocide, nor nihilist Nietzschean cynicism ('human all too human'). Rather, it is a plea for opening the debate to a variety of engagements and discourses because policing any debate is intellectually flawed and counterproductive. Any regulating intervention would result in a 'fascism of representation', Rose argues. 'Holocaust piety' and the privileging (even sanctification) of testimony effectively silence any debate into 'freeze-dried history', while affective engagement might pall into Holocaust fatigue. As Matthew Boswell has argued in his recent book *Holocaust Impiety*, the aesthetic shock of transgressive representation of the Shoah and the violation of discursive rules and ethical consideration may indeed be much more effective in sustaining debate (2011: 6). Michael Handelzalts (2011), writing in *Haaretz.com*, considered the loosening of these rules 'a healthy change' that allows for the display of 'a certain, wary, sense of proportion'.

Today's educational practice and museum culture still subscribe to an arguably rather optimistic, if not idealistic approach to the instrumentalisation of the Shoah (if indeed it is explicitly recognised as such). They often underestimate the politics of commemoration and the ideology of curatorial emplotment. Museums and films are not history, but 'history';

they are representations of the past which, when we encounter them, already present us with a mediated interpretation of history. Surely what kind of history deserves to be commemorated, and which aspects are too difficult, controversial or sensitive to integrate into or make central to national history, is in itself telling. In Britain, it took until the summer of 2012 for the dead of RAF Bomber Command to be honoured in a memorial at the western end of London's Piccadilly; these men had flown the highly dangerous and devastating bombing raids over Germany during the Second World War. Amongst Britain's wartime population who knew what German bombing had done to British cities and citizens, these RAF raids were by no means uncontroversial, and after the war, when the extent of the damage became more widely known through reportage and newsreel, RAF Bomber Command veterans were advised to change their CVs if they hoped to be gainfully employed. The military historian Richard Overy pointed to the paradox underlying the RAF memorial: while it subsumed the crews under the common status of war victims it left unresolved the moral and political accountability of wartime leaders who had legitimised city areas as military targets.[18] The raids themselves remain contentious, and so does the nature of their commemoration. In the USA, the debates in 1995 and 2003 about the *Enola Gay* exhibit (the plane that dropped the nuclear bombs on Hiroshima and Nagasaki) at the Smithsonian Institution illustrate the contested commemorative politics underpinning the curatorial framing of one B-29 aircraft: could photographs of the Japanese casualties of the bombing be displayed? Could the Japanese be acknowledged as victims of US aggression in the Pacific (in contradistinction to the political rhetoric of saving lives and ending the war)? Could the loss of Japanese lives be mourned? It was not before 2010, on the 65th anniversary of the first nuclear attack, that a US representative attended a commemoration in Japan.[19] Only in 2011 could sixty previously classified photographs of Hiroshima be exhibited in at the International Center of Photography in New York.[20] The USA has a Holocaust Museum in its capital but as yet no designated museum to the commemoration of slavery. In the UK such a museum was only inaugurated in Liverpool in 2007 on the bicentenary of the abolition of the British slave trade, therefore overwriting a narrative of exploitation and profiteering with one of liberation and entrepreneurship. Surely it is problematic to instrumentalise the Holocaust as a paradigmatic genocide to create an indirect pedagogical pathway to national history's darker aspects and to teach universal human rights, but this seems to be its cardinal function in contemporary Western classrooms (Donnelly 2006). The key issue in teaching and remembering difficult history is to avoid inducing the pedagogically unproductive feeling of guilt. Short and Reed comment on the ease with which students in Britain and North America can distance themselves from the Holocaust in terms of time and space, but most importantly, they confront it without remorse and guilt as a result of their national affiliation (2004: 29). The link between genocidal continental anti-Semitism and 'mere' racism in contemporary multi-ethnic societies (ostensibly the pedagogical value of teaching the Holocaust) is a 'learning outcome'. It is meant to translate potential guilt (about the international communities' historic indifference; about contemporary racial prejudice) into individual responsibility. Yet, not to put too fine a point on it, to exemplify via the shooting, starving and gassing of millions of Jews seventy years ago that setting a black teenager on fire in the streets of Hackney (Stephen Lawrence) or shooting an Asian student point-blank in Salford (Anuj Bidve) constitutes homicidal racism seems a rather circuitous route.

In German classrooms, Holocaust education has become challenging because contemporary pedagogy appears to demand a mandatory mobilisation of empathy for the victims of fascism. Gudrun Brockhaus suggests that such regimented history classes exert emotional and moral pressure as a result of teachers' insecurity and lack of confidence about the effects of presenting history within a prescribed moral framework (2012: 34–53). There clearly is a reluctance to discuss perpetration: students will have to make a connection between abstract perpetrators and family history, a link teachers often feel imposes an undue sense of guilt. Perhaps more relevant here is the anxiety that perpetration might degenerate into a turn-on in the quagmire of adolescent fantasy, as in Stephen King's novella *Apt Pupil* (also adapted by Bryan Singer). Yet in our media-saturated age of first-person shooter games, porno gonzo close-ups, 'hilarious' horror flicks, and ultra-graphic crime fiction, pious clichés about 'unimaginable horror' simply no longer reach teenage pupils who, according to Brockhaus, appear to have seen quite a lot more than the average adult would care to imagine. Rather than achieving an open and critical discussion of fascism and genocidal anti-Semitism in the German classroom (or in any classroom, for that matter), making empathy with victims imperative and policing classroom debates towards 'required' responses might result in frustration, defensiveness, and even aggressive deflection on the side of students. At worst, students disengage because they perceive that the teacher acts as a moral censor who actively curtails freedom of thought and feeling. In British classrooms, too, history teachers report considerable insecurity about the ability of the historical material to mobilise pedagogical emotions:

When you see . . . some of the more horrific [videos], it will touch some kids. The rest have seen worse in the horror movies – *Nightmare on Elm Street* and that sort of thing. They don't realise that this is actually happening to real people. Lots of them see it as just another video. (Cited in Short and Reed 2004: 63)

Habituation to simulated violence in the media may certainly be one factor in this pedagogical battle for emotional and moral impact, but the medium itself may already be compromised: students apparently struggle to differentiate between real and reel images; between categories of fiction, fantasy and documentary. It seems that the pedagogical insistence on sentient responses and emotional engagement actually reveals an underlying assumption about the absence of any pre-existing ethical framework in youngsters (that is, the guided exposure to genocidal violence is somehow supposed to engender ethical considerations). Such pedagogy is of course highly idealistic, if not delusional. We know that we cannot teach 'required' emotions; we can merely police responses and stimulate thought.

Historiography of the Shoah has also recently turned to a more affective methodology, in its focus on 'sensation' and 'disbelief', casting a violent history that is ostensibly beyond representation into a specific narrative form that departs from the traditional rules of the discipline. Saul Friedländer has prefaced his magisterial second volume on Nazi Germany and the Jews, *The Years of Extermination* by emphasising the affective role of Jewish voices in his narrative:

By its very nature, by dint of its humanness and freedom, an individual voice suddenly arising in the course of an ordinary historical narrative of events such as those presented here can tear through seamless interpretation and pierce the (mostly involuntary) smugness of scholarly detachment and 'objectivity'. Such a disruptive function would hardly be necessary in a history of the price of wheat on the eve of the French Revolution, but it is essential to the historical representation of mass extermination and other sequences of mass suffering that 'business as usual historiography' necessarily domesticates and 'flattens'. (2007: xxvi)

The premise here is that ordinary historiography (and sober narrative) does not do justice to the event being described, analysed and conceptualised. In fact, the rules of the discipline with its established rhetoric suggest an ostensibly inappropriate ability to fathom and master the Shoah, and would thus violate some of the crucial discursive rules surrounding it: non-representability, uniqueness, incomprehensibility. Therefore, the rules of the discipline must be adjusted towards a more affective engagement *of the reader* with the material. Historical excess can only be met with historiographical transgression. Crucial here is also perhaps the anxiety that the passing of time will silence the voices of the survivors and with the palling of the immediacy of the events, the Shoah might sink into a historical continuum of genocide in which its status degenerates from unique to merely extreme. Whether this new turn in Holocaust historiography lives up to its affective and empathic agenda remains a matter of debate (Confino 2009; LaCapra 2011).

For Landsberg, the passing of time is a clear reason to encourage sensation in a variety of representations suggesting that historical trauma requires temporal distance to be properly conceptualised and 'felt'. Precisely how affect is conceived and ethically regulated, however, poses a problem. In my view, the privileging of affect over intellect in the encounter with violent history is rather worrying:

> Prosthetic memories are neither purely individual not entirely collective but develop at the interface of individual and collective experience. They are privately felt public memories that develop after an encounter with a mass cultural presentation of the past, when new images and ideas come into contact with a person's own archive of experience. Just as prosthetic memories blur the boundary between individual and collective memory, they also complicate the distinction between memory and history. (Landsberg 2004: 19)

Is it really desirable and productive that the relationship between history, 'history' and memory should be so complex? In fact, the blurring of such boundaries is increasingly alarming to professional historians who fear that the emotional or dramatic emplotment of history in 'faction', docu-dramas or exhibitions takes too many postmodern liberties with hard facts or, conversely, that survivor testimonies have been elevated into fact (Beevor 2011; Evans 2011: 12). For all the emphasis on the external nature of suturing and prosthesis, it is hard to see how 'privately felt public memories' are not the result of internalisation through appropriation or identification. Dominick LaCapra offers an even more differentiated notion of 'empathic unsettlement': 'In the virtual (in contrast to the vicarious) experience of trauma, one may imaginatively put oneself in the victim's position while respecting the difference between self and other and recognising that one cannot take the victim's place or speak in the victim's voice' (2004: 125). Such refined attempts at negotiating positions and places originate in the moral prohibition of identification through which the victim's experience would get overwritten with one's own solipsistic concerns and questions. In practice, the distinction between identification and empathy is perhaps impossible to regulate. The debate about how to represent the Holocaust and how to respond to its representation is, however, indicative of an *impasse* in several disciplines. If 'Holocaust piety' prohibits understanding of traumatic history (rejecting the enlightenment project), the mobilisation of affect is drawn upon to approach and approximate it (note LaCapra's 'virtual experience') as a form of acceptable ethical simulation. Even for Friedländer, knowledge is not only not enough but actually obstructive and should not precede affect: 'disbelief is a quasivisceral reaction, one that occurs before knowledge rushes in to smother it' (2007: xxvi). Rarely has knowledge been described as so counter-productive to understanding. Here affect is also subject to ethical regulation, and this may just be too much for the average libidinal economy.

If the audience of mass cultural experiences of 'history' are indeed able to fashion a creative and independent response to what they are presented with, there is in turn little guarantee about what role they choose vis-à-vis traumatic history or with whom they wish to empathise in this affective framework, if they don't altogether reject it. In Chapter 2 I discuss a number of scenes from Ian McEwan's novel *Black Dogs* where the spectator role is foregrounded as a position from which empathy or sympathy with the victims of atrocity cannot be generated. Since the technologies of memory now make it harder to own history or lay claim to 'heritage', it is correspondingly easier to empathise with, appropriate and inhabit others' history. The recent turn of fictional and cinematic attention to perpetrators could perhaps also be seen as a recalcitrant reaction to the demands of empathetic 'history' or as a rejection of the potential of such an affective framework to enable understanding and analysis.

Perhaps the most forceful refutations of Landsberg's notion of prosthetic memory as a facilitator of empathetic historical consciousness are three exhibitions about 'fascism' that explicitly preclude empathetic positions and that were attacked for doing just that: Pjotr Uklański's photo frieze *Untitled (The Nazis)* at the Photographer's Gallery in London (1998); the group exhibition *Mirroring Evil: Nazi Imagery/Recent Art*, curated by Norman Kleeblatt at the Jewish Museum in New York in 2002; and the work of the Chapman Brothers at the White Cube Gallery, London, specifically *Hell* (1999–2000), *Fucking Hell* (2008), and *Jake or Dinos Chapman* (2011). Not only did contemporary artists argue that the lines between 'fascism' and fascism had become permeable; the public's sceptical and occasionally angry response to their artworks also demonstrated an erosion of the ability to distinguish between an endorsement of fascism and a critique of 'fascism'. This confusion between 'fascism' and fascism, history and 'history', seemed to prove the artists' points about the power of the photographic and cinematic 'iconography of evil' to replace the historical face of fascism. As a mass medium it would remain the chief vehicle for the popular construction of a historical imaginary.

Another difficulty in the construction of empathetic historical consciousness is the fact that not all mass cultural representations of history encourage this position. In *The Hollywood War Machine* (2007), Carl Boggs and Tom Pollard argued that US popular culture has taken on a more combative strain since the 1980s. They point to the strict controls the Pentagon exerts over the culture industry and the representation of its military forces that play into right-wing agendas. Roger Stahl's *Militainment, Inc.* suggests that this combative mode is part of a larger cultural trend that makes war consumable as entertainment through sophisticated, interactive first-person shooter games, war movies, real-time TV coverage, and the practice of embedded reporting. Such technowar allows the audience to fantasise themselves into battle. It also acclimatises the ordinary civilian to a high level of (simulated) violence and serves to erode the traditional distance between the soldier and the civilian; they reconnect and this transforms the 'citizen-spectator' into 'the virtual citizen-soldier' (Stahl 2010: 20–49). In this climate of spectacular mediated violence, the willingness of the citizen to commit or tolerate ideologically motivated violence is of particular interest, whether it is to defend his country and its values or to attack another's.

The fascist flâneur

Empathy is of course not a modern concept in the (neo-)historical encounter but has always been the creative strategy of historical fiction, a kind of 'empathetic fallacy' that enabled time-travel. In the words of Georg Lukács:

> What matters . . . in the historical novel is not the retelling of great historical events, but the poetic awakening of the people who figured in those events. What matters is that we should re-experience the social and human motives which led men to think, feel and act just as they did in historical reality. ([1936] 1969: 42)

In other words, the historical novelist needs to create a protagonist with whom the reader willingly identifies; whose 'social and human motives' are dramatised as a set of inescapable dilemmas. Lukács does not encumber his study with reflections on the moral appropriateness, let alone possibility, of *re-experiencing* another's psychology. For him, historical fiction is an imaginative conduit into the past that can only be achieved through inhabiting the construct of an average man (*l'homme moyen*).

If that protagonist is a German in the Third Reich, the elect framework of the popular Anglo-American imagination vis-à-vis historical fascism requires that the reader is provided with a simulacrum of oppression that simultaneously incriminates *and* exculpates. The result is either the morally ambiguous anti-hero of hardboiled crime or the splitting of the protagonist into a Good German and an evil Nazi. The problematic construction of the 'Good Nazi' which often serves to legitimise 'fascism' in the first place, runs through several chapters of this book, and is brought into particular focus in Chapter 2. It involves a range of positions from passive collaboration to coercive collusion to active resistance to Nazism. Whatever gradation of involvement is chosen, 'fascism' often reduces its neo-historical world to an exotic atrocity exhibition the reader or the audience can visit and leave behind in a form of ideological flânerie. At the heart of such an attitude are deeply contradictory desires: to 're-experience' fascism and yet to remain untouched by it.

A more literal form of flânerie and tourism has become possible since the fall of the Iron Curtain in 1989. Eastern Europe and its wartime historical legacies are accessible again.[21] Both Holocaust sites and Third Reich tours are increasingly popular 'optional' extras of itineraries in Central Europe: historic Krakow includes a visit to Auschwitz; Dresden 'comes with' Colditz Castle; a weekend in classical Weimar might allow for an afternoon at Buchenwald camp; Plötzensee Prison is part of the historic Berlin tour. Although it is a favoured location for 'fascism', Berlin in fact never supported the fascist movement in the manner of, say, Munich, but its urban topography is a singularly compressed landscape of momentous twentieth-century history: the setting for Weimar decadence, Speer's monumentalist architecture, spectacular wartime devastation, Cold War division and democratic change. Berlin has become a popular psychogeography of fascism. The relationship between politics and the map seems more direct: one can walk the course of the Wall, wander around the ruins of the Gestapo headquarters in Wilhelmstraße, or trace the Cyrillic graffiti left by Soviet soldiers that still marks the staircase of the Reichstag. Small wonder that the Berlin tourist office markets the city's tangible historicity as one of its main attractions. Yet as its regular window displays of English-language fiction about Berlin demonstrate, this is a particularly British view of the capital as an ideological faultline: the tourists only see what they already know from the novels of Christopher Isherwood, John LeCarré and Philip Kerr, and more recently, Louise Welsh, Beatrice Colin or Ida Hattemer-Higgins. They encounter 'Berlin' rather than Berlin.

Crime writers like Philip Kerr even assume the position of historical tour guides in interviews, laying claim to the fictionalised terrain. In an interview Kerr elaborated on the attraction that Berlin has long held for him:

> I've been interested in Berlin ever since I was a student . . . I've been making visits there since 1988 when it was more exciting and very Le Carré because of the wall. Visiting the east and dodging the Stasi was always quite a thrill. And of course the state of Berlin even in 1988 was a living link with the fall of Berlin. The place was still a ruin and it was possible easily to imagine that the Red Army had just left. Berlin is so different today. I often stay at the Adlon which has a fine view of the Brandenburg Gate and it still seems hard to imagine that the whole area was one large mine field. (cited in Jones 2010)

Kerr's approach to cataclysmic history is that of the flâneur whose thrills are an entirely fictitious – and fictional – frisson with totalitarian ideology; one recalls here Richard Evans's notion of Nazism as 'dramatic' history. The interviews that comprise the special features for the DVD release of Singer's *Valkyrie* display a similarly touristic attitude masquerading as a search for authenticity or even historical sensitivity. There is a noticeable nostalgia here for a lost sentient topography that served as a vicarious experience of history (or what Henry James called 'the visitable past'). In fact, 'fascism' here seems refracted through Cold War spy fiction. The reality and pace of post-communist political change made the Cold War aesthetic obsolete overnight but it also resuscitated the conventional gothic tropes of the perilous European past that form the marketing clichés on DVD covers or jacket blurbs, alongside swastikas and gothic script. Guy Walters, author of four popular novels set during the Third Reich, summarised the formula with which such genre fiction (or film) operates:

> What readers expect from Third Reich fiction certainly is – they really do want to have the sense that they're there in the Third Reich. People love the idea of being in Berlin during the war. It's kind of 'that's where you wanna be'. They want to be able to see the big red Swastika flags hanging from these Albert Speer-designed buildings. They want all the pageantry. And they want to see Nazis. They wanna meet them, and I guess they want their Nazis to be from central casting: you've got your sort of trusty German corporal figure, who's a kind of likable chap and he's a bit of a victim of the Nazi regime. Then you've got maybe a junior SS officer, probably with the rank of Captain, who is a maniac, and loves killing people all the time. Because people *want* violence. They want gore, glamorous people committing – you know – hideous acts. And they also probably almost certainly want a prostitute with a heart of gold who sleeps with Nazis and is really sexy and looks a bit like Charlotte Rampling in *The Night Porter*. So I think you've got to touch all those bases. And once you've done that you should be down to the bank and cashing in your advance cheque. (Anderson 2011)

All those bases cover the already known of 'fascism': its cinematic familiarity, its stereotypical settings and split protagonists, its graphic violence and its eroticisation. What the reader 'wants' is what he has already seen or read before. *This* truly is a 'freeze-dried version of history' in Susan Sontag's words, not imposed from above by an autocratic regime but replicated ad infinitum by the desires of a predominantly British and American audience that continues to fill an experiential gap with a cultural fantasy. In this sense, 'fascism' is to history what hardcore pornography is to real sexual experience: something kinky to look at (but perhaps not try out oneself).

If the agents in LeCarré's spy fiction were the reader's Cold War contemporaries, the serial protagonists of neo-historical crime are the reader's 'living link' to the Third Reich:

> It is certainly, for my money, the most important historical event of the millennium, certainly since the reformation anyway . . . It's only 50, 60, 70 years [ago] – which is nothing in historical terms, nothing at all . . . [It is] a fantastically epochal moment in history which is just going on. That just sort of makes the whole thing have a greater resonance. (Kerr cited in Westervelt 2009)

What is more interesting here than Kerr's hyperbolical taxonomy of historical events is his lucrative insistence of the presence of that past: for his money, this will indeed be going on and on. 'Fascism' easily piggybacks on the moral imperatives of contemporary memorial discourses that insist on keeping the past near. Even the most arcane aspects of fascism (*A Guide to Third Reich Cutlery*) pass as occult historiography and allegedly contribute to keeping the memory of that era alive as 'a warning from history'. 'Fascism' makes very complex history readable by refracting ideology through narrative formulas (communism through spy fiction; fascism through noir) while reducing some of the crucial ambivalences and ambiguities that originally made these genres such apt critiques of the socio-political and economic climates to which they responded. It offers commodified, consumable history, what Jake Chapman called 'having your Nazi cake and eating it' and Tony Barta criticised as complacent historical voyeurism (1998: 144). It is what one might term Adlon fascism: a fine view, from a safe distance. To understand the prisms through which this view is currently constructed remains the task of this book.

Notes

1. Available at <http://www.catsthatlooklikehitler.com/cgi-bin/seigbest.pl> (last accessed 31 March 2011); kwadelupi, *Build Concentration Camp with Lego*, <http://www.youtube.com/watch?v=k8JiGc-QDoI&feature=related>; see also luvendraw who produced this as a seventh grade school project: *Lego Auschwitz*, <http://www.youtube.com/watch?v=TasoEf08UB0>; AlexnBasti, *The Final Solution: Lego Version*, <http://www.youtube.com/watch?v=4xZdIcGqkHw&feature=related> (all last accessed 31 March 2011).

2. Churchill 1941: 234. Similarly, the 'template' for the American response to the terrorist attacks on the Twin Towers in New York and the Pentagon in Washington DC on 11 September 2001 was the Japanese attack on Pearl Harbour: what followed was a declaration of war even if the enemy in this 'war on terror' was rather opaque.

3. For the problematics of a multi-ethnic country fighting a war against both Asian and European enemies see, for instance, Blum 1976, Dower 1986, Fox 1990 and more recently Takaki 2000.

4. For an illuminating discussion of different templates of historical fascists and their cultural impact (Eichmann versus Speer) see Torgovnik 2005: 45–71.

5. Challenged by a German TV journalist about whether the invasion of Iraq did not constitute a form of aggressive neo-imperialism, the National Security Adviser Condoleezza Rice responded with another analogy: the re-education of Germany in the postwar years validated the export of the American way of democracy: 'I think rather of what happened after World War II, when the United States . . . came back to Europe and helped to create a whole set of institutions . . . and to contribute to the creation of a new kind of Germany that became an anchor for a democratic Europe. We're now trying to do that, in a sense, in the Middle East, with Iraq and with the Palestinian state and with what we've done in Afghanistan'. Interview with ZDF, 31 July 2003. For a more extensive discussion of this fallacious analogy see Fay 2006.

6. Indeed the more comprehensive assessment of the Second World War in recent years could already be seen in, for instance, the journalism of Rebecca West, who noted many of these instances in her reportage on the Nuremberg Trials and postwar Germany, *Greenhouse with Cyclamens*.

7. *Gott im Himmel* (Heavens above! Good Lord!, literally: God in Heaven) is also a frequently cited phrase denoting Teutonic exasperation although one would struggle to hear it from the mouths of native speakers in the twentieth century.

8. For the problematics of cinematic treatments alone see for instance Kuhlbrodt 2006 and Fröhlich, Schneider and Visarius 2007.

9. Amongst the many publications on this topic, one might want to begin with Claudia Brunner and Uwe von Seltmann's *Schweigen die Täter, reden die Enkel* (2004); Norbert Lebert and Stephan Lebert, *Denn Du trägst meinen Namen* (2000); Christoph Meckel, *Suchbild: Über meinen Vater* (1983); Thomas Medicus, *In den Augen meines Großvaters* (2004); Dagmar Leupold, *Nach den Kriegen* (2004); Ulla Hahn, *Unscharfe Bilder* (2003); Ute Scheub, *Das falsche Leben* (2007).

10. For some of the sensitive issues involved see Paris 2000: 312–46. Neither Michael Bay's *Pearl Harbour* (2001) nor Jonathan Mostow's *U-571* (2001) adhered to the accuracies of wartime history but reshaped it to construct national heroes in a year of national emergency: the former altered military history to showcase US fighter pilots, the latter credited the Americans with the cracking of the German enigma code.

11. Sporting reportage can be a sounding board for international relations. In the British tabloid press any football encounter between England and the German team evokes military metaphors and national stereotypes; for the Germans the arch enemy on the pitch is Holland. Germany's victory over England in the 2010 world cup in South Africa carried connotations of the 1966 World Cup at Wembley. In 1966 the Germans disputed the second English goal as not having crossed the line – and went on to lose 2:4; in 2010 the English had their second goal disallowed despite clear video evidence that it had crossed the line – and went on to lose 1:4.

12. The Germans, too, produced historical crime novels in the 1990s, with serial detectives or private eyes that investigated regular crime in the volatile 1920s and 1930s, most notably Robert Hültner's Kajetan series.

13. Far-fetched as it may sound, the novelist also gave a speech at the Museum of Tolerance in Los Angeles in which he accused Bin Laden of having Hitler's mentality. For an analysis of this novel see Butter 2009: 131–41.

14. There are certainly plenty of recent films in which serviceable Cold War villains have been updated with rogue tyrants, suicide bombers, Muslim fundamentalists or drug traffickers from the Middle East or South America. The cinematic epic saw a revival, in which the enlightened forces of a US-accented antique civilisation fight against bearded, olive-skinned Persians, as in *300* (2007) or *Troy* (2004). A more veiled working through of US policy could be seen in the TV series *Rome*, which portrayed a decadent empire in its last throes. The survival of a highly evolved civilisation is also at stake in the TV series *Battlestar Galactica* (2004–7) as a result of genocidal war with an independently minded robot army that has a surprisingly human appearance. Both worked through the hubris of imperialist politics that depended on clear images of alterity (racial others, machines, aliens) but had to evolve to a more complex understanding of shared responsibilities and commonalities with all living forms. But they also suggested that we have to take responsibility for the conduct that creates the enemies we profess to fight.

15. Syberberg became a controversial figure after re-unification, notably after his essay collection *Vom Unglück und Glück der Kunst in Deutschland nach dem letzten Kriege* (1990) and a number of embarrassing public appearances in which he voiced reactionary opinions. See for instance Buruma 1990, and for a critique of Syberberg's politics as 'obscene' Santner 1992, Elsaesser (1981/2).

16. A recent British scandal suggests that neither context nor taste seem to have changed since then: in 2008 Max Mosley, son of the former leader of the British Union of Fascists Sir Oswald Mosley and president of the International Automobile Federation, sued the *News of the World* for damages after the paper had alleged that Mosley had hired five prostitutes to enact a 'Nazi sex orgy', one of whom had secretly filmed the rendezvous

and passed on the footage. Mosley's libel suit primarily revolved around the violation of privacy, but an important element of his case was the rebuttal that any aspect of the filmed scenario made unequivocal reference to Nazism but merely involved generic S&M conventions. See Ben Dowell, 'Max Mosley v *News of the World* timeline', 24 August 2008, available at <http://www.guardian.co.uk/media/2008/jul/24/privacy.newsoftheworld> (last accessed 30 January 2011); 'Mosley vs. News Group Newspapers', Royal Courts of Justice, 24 July 2008, case No: HQ08X01303, available at <http://news.bbc.co.uk/1/shared/bsp/hi/pdfs/24_07_08mosleyvnewsgroup. pdf> (last accessed 31 January 2011). 'Women deny Mosley Nazi theme', *BBC News*, 8 July 2008, available at <http://news.bbc.co.uk/1/hi/ uk/7495604.stm> (last accessed 29 January 2011).

17. Edmonds's *Ilsa* has become notorious for its sexploitation but remains a 'must-buy' for fans of so-called euro-sleaze, according to knowing amazon reviewers. The emphasis on the geographical origin of such material rather quaintly comes with the reassurance of English subtitles (as if the consumer of such films were interested in the nuances of the dialogue). See for instance <http://www.amazon.co.uk/Ilsa-She-Wolf-SS-DVD/dp/B000JMKA7M/ref =sr_1_1?s=dvd&ie=UTF8&qid=1296321372&sr=1–1> (last accessed 31 January 2011).

18. Overy 2012: 38. The controversy over both area bombing and its commemoration continues not just in historiography and philosophy but also on the letters pages and the online comments section triggered by such articles. See, for instance, Richard Gott's less nuanced article 'This flurry of memorials discourages deeper analysis of the war' in the *Guardian*, 21 June 2012, and the flurry of commentary this feature provoked. Both are available at <http://www.guardian.co.uk/commentisfree/2012/jun/21/ memorials-cost-of-war-bomber-command> (last accessed 7 October 2012). Similarly emotional are the responses to Rowan Moore's sceptical review of the aesthetics of the Bomber Command memorial as 'defiant and triumphant' in tone rather than 'offering some recognition of moral complexity, some regret, some invitation to reflection' along the lines of Maya Lin's reflective wall of names for the Vietnam memorial in Washington, DC. 'Bomber Command Memorial – Review', *Observer*, 24 June 2012, available at <http://www.guardian.co.uk/artanddesign/2012/jun/24/bomber-command-memorial-london-review?INTCMP=ILCNETTXT3487> (last accessed 7 October 2012).

19. 'US attends first Hiroshima bomb anniversary', *BBC News*, 6 August 2010, available at <http://www.bbc.co.uk/news/world-asia-pacific-10888571> (last accessed 6 August 2011).

20. Exhibition website is available at <http://www.icp.org/museum/exhibitions/ hiroshima-ground-zero-1945> (last accessed 6 August 2011). See Bird and Lifschultz 1998 and Barnett and Mariani 2011. See also Elizabeth Olson, 'Enola Gay Reassembled for Revised Museum Show', *New York Times*, 19 August 2003, p. 16, available at <http://www.nytimes.com/2003/08/19/ national/19MUSE.html> (last accessed 18 March 2011).

21. See for instance Max Egremont, *Forgotten Land: Journeys Among the Ghosts of East Prussia* (2011), James Charles Roy, *The Vanished Kingdom: Travels Through the History of Prussia* (1999), Martin Gilbert, *Holocaust*

Journey (1997), Eva Hoffman, *Exit into History: A Journey Through the New Eastern Europe* (1994), Tina Rosenberg, *The Haunted Land: Facing Europe's Ghosts After Communism* (1995), and Rory MacLean, *Stalin's Nose: Across the Face of Europe* (1993).

Chapter 1

Nazi Noir: Hardboiled Masculinity and Fascist Sensibility from Ambler and Greene to Philip Kerr

One of the hallmarks of both the classic hardboiled novel and film noir is the level of graphic violence meted out either to or by the detective. The body count in Hammett's *Red Harvest* (1929) is staggering; the torture scene in *The Glass Key* (1931) even suggests a certain masochistic propensity for voluptuous anguish in the detective. The fascination with, even admiration of, violent crime (and, concomitantly, the new type of crime fiction) worried a number of intellectuals in the 1940s.[1] For J.B. Priestley, hardboiled fiction was a foreign import about a 'particular America', 'a fungus world, of greed, of calculated violence and a cold sensuality' whose existence appalled him. Yet he conceded that such sensibility increasingly permeated contemporary fiction and film precisely because its aesthetics offered uncomfortable truths about modern urban life (1940: 75–6). Both George Orwell and Bertolt Brecht saw the popular turn to crime and violence as a symptom of moral equivocation that helped to glorify the pursuit of power. They equated capitalism and fascism through the violence both generated and exploited. In Brecht's *Der aufhaltsame Aufstieg des Arturo Ui* (*The Resistible Rise of Arturo Ui*, 1941) Al Capone's mafia becomes the template for a gangster version of fascism. Taking the example of James Hadley Chase's *No Orchids for Miss Blandish* (1939), Orwell dismissed the genre as pornographic, vulgar pulp, penned in almost incomprehensible gangster argot.

Perhaps more interesting than the moral panic about literary values and mass culture is Orwell's concern that the popularity of hardboiled fiction indicated a fascist sensibility in the average reader.[2] The 'simple story' they were offered resembled 'a distilled version of the modern political scene': 'it is a daydream appropriate to a totalitarian age'. In suggesting that the genre offered an 'interconnexion between sadism, masochism, success-worship, power-worship, nationalism and totalitarianism', he offered an astute critique of how fascist aesthetics had permeated popular fiction ([1944] 1975: 78). For Orwell, then, hardboiled fiction had a certain nasty 'Naziness' even when it seemed to have absolutely nothing to do with Nazis, and it spoke of a certain transnational appetite for fascism repackaged as transatlantic crime. Bethany Ogdon has argued that early hardboiled fiction operated according to a core ideology alarmingly similar to that of popular *Freikorps* literature (precisely the corpus that formed the basis of Klaus Theweleit's study of fascist masculinity in *Male Fantasies*). Both privileged straight white men pitched against a range of threatening subalterns whose vile bodies provoke disgust and must be destroyed: foreigners, racial Others, homosexuals and women; in other words, the hardboiled detective and the early fascist shared a sensibility from the outset although they operated in different spheres (Ogdon 1992: 80).

The French surrealist Léo Malet was the first fiction writer to import the American hardboiled style into the European context of war. His *roman noir* series featuring the private eye Nestor Burma started in 1943 with *120, Rue de la Gare*. In these books Malet asked important questions about the nature of crime and criminality, pitching the brutish Nazi occupation against the questionable behaviour of his fellow citizens. In the early postwar years, the commercial success of hardboiled fiction and noir film in France and beyond seemed to capture a European sense of political and ethical dislocation that could even infect the Allies, as in Carol Reed's *The Third Man* (1949) or Jules Dassin's *Night and the City* (1950). The moral and psychological disorientation of the hardboiled hero and the erotic assertiveness of the *femme fatale* struck a nerve with existentialist views of the individual. For Jean-Paul Sartre, these characters were 'swamped, lost in too large a continent, as we were in history, and who tried, without traditions, with the means available, to render their stupor and forlornness in the midst of incomprehensible events' ([1947] 1966: 156). While noir and hardboiled aesthetics showed – more or less – common characteristics (alienated characters; eroticised violence; anarcho-leftist critique of bourgeois ideology; flashbacks and notions of discontinuity; an intermingling of social realism with oneiricism), for the European audience these seemed informed by a wartime sensibility. Some classic film noir plots also employed Nazi villains, such as Hitchcock's *Notorious* (1946) or Charles Vidor's *Gilda* (1946). At the very least the genre allowed for a transnational working through of psychologically dark aspects of the European war (occupation, collaboration and betrayal) even if, or particularly when, the story had little to do with the recent violent past.

From the very beginning, fascist sensibilities have been refracted through transnational modes of reading crime and crime writing. Brecht and Orwell's Marxist readings of American crime indicated similarities in capitalist and fascist modes of thinking that tapped into readers' reprehensible fantasies. Malet and his compatriots, on the other hand, worked through their own country's complex situation, by exploiting the moral erosion that was already part of the hardboiled template. It is perhaps more puzzling why, decades after fascism has been vanquished, this transnational negotiation was resuscitated by the contemporary Scottish crime writer Philip Kerr who merged historical fiction and hardboiled style for dramatising and exoticising fascist Germany. Kerr's publisher Penguin was quick to market his first three crime novels as the *Berlin Noir* trilogy: *March Violets* (1989), *The Pale Criminal* (1990) and *A German Requiem* (1991). Rather than indulge in fantasies of men in Nazi uniforms, Kerr's imagination produced 'a weather-beaten man in a crumpled overcoat' – the serial PI Bernie Gunther (Kerr 1992: 487). Skipping the war years, the novels were set in 1936, 1938 and 1947 respectively, and their aesthetics fused a hardboiled literary style with the atmosphere of noir cinema into metaphysical detective stories overtly conscious of their literary and cinematic heritage. Kerr's hybrid formula was commercially so successful that he revived the series in 2007. By that time Alan Furst, Robert Wilson, Jonathan Rabb, Robert J. Janes and David Downing had extended and further established the subgenre of historical noir set in the 1930s or in the war years, and their books were also marketed with chiaroscuro covers. Crime fiction set in the Weimar Republic, in Nazi Germany or Nazi-occupied Europe seemed to plug the gap left by the suddenly outdated Cold War spy thriller. In the uncertain post-communist era Nazi noir offered a nostalgic return to the old certainties of historically well-documented fascist evil.

If, according to Orwell, the contemporaneous British reader was receptive to fascist tales clad in the guise of hyper-violent crime novels, we might want to ask why the contemporary reader should still be susceptible to such an aesthetic. How should one read this retro style? Is it the symptom of a postmodern exhaustion with historicity, 'an alarming and pathological symptom of a society that has become incapable of dealing with time and history', as Fredric Jameson argued (1983: 117)? Or, as I am more inclined to argue, is it a retroactive fantasy in which historicity and genre function as a double disavowal, similar to the manner in which a member of an WW2 re-enactment society proclaims historical interest before he orders his replica SS uniform from eBay? Are such books as Kerr's *Berlin Noir* trilogy and their never-ending sequels not really expressions of a fascist sensibility that uses genre as way of 'having your Nazi cake and eating it'? Had *Berlin Noir* not better be called Nazi noir? In this chapter I want to examine the cultural function of Nazi noir for its predominantly male audience: what does this genre reveal about the Anglo-American relationship to the German history it purports to illustrate? What kind of (contemporary) fantasies does Nazi noir dramatise about the common man in a totalitarian regime? How does Kerr construct the masculinity of his protagonist against the fascist Aryan on the one hand and fascism's subalterns on the other? Perhaps most importantly, since the first-person perspective of the novels invites us to share and inhabit the protagonist's position, what moral compass does this assign the reader in a genre in which the boundaries between perpetrators, victims and bystanders are habitually blurred? Exploring the affinities between early hardboiled fiction (particularly the British pre-war thrillers of Graham Greene and Eric Ambler) and contemporary historical Nazi noir such as Kerr's novels will point us to the problematics of using this style for the articulation of a fascist sensibility.

Hardboiled style and ordinary masculinity

Early twentieth-century hardboiled fiction has been read as a modern version of a national heroic myth, translated into an urban setting (Porter 1981: 172; 179). In the USA, the hunter, scout or frontiersman became the lonely private eye who, when paid handsomely, descended from his shabby office to prowl the mean streets of a corrupt or depression-ridden city. Armed with a gun, physical endurance and ostentatious similes, the tough guy had a singular capacity for independence. Yet while he remained on the margins – of wealth and power, domesticity, romance and the law – he was also always implicated in the very corruption of the society and the institutions he investigated with such irreverent detachment. At best he could expose the criminality of the society in which he operated and which forced him to resort to equally criminal means to survive. In hardboiled fiction, crime is not a unique disruption of the bourgeois order which the amateur detective (as opposed to the professional police inspector) can restore; it is a mode of living. However, this verdict is not unique to this genre but also present in narratives whose vision of contemporary society, whether continental, British or American, is on the bleaker side. Alfred Döblin, in his afterword to *Berlin Alexanderplatz*, commented on the world the novel depicted as 'von Kriminalität unterwühlt': a society hollowed out by criminality ([1932] 1961: 527). In Joseph Conrad's bleak view, 'crime is a necessary condition for all types of organisations. Society is essentially criminal – or it would not exist' (cited in Naremore 2008: 46). Small wonder, then, that the foundational texts for literary noir – *Heart of Darkness* (1900), *The Secret Agent* (1907), T.S. Eliot's *The*

Waste Land (1922) – see the world as underworld. This mood is also refracted through the political thrillers of the 1930s, notably the work of Eric Ambler and Graham Greene, who both self-consciously respond to earlier modes of adventure fiction and the classic detective story. More importantly, they habitually cast their ordinary male protagonists into the maelstrom of history as a testing ground for their integrity and their masculinity. But what does 'ordinary' mean at a time when masculinity is also redefined ideologically through fascism and communism?

Ordinary men are crucial for hardboiled fiction and noir since they are social mirrors for their intended audience, other ordinary men. As Jerome de Groot has argued, male genre fiction constructs masculinity through a quintessential potential for action and agency (war, adventure, crime, espionage), however curtailed by class, circumstance or community (2010: 79). The ordinariness of the protagonist allows for greater identification and achieves a certain degree of realism. Writers such as Hammett and Spillane often had a series of odd jobs before they became successful, and the narratives themselves are populated with insurance clerks, petrol station attendants, travelling salesmen, even barbers. The detective too (who sometimes works for an insurance agency) is supposedly ordinary. Quite where we position this collective ordinariness on the spectrum of masculinity and morality is what Raymond Chandler struggled with in his essay 'The Simple Art of Murder' (1944), in which he offered the well-known definition of the hardboiled detective and his world:

> It is not a fragrant world, but it is the world you live in . . . Down these mean streets a man must go who is not himself mean, who is neither tarnished nor afraid. The detective in this kind of story must be such a man. He is the hero; he is everything. He must be a complete man and a common man and yet an unusual man. He must be, to use a rather weathered phrase, a man of honor – by instinct, by inevitability, without thought of it, and certainly without saying it. He must be the best man in his world and a good enough man for any world. ([1950] 1988: 18)

Both 'common' and 'unusual', this 'hero' lives in a thoroughly unheroic world, but one which he claims to share with a presumably more innocent reader for whom he serves as a prism. In many ways this passage seeks to negotiate what such an unfragrant world does to 'a man of honor'; what precisely does it mean to be 'good enough'? Gill Plain has argued that Chandler's detective does not so much embody 'the best man' but is perennially engaged in a quest to find that man, which accounts for the homoerotic subtext of so many hardboiled plots (2001: 65). As we shall see, Kerr's Bernie Gunther is a more literal interpretation of Chandler's definition of the hardboiled investigator whose moral equivocation is self-consciously manipulated to enable (male) reader identification.

In his essay 'Raffles and Miss Blandish', published in the same year, George Orwell offered a scathing critique of hardboiled fiction and its pernicious effect on the reader's moral compass. His common man was unwilling to be politically engaged: 'the average man is not directly interested in politics, and when he reads, he wants the current struggles of the world to be translated into a simple story about individuals' ([1944] 1975: 78). This comment located the popular success of the genre in its *translation* of the political climate into 'a simple story'. For politics to be relevant they had to affect the individual, and it was the narrative's task to demonstrate this. This strategy was not just a feature of tough crime fiction. Average in the sense of 'mediocre' or 'prosaic' was how Lukács had read Scott's heroes in his groundbreaking study *The Historical Novel* (1936). A 'living embodiment to historico-social types', Scott's average man appealed to a middle-class readership precisely because he became an identificatory template and served as a mediator between extremes (of passion or political intention) while steering clear of those extremes himself ([1936] 1969: 32, 24, 36–8). For Lukács this type of hero perfectly illustrated a national moment of crisis (civil unrest, revolution, war) because the hero represented a middle way of compromise or negotiation while the historical dramatis personae carried the weight of a political or cultural Zeitgeist in essence.[3] The reader was ideologically closer to the prosaic protagonist than to those at the extremes of power and passion. Combining the historical novel and hardboiled fiction, then, is precisely the hybrid formula of Nazi noir which promises the reader first-person access to an ordinary man in a time of ideological, national and international crisis. It also means that this protagonist's masculinity must also be situated between the extremes of power and powerlessness, fascist agency on the one side and on the other the disempowerment and persecution of fascism's victims.

However, the positioning of the 'ordinary man' between the hypermasculine Nazis and the disempowered fascist subaltern raises questions of masculine agency and individual culpability. In her study *Forever England* (1991), Alison Light identified a crucial recalibration of English masculinity after the First World War, which suggested a reorientation towards the more domestic and introverted. According to the historian Sonya Rose, by the outbreak of war in 1939, this conservative version of middle-class hegemonic masculinity had to be rearticulated as a form of temperate masculinity deliberately set against effeminate pacifism on the one hand and violent fascist hypermasculinity on the other (2004:

151–97). However, as I have argued elsewhere, in the 1930s fascist masculinity was also often admired as a powerful counterconstruct to the perception of an economically and physically decrepit Britain (Rau 2009a: 149–83). Fascists got things done, even if their means weren't always legal or their aims laudable. Paramilitary violence and criminality seemed preferable to inaction or disorder, and was increasingly seen as an expression of regenerative masculinity; fascists were virile, and had muscular, hard bodies to prove it.

The popularity of the *roman policier americain* with French existentialists like Albert Camus lay in the fact that this genre represented a departure from, even a reversal of, modernist interiority: American tough guy realism treated 'the supposedly average man studied from the pathological point of view'; unlike Proust's Swann, these heroes were 'men without memory' reduced to 'the life of the body' in an 'abstract and gratuitous universe' (Camus [1951] 2006: 230–1). The first-person perspective of these novels offered such reification as interior life: the manner of the hero's observations as well as his actions *were* his inner life (Knight 1980: 148). Such fast-paced, plot-driven action also departed from the pattern of classic crime fiction. Its extraordinary and extraordinarily eccentric detectives (Sherlock Holmes, Lord Peter Wimsey, Hercule Poirot) were a class above 'the common man' and 'the average reader'. Such cerebral activity, however, often came at the expense of virility: none of these classic detectives are what a character in Greene's *A Gun for Sale* would have called 'he-men' ([1936] 2009: 38). Chandler's 'complete' common man must be a man *capable of* phallic action, whether this be violence or sex. Yet his actions and wisecracks are a way of *negotiating* (rather than re-ordering) a morally equivocal world (Christianson 1989). In the final instance his violent agency has to be curbed to distinguish him from the proper gangsters through romantic (rather than sexual) failure, through subordination under a more powerful (father) figure, such as the Old Man in Hammett's Continental Op narratives, or through the revelation of the original mission as a dead end. The hardboiled detective and the noir 'hero' thus regularly inhabit a liminal position of *curtailed* male agency. Such male genre fiction of the 1930s, then, seems to be much more about the *search* for a tenable masculine position for the hero in a society in which gender and ideology are already linked, rather than a formulation of masculinity itself.

'There's always been a war for me': the ugly world of Ambler and Greene

The British pre-war thriller offered as bleak a vision of contemporary society and the interplay between capitalism and (international) politics, crime and social environment as could be found in the more localised versions of Hammett's 'Poisonville' or in Chandler's Los Angeles. As Graham Greene commented about the moral climate of the 1930s, 'the hunger marchers were more real than the politicians' ([1980] 1999: 69). An often self-conscious genre that deliberately set itself against its predecessors (Snyder 2009), the pre-war thriller often showed the characteristics of the metaphysical detective story, a term coined by Howard Haycroft in 1941. The sleuth – both amateur and professional – habitually failed; individuals went missing without being missed; identities were lost, stolen or exchanged but never fixed; clues were ubiquitous but meaningless or turned out to be red herrings (Merivale and Sweeney 1998: 18). The protagonists, often naïfs or hapless bystanders, were drawn into complicated plots they never fully understood. The high level of dramatic irony conveyed a sense of a world that had become unknowable and unreadable.

Ambler's impenetrable universe is often reduced to the continent, where war and shifting geopolitical boundaries created political instability and dislocated identities, as in *Epitaph for A Spy* (1938) where as a result of the Versailles Treaty (rather than their own wishes) characters change nationality or become stateless. Europe is full of deracinated others, and patriotism seems not just quaintly outdated (as it did to Greene) but gets in the way of survival. In *Uncommon Danger* (1937), the journalist Kenton hopes to earn quick money with a one-off courier service across the German-Austrian border, but this job opportunity soon sets Rumanian fascists and Soviet spies on his heels. Pursued by Austrian police for a murder he did not commit, Kenton is helped across the Czech border by a fellow Englishman, the continental sales rep Mr Hodgkin. After fifteen years of continental food, continental hotels and continental competition, Mr Hodgkin justifies his qualified empathy with a man whom he believes to be a cold-blooded murderer with a dyspeptic rant about the essence of continental otherness:

> They say the British are all stuck up about foreigners, that we're all men and women just the same, that they've got a lot of good points that we haven't. It's all lies, and when you've been away from home as long as I have, you'll know it, too. They're not like us, not at all. People come over here for a fortnight's holiday and see a lot of pretty *châlets* and *châteaux* and *Schlösser* and say what a fine place it is to live in. They don't know what they're talking

about. They don't see the real differences. They don't see behind the scenes. They don't see them when their blood's up. I've seen them all right. I was in sunny Italy when the Fascisti went for the freemasons in twenty-five. Florence it was. Night after night of it with shooting and beating and screams, till you felt like vomiting. I was in Vienna in thirty-four when they turned the guns on the municipal flats with the women and children inside them. A lot of the men they strung up afterwards had to be lifted on to the gallows because of their wounds. I saw the Paris riots with the *garde mobile* shooting down the crowd like flies and everyone howling '*mort aux vaches*' like lunatics. I saw the Nazis in Frankfurt kick a man to death in his front garden . . . In Spain, they tell me, they doused men with petrol and set light to them . . . They don't talk the same language as us. I don't mean that they don't speak English, but that their minds are different. They're like animals. (Ambler [1937] 1960: 137–8)

For Hodgkin fascism is less an ideology than an expression of continental collective character, a manifestation of violence slumbering beneath the veneer of a civilised and cultured exterior. Fascism is always latent 'behind the scenes'. English men and women don't respond to conflict with the same passion and brutality; their blood, in other words, is never 'up'. Unless they are in a desperate situation that leaves no alternative – as in *Journey into Fear* (1940) – the British do not resort to violence. Ambler makes clear, however, that his Little Englander Hodgkin is out of touch with the reality of Little England which is not immune from such continental menace. 'Behind the scenes' in Britain are those who turn a blind eye to politics in order to further Big Business or, worse, manufacture political conflict to sell arms. In *Uncommon Danger* and in Graham Greene's *A Gun for Sale* (1936), the powers behind such sinister plots are business magnates of vaguely 'Eastern' origin: naturalised Armenians, Greeks, Jews, Turks, 'gypsies'. British industry is already in the hands of foreign interests, or at least part of an international cartel of criminal capitalists. The Marxist conflation of crime, fascism and capitalism is characteristic of its time, and has a particularly xenophobic inflection in these books, but it also speaks of an imperialist nostalgia for a time when Great Britain was important, a global force as well as a global economic powerhouse. Such plotlines are indicative of a sense of anxiety about the continent as well as Britain's place and purpose in the world.

Perhaps equally interesting is the fact that the most brutal characters in these thrillers are the products of British educational bodies and their institutionalised violence. Ambler's truncheon-wielding thug in *Uncommon Danger* is the public-school educated Captain Mailler, whose subsequent career involved the Black-and-Tans, professional strikebreaking in America, and racist murder. One is reminded here of

W.H. Auden's essay 'The Liberal Fascist' (1934) in which he likened the very institution traditionally held to shape and epitomise British virtues to the 'Fascist State' ([1934] 1977: 325). For Ambler, the Maillers of this world are a throwback to 'the stupid, fumbling, brutish forces of the primeval swamp' ([1937] 1960: 75). Greene offers us a similar character in *A Gun for Sale* – the sexually timid, mediocre medical student Buddy Fergusson, who graduated from 'one of the obscurer public schools' ([1936] 2009: 145). Fergusson is keen to be 'a leader of men' (175) and can't wait for war to give him an opportunity for 'action'. He uses a mock air raid as cover for a lawless 'rag', a bullying campaign against a fellow student.

A Gun for Sale is Greene's most savage indictment of pre-war Britain, more caustic than *It's a Battlefield* (1934) and more sweeping in its social panorama than *Brighton Rock* (1938). This is as close to noir as the British pre-war thriller would come, seething with violence. Like Conrad's *The Secret Agent*, Greene's novel presents the capital as a landscape of seedy rented lodgings, porn shops masquerading as tobacconists, basement gambling rooms and backstreet abortionists: the rot sits deep. Its array of grotesque physiques acts as a metaphor for a deformed society in which corruption permeates all institutions. The hare-lipped assassin Raven is a singularly dark and ruthless character, yet Greene makes his villain entirely the product of this 'ugly' world – a word that is repeated throughout the novel and refracted countlessly in Greene's portrayal of so-called respectable people's lives who think of Raven as 'a wild animal' or as a social 'waste product' ([1936] 2009: 128, 106). Raven is of course a symptom of this ugly world, its most violent manifestation.

In the novel's key scene the professional assassin is under siege from pursuing police and spends the night hiding in a steel yard with Anne Cowder, a young woman he has entangled in his own pursuit of those who double-crossed him. In the course of the night he tells her about his past in a narrative that radically reinterprets the values and virtues of 'home' and 'education':

> 'Three minutes in bed or against a wall, and then a lifetime for the one that's born. Mother love,' he began to laugh, seeing quite clearly the kitchen table, the carving knife on the linoleum, the blood all over his mother's dress. He explained, 'You see I'm educated. In one of His Majesty's own homes. They call them that – homes. What do you think a home means? ... You are wrong. You think it means a husband in work, a nice gas cooker and a double-bed, carpet slippers and cradles and the rest. That's not a home. A home's solitary confinement for a kid that's caught talking in the chapel and the birch for almost anything you do. Bread and water. A sergeant knocking you around if you try to lark a bit. That's a home. ([1936] 2009: 117–18)

Greene is as sceptical as Ambler about the values of British education in the guise of institutionalised violence, whether it serves the top echelons or the bottom tier. Raven's embittered deconstruction of domesticity is only one in a series of revaluations of middle-class ideals and social institutions, from romantic love to loyalty; from policing to war. In an ugly society, someone with a facial disfigurement, raised on poverty and pain, has always been under siege, not just when he is surrounded by police for a crime he did not commit. That he was hired for an assassination in order to provoke a war is of little interest to him: 'There's always been a war for me' ([1936] 2009: 43; 125), he comments on Anne's sentimental sympathy for the civilian victims of conflict. Raven's world is smaller than the global network of Big Business and politics in which war means rising share prices. His war is a class war between rich and poor; his quest is for justice. The plot separates law and justice into (literally) different pursuits and thus suggests to the reader that they have little to do with each other.

The suspense of the novel revolves around whether the assassin or the detective can piece together the causal chain that links the assassinated Czech Minister of War and Sir Marcus the Nottwich industrialist, who ordered his death. Anne, the chorus girl bystander who is immediately turned into a 'moll' once associated with Raven, is the only one who manages to get an inkling of these international connections, but only after she has been through the ordeal of two abductions and two attempted murders. In Greene's world, men with agency remain in the fug of partial knowledge, not least because their masculinity is deeply compromised; for them, women are a symptom of their failure because they possess knowledge about this compromised masculinity. Raven knows countless tales of criminals whose downfall was caused by 'going soft on a skirt'. Fergusson, who has bragged about his erotic conquests to his fellow students, cannot even buy the local prostitute. The Chief Constable is a henpecked husband plagued by missing out on active war service. The middle-man Davis/Cholmondeley has to try to strangle his theatre girl who knows too much rather than take her to bed. The misogyny underlying these heterosexual relationships often assign women physical punishment for superior knowledge or agency. In fact, in *A Gun for Sale* and in *Brighton Rock* (1938), Greene suggests that men define masculinity through their capacity for violence. It becomes a substitute for erotic success with women; it may even be a symptom of their fear of women and their disgust with sex. Raven says, 'It takes a man to kill', while the would-be leader of men Fergusson 'strained for action', for 'complete freedom from control' ([1936] 2009: 114; 137; 136).

The masculinity of Greene's violent men, Raven in *A Gun for Sale* and Pinkie in *Brighton Rock*, contains a powerful paranoid streak: the outlaw of justice 'is pursued by the Others. The others have committed worse crimes and flourish. The world is full of Others who wear the masks of Success, or a Happy Family' (Greene [1980] 1999: 72). His villains can be read as fascist characters because their resentment is so strangely persistent and old-fashioned ('a morality which once belonged to another place'), and their grudge reminiscent of fascist self-justification ([1980] 1999: 72). But we also need to bear in mind that Greene distinguishes between criminals with fascist tendencies such as Pinkie and Raven who are fully contextualised with a coherent psychology and those Jewish criminal masterminds who are merely motivated by power and greed. In fact, as in Ambler's novels, the world of *A Gun for Sale*, from Nottwich to Czechoslovakia, is ruled by the likes of Sir Marcus and those in his pay as if it were some vast Jewish capitalist conspiracy. Arguably the reader's sympathy is steered towards the fascist assassin (who manages to kill the Jew) and is therefore brought periously close to a fascist worldview. The 'simple story' of these thrillers certainly personifies fascist threats but in contextualising them also provides a *rationale* for fascism to which the reader is encouraged to relate.

In her analysis of noir, Lee Horsley has argued that the pre-war British thriller often cast gangsters as fascist thugs who presented the protagonist with the unpalatable choice between passive victimisation or violent intervention that would abolish the very difference between them and their foe: 'The kind of division one sees here, between an essentially non-violent man . . . and the twisted, violent psychopath, was a crucial one for British thriller-writers of the late thirties and early forties . . . There was a deep-seated sense that violence and criminality were inherently un-British' (2001: 61). As we have seen, Greene certainly challenges the notion of the 'essentially non-violent' British man. *A Gun for Sale* is full of violent yet disempowered male characters who rage against the hegemonic order and who, given the opportunity, behave like fascists. Although the novel ends on the word 'home' we know that the policeman and his rescued wife-to-be are on borrowed time and that 'homey stuff' is anything but homely. As Raven says, 'This isn't a world I'd bring children into' (Greene [1936] 2009: 123; 117). Ambler's Mr Hodgkin may have been away from home for fifteen years but any reader of Greene could have told him that in the meantime the British social fabric seems to have become continental behind the scenes. Raven's brutality becomes more understandable with every chapter because it is merely the crudest manifestation of the violence inherent in and enabled by his socio-economic environment. The hired assassin is merely a more 'masculine' version of the would-be 'leader of men' who bullies colleagues and for whom a 'rag' is a welcome release from social niceties; of the Chief Constable whose defining war experience consisted in 'the fun it had all been giving hell to the conchies'; of the frail industrial magnate who orders men to be shot on sight; of the woman who is not averse to the retributive violence she finds so repulsive in the hired assassin: 'there are killings *and* killings' (Greene [1936] 2009: 101; 117). This is an ugly world, an unfragrant world, a proto-noir world, but it is the fascist world you live in, Greene suggests. 'Behind the scenes', there are no 'real differences' between the 'animals' on the continent and the home-grown 'wild animals', but perhaps the veneer of civilised behaviour is a little less brittle at home. For Greene, 'the war' would be a logical culmination of a society simmering with violence in all its strata.

Importantly, such articulation of violence as virility also commands male admiration and female attention. Anne concedes, 'I like he-men' ([1936] 2009: 38) as she is abducted by Raven. The plot appears to position woman between two types of masculinity (one erotic and violent, one temperate and domestic) yet they actually turn out to be two different expressions of fascistoid temperaments. True enough, in *Uncommon Danger* Kenton has to let the villain go rather than shoot him: 'The Anglo-Saxon sense of humour . . . is one of the most emasculating influences known to mankind.' Sense of humour here stands for moral superiority, 'character' and for a determination to rise above the 'brutish forces of the primeval swamp' (Ambler [1937] 1960: 220; 75), but this comes at the expense of virility and masculinity. The decent police inspector Mather in *A Gun for Sale* cannot be allowed to kill either. Even in the final shootout his hands can't find a gun. If Greene's and Ambler's detectives are unheroically immobilised, their emasculation captures the political paralysis of the 1930s, but this should not detract from the finer points of their characterisations which identify the society these protagonists defend as producing fascist worldviews. As Bethany Ogdon has argued, 'The hardboiled detective describes a world in which he is the sole "normal" person; he describes a world in which he is constantly under siege' (1992: 76–7). Camus, we remember, described this position as 'pathological'. Greene's detective Mather deserves just as much attention as his mythologised villains because he too is cast as a typically average man and he too is under siege from a world given over to crime. Even for Anne his ordinariness is indicative of a politically disengaged, compartmentalising mentality:

war might be declared before they met again. He would go to it; he always did what other people did, she told herself with irritation, although she knew it was his reliability she loved. She wouldn't have loved him if he'd been eccentric, had his own opinion about things ... She wanted her man to be ordinary, she wanted to be able to know what he'd say next. (Greene [1936] 2009: 20)

Mather's predictability may be an insurance policy for matrimonial quietude (as opposed to the He-Man fantasy Raven briefly fulfils) but his conformity and his lack of critical thinking suggest the mentality of a sleepwalker (the soubriquet Hitler gave the German people). Mather, whose investigative skill consists in repeating to himself phrases that might have seeped out of detective fiction as if they were some magic formula, is a police officer because he needs a concrete sense of purpose:

> he was part of an organization. He did not want to be a leader, he did not even wish to give himself up to some god-sent fanatic or leader, he liked to feel that he was one of thousands more or less equal working for a concrete end – not equality of opportunity, not government by the people or by the richest or by the best, but simply to do away with crime which meant uncertainty. He liked to be certain, to feel that one day quite inevitably he would marry Anne Crowder. (Greene [1936] 2009: 34)

Mather's purely abstract goal – 'to do away with crime' – is reminiscent of the incompetent police officers in classic detective fiction (Conan Doyle's Lestrade and Christie's Japp), who always mismatch signifier and signified. This curious passage of free indirect discourse is rather vague. Mather appears to reject totalitarianism only to rephrase his need for a collective purpose as leading to a domestic, private goal. In fact, his reasoning attempts to depoliticise the police as agents of the hegemonic order (of which the Chief Constable in the novel leaves no doubt). Crime disrupts a conventional bourgeois order merely as an invasion of privacy; with this thinking, Mather really belongs in the classic clue-puzzle detective story. Like Ambler's Hodgkin, he fulfils the role of the Little Englander out of touch with the country whose outdated values he defends. We need to read 'certainty' here not as merely encapsulating the domestic happiness of a petit bourgeois couple, but as a desire for the status quo of the politically disinterested private individual, the insular Briton for whom anti-Semitism is a matter of foreign domestic politics; for whom Czechoslovakia is as remote as the Belgian Congo and as incomprehensible. We may be tempted here to read *A Gun for Sale* as a novel about the impossibility of privacy in a time of political crisis; about the naiveté of believing that 'neutrality' and inaction are not a political acts; about conformity as the kind of wilful blindness that *enables* totalitarianism. *A Gun for Sale* is as much about the folly of appeasement as it is about holding up the mirror to a society that is not that dissimilar to what it professes to see looming across the Channel. Like the later cinematic version of noir across the Atlantic, the 1930s British thriller is therefore clearly an avenue of social and political expression in which Britain can see its violence simultaneously unmasked and submerged.[4]

It takes a while before the policeman can become a credible protagonist in crime fiction or in any fiction, for that matter. In the early hardboiled thrillers of Hammett and Chandler, the police are often presented as part of the problem of endemic capitalist corruption. The private investigator, on the margins of that shady society, represents an omnicompetence suitable for an economically tough climate. He is as resourceful as the pioneer. In British fiction, policemen are too ordinary, that is: lower-middle-class professionals (Knight 1980: 156). In both cases though, the police are an integral part of the dominant ideology. For historical Nazi noir, the policeman protagonist offers a particularly piquant position.[5] He operates in a regime that has redefined crime along ideological lines, but even those lines constantly shift as the police force is integrated into the SS. How then does Nazi noir negotiate the notion of ordinariness, when the protagonist cannot be a hypermasculine Nazi gangster nor a disempowered victim but must constitute a credible figure with whom the male reader can empathise and who embodies the compromised integrity of the average citizen in a totalitarian regime: how to create a common man, a man of honour, untarnished by his environment, in Nazi Germany?

Grey ideas: Philip Kerr's exculpatory strategies

Philip Kerr's protagonist Bernie Gunther is a deeply problematic investigator. The eight novels of this series stretch from 1932 to 1954,[6] and those parts set in 1930s Berlin focus on Gunther's career inside *Kripo* (*Kriminalpolizei*, the department dealing with ordinary and capital crime), his time as an in-house detective in Berlin's finest Adlon Hotel, and as a private eye. Over the course of the series, Kerr struggles to maintain Gunther's 'ordinariness', not least because historical research about 'ordinary men' delivers alarming conclusions about the average man's propensity to kill. In *March Violets*, Gunther works as a private detective investigating a jewellery theft. In *The Pale Criminal* he is redrafted into *Kripo* to help solve a case of gruesome serial murders of teenage girls. In *A German Requiem*, the PI finds himself in a bleak early Cold War Central Europe where Nazi war criminals construct new identities while Soviet and US occupation forces spy on each other to increase political influence in Europe and scour for Nazi scientists for their own armaments projects. So while we start out with a protagonist who appears to have opted out of an organisation in cahoots with the regime, Kerr makes it clear on the very first pages that Gunther has much in common with other 'March violets' (opportunists who joined the party late to further their career or gain advantages): the 'best man' in this ugly world makes a living from looking for those the regime 'disappears'. His promptly paying customers are Jews inquiring after missing persons who usually surface as corpses in Berlin's *Landwehrkanal* or as inmates in concentration camps.

The Pale Criminal is perhaps Kerr's most self-conscious attempt at the metaphysical detective story since he constructs his PI as an Chandleresque everyman:

> I'm no knight in shining armour. Just a weather-beaten man in a crumpled overcoat on a street corner with only a grey idea of something you might as well go ahead and call Morality. Sure, I'm none too scrupulous about the things that might benefit my pocket, and I could no more inspire a bunch of young thugs to do good works than I could stand up and sing a solo in the church choir. But of one thing I was sure. I was through with looking at my fingernails when there were thieves in the store. (1992: 487)

'A grey idea' is as good as it gets for justice and the law in this shady Nazi universe. This self-reflective comment of mixed metaphors precedes Gunther's reckoning with the criminal gang in the novel, but it is perhaps the closest version of Chandler's 'common man', not just an admission that the 'world we live in' corrupts everyone, but that the potential for agency is really limited to exceptional moments; other than that looking the other way is the common option. So what does agency involve in this novel?

Gunther finds out that the serial killings of Aryan teenage girls are organised by a Dr Kindermann and their purpose is to make them look like ritual killings in order to provoke an anti-Semitic pogrom. This knowledge comes at a cost. In the course of the investigation Kindermann's gang deprives Gunther of heterosexual and homosocial objects of desire by accidentally killing his lover Inge with a drug overdose, and by stabbing his associate Bruno Stahlecker. With the evidence against Kindermann piling up, Gunther moves into the territory of Ambler and Greene. He executes Kindermann in a scene reminiscent of the confrontation with the villain in the forest in *Uncommon Danger*. While Ambler's protagonist was emasculated by Anglo-Saxon humour, Kerr's detective takes the law into his own hands. As in Greene's *A Gun for Sale*, law and justice are seen as different concerns. We recall Anne Crowder's equivocal statement, 'But there are killings *and* killings. . . .

I'd let you shoot [the political assassin] without raising a finger' (Greene [1936] 2009: 117). Kindermann's execution is one of those 'killings' about which the reader is not supposed to raise an eyebrow. However, this 'killing' is not merely made meaningless by the fact that the so-called '*Reichskristallnacht*' takes place regardless, albeit for different reasons. It also suggests that in order to beat the Nazis, or at least contain them, one has to resort to their methods of dispensing violent 'force' (Kerr 1992: 501).[7]

By 1947, the time of *A German Requiem*, executions of unarmed civilians in forests are reminiscent of the systematic war of extermination on the Eastern Front. As an SS-*Obersturmführer* Gunther becomes part of the *Einsatzgruppen* who in 1941 follow the frontline to murder Jewish civilians and 'partisans'. Kerr makes him a witness to, rather than an active participant in, mass executions in White Russia. Here too the protagonist is allowed agency, not by exceptionally resorting to fascist violence, but by avoiding it. The 'man of honour' requests a transfer to the *Wehrmacht* rather than risk being shot for refusing to obey orders (a convenient myth of *Befehlsnotstand* [duty to follow orders] not borne out by historical evidence, as we know from Christopher Browning's study of one such group, reserve police battalion 101; 2001: 170). What made ordinary men kill unarmed civilians on such a scale and with such compliance, according to Browning, was a complex nexus of psychosocial factors:

> Those within the hierarchy adopt the authority's perspective or 'definition of the situation' . . . The notions of 'loyalty, duty, discipline,' requiring competent performance in the eyes of authority, become moral imperatives overriding any identification with the victim. Normal individuals enter [what Stanley Milgram called] an 'agentic state' in which they are the instrument of another's will. In such a state they no longer feel personally responsible for the content of their actions but only for how well they perform. (2001: 173)

Browning draws on Stanley Milgram's *Obedience to Authority* (1974) which also informed Zygmunt Bauman's *Modernity and the Holocaust* (1989). The disturbing conclusions of these studies confirmed an earlier verdict by the eminent Holocaust historian Raul Hilberg that perpetrators 'were not different in their moral makeup from the rest of the population. The German perpetrator was not a special kind of German' (2003: 1084). Nor, according to Browning, were those 10 to 20 per cent who refused to participate in or continue with the killings, special Germans either. This is one instance where history makes it very difficult for Nazi noir to distinguish between 'killings *and* killings'. How 'ordinary' can Kerr allow Gunther to be before the reader becomes profoundly uncomfortable with the colluding first-person perspective that noir habitually assumes (Ogdon 1992: 84)? He can have all manner of grey ideas including the financial exploitation of persecuted Jews, but he can be allowed neither heroic opposition, as in Cartwright's *The Song Before It Is Sung* or Joseph Kanon's *The Good German* (2001), nor complete collusion as in Littell's *The Kindly Ones*. He must feel the full force of claustrophobic totalitarian oppression without being fully corrupted by it. Nazi noir offers the reader simulation without too much incrimination.

Throughout the series Gunther can enact the 'grey idea' as long as he kills Nazis or criminals. He can be a killer (as he is in the sixth novel which opens with the manslaughter of a police detective and concludes with the carefully planned assassination of a racketeer) but he must never be an 'ordinary' mass murderer. In fact he cannot even be allowed to be an ordinary soldier since *Berlin Noir* skips the war years and later books only flesh out those war experiences that show him as a Soviet prisoner of war. For Achim Saupe the narrative gaps that omit the height of Nazi extermination policy amount to a veritable exculpatory strategy (2009: 307). This constant adjustment of the moral framework between violent justice and brutal force, between the common man and the unusual individual, between oppositional agency and institutionalised brutality enacts on the level of plot and character the semantic shifts fascist usage imposed on common language, according to the Romanist Victor Klemperer (1970). Paradoxically, Gunther's killings are supposed to sustain his masculinity and underline his fundamental decency. But what does it mean to be a decent man in Nazi Germany? Decency, like the 'home' in Greene's novel, means different things for different people. Its most infamous definition was delivered by Heinrich Himmler in his address to senior SS officers in Posen (Poznan) on 4 October 1943:

> Most of you know what it means when one hundred corpses are lying side by side. Or five hundred. Or one thousand. To have stuck it out and at the same time – apart from some exceptions caused by human weakness – to have remained decent fellows, that is what has made us hard.[8]

Decency is not an adjective one expects in this context and yet it is used to suggest that ideologically motivated killing of unarmed civilians and criminal mass murder are not the same thing. It is one of those words (like education, home, certainty or loyalty) that fascism radically redefines. The fantasy of remaining untarnished follows precisely the fascist logic that there are 'killings *and* killings', one of which does not constitute an immoral act but is instead merely special treatment (*Sonderbehandlung*). Rather than offer Gunther the 'agentic state' that 'normal' individuals fall into, he must be given a level of agency that allows him an exit from such incriminating ordinariness.

Voluptuous anguish: sexual violence and the fascist subaltern

To remain 'ordinary' the detective must also reassure the reader of his heterosexual normativity and his *limited* agency. His is a temperate masculinity situated between the powerful, hypermasculine (and often historic) Nazis on the one side and the disgusting bodies of the fascist subaltern on the other: Jews, Sinti and Roma, homosexuals, communists, religiously motivated opponents, the disabled and the 'asocial'. From the outset, Gunther is a wounded man, who must remain a romantic, deprived of the 'certainty' of domestic bliss. A First World War veteran, he lost his first wife to the influenza epidemic. His second wife supplements the pantry with army rations earned through sexual favours to GIs but dies as a result of dubious medical experiments. Hardboiled fiction from Hammett to Spillane regularly makes woman 'the mystery beyond the capacity of the detective' (O'Brien 1997: 108). In Kerr's novels too, women characters are merely narrative functions rather than rounded characters, bodies with an (erotic) effect on the detective. Secretaries, prostitutes, or rape victims, many of them don't make the final page alive or walk out of the plot into someone else's arms. *March Violets* begins with such a romantic foreclosure when Gunther's capable secretary Dagmarr [sic] walks up the aisle with a fighter pilot, 'the epitome of the dashing young Aryan male' (1992: 4). Gunther puts on a brave face and a fine grey flannel suit for the wedding party, and quips at the uniformed groom: 'I'd have asked her to marry me, only I don't think I look as good as you in uniform . . . I guess we've all done well out of National Socialism, haven't we? Proper March Violets' (1992: 5–6). Erotic success, Gunther suggests to the groom, is not a result of some form of inherent dominant maleness but of the opportunistic, ideological packaging of masculinity as He-Man fantasy. Like Greene and Harris, Kerr sees the semiotics of power as a greater stimulant than male physique.

According to Jerome de Groot, conventional male genre fiction (including the historical novel) tends to offer relatively conservative, unreconstructed versions of masculinity (violent, heroic, rugged). Key to the reader's enjoyment is the protagonist's *possibility* of agency and self-expression as well as realistic detail (Groot 2010: 79–85). The commercial success of Nazi noir suggests that neither its limited male agency nor its scenes of spectatorial sexual violence are perceived as offensive, confused or problematical, but as part of the authentic fallacy historical fiction utilises, on the same level as say, meticulous descriptions of German car makes, transliterations of Berlin slang, details of uniforms and military ranks, or the urban topography of pre-war Berlin. As Jerome de Groot argues, the male demographic of such historical novels is conservative and demands serial and authorial brand coherence (2010: 81).[9] Guy Walters, another practitioner of Nazi noir, reassures us: 'the reader wants violence' as long as it is (literally) contained in a specific narrative structure and logic (Anderson 2011).

While the plot regularly exhibits Gunther's virility to reassure the reader of his heterosexuality (and often translates 'romance' into sexual attentiveness), it equally regularly rehearses his emasculation in scenes in which the protagonist is entirely deprived of agency or reduced to a passive witness of fascist violence. In *A Pale Criminal*, Gunther starts an affair with Hildegarde [sic], the stepmother of a murder victim.[10] At one stage in the affair, Hildegarde asks Gunther to roughen up his sexual technique. When he rejects this, she retorts 'If you were a man you'd rape me. But you haven't got it in you, have you' (1992: 486). The serial rapists loose on the streets of Berlin are of course fanatical Nazis, and the narrative cannot allow the protagonist to cross over into their territory in the bedroom. When, having solved the crime, he returns to Hildegarde's flat some weeks later, his place has been taken by a young SS major of hypermasculine Aryan type who opens the door:

> His tunic was unbuttoned, his tie was loose and it didn't look like he was there to sell copies of the SS magazine ... Perhaps he made a better job of slapping her around than I had, him being in the SS and all. Whatever the reason, they made a handsome-looking couple, which was the way they faced me off, Hildegard threading her arm eloquently through his.
> I nodded slowly ... and then handed her back the keys. (1992: 522–3)

The heavy-handed symbolism here of course suggests a moment in which the woman is formally exchanged between two men, and in this triangulation the less powerful man in a crumpled overcoat acquiesces *post factum* in this exchange by handing over the symbol of unrestricted access. In Greene's *A Gun for Sale*, the policeman Mather also conceded his girlfriend to the criminal. She was quickly demoted to a 'moll' as soon as she had been seen with Raven who merely abducted her. For Greene, women gravitate towards he-men, but in the political economy of Kerr's plots losing women is the price of retributive violence against fascists.

When Gunther executes Dr Kindermann, he has also 'earned' this retributive act of violence at the end of the novel by remaining stock-still behind a curtain while enduring 'the sound of two men engaged in a homosexual act', which leaves him 'feeling utterly nauseated' (1992: 470). Homosexual panic is as much a response to the protagonist's constantly frustrated desire for male friendship as it is a paranoid reassertion of heterosexual normativity. Since William Shirer's bestselling *The Rise and Fall of the Third Reich* the ostensible 'unnatural sexual inclinations' of fascists have become a cliché despite the well-known persecution of homosexuals under the Nazi regime (1962: 172). To kill in crime fiction is to encounter the other, as Gill Plain has argued (2001: 226). Yet in those moments of permitted violent transgression – of a kind of consensual perpetration – we seem to be entering a different territory altogether, that of fantasy in a historical setting (similar to Tarantino's guerrilla scalpists and Jewish avengers in *Inglourious Basterds*): to kill a homosexual Nazi rapist offers both an emotionally satisfying fantasy of retributive antifascist violence[11] and a simultaneous reassurance of the protagonist's sexual and moral (and political!) normality. This representational strategy grafts itself onto the relationship between sexual fantasy and political ideology that Laura Frost has identified as a legacy of modernist Germanophobic fantasies of fascism, in which what is politically prohibited is dramatised through forms of transgressive sexuality: 'Sexually deviant fascism secures sexual normativity and democracy' (2002: 159). The formula for emasculation and remasculation (or vice versa: virility and subsequent castration) in Kerr's noir series is 'you lose the girl – but you get to kill a Nazi'. In other words, the loss of sexual pleasure is *compensated with* a moment of legitimised fascist violence against fascists.

Emasculation in the face of violent fascist agency also often reduces the detective to a passive bystander, but the first-person perspective from which these scenes are described, I would argue, severely compromises both investigator and reader. This perspective frames the scenes in a different way from the first-person perpetrator viewpoint in Jonathan Littell's *The Kindly Ones* or the third-person fantasy or testimony in Ian McEwan's *Black Dogs*, discussed in the following two chapters. Ostensibly spectatorship is presented as a form of witnessing through which the fascist menace is exemplified, although the bystander position is by no means morally unequivocal and holds the potential for passive collusion or voyeurism. Such violence is supposedly sanctioned by the contiguity principle: because there is historic evidence of Nazis committing acts of callous brutality, one can reasonably invent similar acts to illustrate their evildoing. Through a scene of witnessing, invention can masquerade as testimony.

A scene in *March Violets* illustrates this point and is worth quoting in full. Gunther finds a set of missing jewels and a missing woman but a group of Nazi thugs get to her first:

'Franz. Where the fuck are you?' We heard a soft groan, and the slap of flesh against flesh. Then we saw them: an enormous figure of a man, his trousers round his ankles, bent over the silent and naked body of Hermann Six's daughter, tied face down over an upturned boat.

'Get away from her, you big ugly bastard,' yelled Red.

The man, who was the size of a luggage locker, made no move to obey the order, not even when it was repeated at greater volume and at closer range. Eyes shut, his shoe box of a head lying back on the parapet that was his shoulders, his enormous penis squeezing in and out of Grete Pfarr's anus almost convulsively, his knees bent like a man whose horse had escaped from underneath him, Franz stood his ground.

Red punched him hard on the side of the head. He might as well have been hitting a locomotive. The very next second he pulled out a gun and almost casually blew his man's brains out.

Franz dropped cross-legged to the ground, a collapsing chimney of a man, his head spiriting a smoke-plume of burgundy, his still erect penis leaning to one side like the mainmast of a ship that has crashed onto the rocks.

Red pushed the body to one side with the toe of his shoe as I started to untie Grete. Several times he glanced awkwardly at the stripes that had been cut deep into her buttocks and thighs with a short whip. Her skin was cold, and she smelt strongly of semen. There was no telling how many times she had been raped.

'Fuck, look at the state of her,' groaned Red, shaking his head. (1992: 215)[12]

The first-person plural here includes both male spectators in this over-determined, pornographic scenario which reads like a more explicit version of a script by James Hadley Chase or Mickey Spillane (note that guns and mainmasts function like the keys in *The Pale Criminal*). Perhaps more worryingly, the first-person perspective easily incorporates the reader who – again – loses the girl and gets to kill a Nazi. The way in which the perspective pans through the scene offers the reader three positions: that of the raping perpetrator Franz (whose fascist hypermasculinity apparently survives death); that of the voyeuristic impassive bystander Gunther; and that of the executioner Red whose equally phallic response services the fantasy of legitimised retributive violence. The violence meted out to thugs and Nazis is certainly a confrontation with 'the darkness that dwelt within me . . . that dwells within us all' (Kerr 2008: 286). We too only 'glance awkwardly' at the prostrate victim whose torturous position remains shameful, isolated, exploited. In her essay on Syberberg's *Hitler*, Susan Sontag argued that 'this exercise in the art of empathy produces a voluptuous anguish'

([1980] 1996: 164). Empathy with fascist victims is not really the point of such scenes; it is the vicarious pleasure of watching the exertion of and submission to unrestrained power. Witnessing, as we shall see in the next chapter, does not necessarily have the function of testimonial but can simply become an alibi for both the writer's and the reader's reprehensible pleasure in violence.

Scenes of torture or observed sexualised violence are *de rigeur* in representations of fascism, whether they are thrillers or literary fiction. How they are represented and what function they are made to fulfil, however, varies considerably. In Nazi noir sadism operates in a veritable free-range zone of sexual fantasy. David Downing's *Zoo Station* gives us genital mutilation and defenestration. Robert J. Janes's *Mayhem* delivers mutilated female partisans, and vile Gestapo agents indulging in pornographic surveillance and torture. Robert Wilson's *A Small Death in Lisbon* features anal rape, and beatings with wire. These scenarios dramatise, like the decoded grammar of fantasy in Freud's essay 'A Child is Being Beaten', a range of subject positions vis-à-vis a figure of absolute power and authority. The bystander position exists precisely to negotiate the problematics of male agency for the 'ordinary man' in a society in which that agency is associated with fascist supremacy. So while noir looks like 'macho stuff' (as Kerr refers to his Bernie Gunther series),[13] it actually offers us narratives of exculpatory emasculation.

It is one of the hallmarks of classic noir that the roles of the male protagonist shift between investigator, victim and transgressor. Postmodern historiographical metafiction challenges the master narratives of key moments in history (Kim 2005; Pearson and Singer 2009), and the hybrid genre of historical noir has the potential of appropriating the hardboiled formula in order to inhabit the position of the subaltern. Walter Mosley's Easy Rawlins novels, for instance, offer a critique of white supremacist society from the perspective of his African-American protagonist. However, Kerr's positioning of his hero vis-à-vis the fascist subaltern is highly disturbing. The woman raped in *March Violets* is a murderess, but she is also the daughter of a 'gypsy'. *The Pale Criminal* delivers forensic detail about sexual violation that is supposed to underline the brutality of the perpetrators but perhaps also suggests a gratuitous imagination (this is after all a novel in which the step-mothers of rape victims desire to be raped). *A German Requiem* presents an equally pornographic scene in which a Czech Jewess is stripped of her blouse and tortured with a corkscrew before she is murdered in a winepress.[14] Noir is of course well known for its 'foundational misogyny' and for the racism and homophobia that the first-person perspective invites and assumes the reader to share with the protagonist (Plain 2001: 221;

Ogdon 1992: 76–8). By the same token, since the 1970s sexual perversion has been an explicatory narrative for fascism on the basis of scant evidence. In Nazi noir questionable ideology is 'merely' part of the period detail without the slightest metafictional problematisation.

Equally worrying is Kerr's strategy of making his detective increasingly violent *and* increasingly Jewish over the series, accruing several Jewish lovers and a Jewish grandmother. In his analysis of the *Berlin Noir* trilogy, Brian Diemert has justifiably asked whether the noir formula can carry the burden of history when it comes to the Holocaust (2002: 347). In *March Violets*, Gunther is sent to Dachau as if the full force of fascism could only be experienced in a camp (obviously an experience most Germans did not have but feared); in *A German Requiem* he finds himself kneeling at the edge of a trench in the manner of the *Einsatzgruppen* victims. When Kerr continues the series fifteen years later he takes his protagonist through a disused gas chamber in a putatively fictitious extermination camp in the Argentine hinterland. Gunther's relativism towards fascism's subalterns runs like a refrain through *A Quiet Flame*: 'it wasn't that I liked queers. I just didn't dislike them as much as she did'. And 'it's not that I love Jews. It's that I love anti-Semites just a little bit less' (2008: 62; 181). While we should certainly not read the serial protagonist as the author's mouthpiece, we do need to bear in mind that the first-person perspective in hardboiled fiction, at least for the time of the reading process, constructs and depends on what Bethany Ogden has identified as 'a pre-existing colluding perspective'; anyone who has problems with Gunther's grey ideas or with Kerr's emplotment of his detective will find these books virtually unreadable (1992: 84). If racism, misogyny and homophobia are indeed part of being 'ordinary' in the historic setting of Nazi Germany (and, by a lesser degree, the 1930s British thriller), the attraction of these books is surely that such unpalatable qualities become historicised and relativised, and therefore excusable. And as Kerr keeps emphasising when challenged by female readers: he is not 'glamorising an almost Nazi', 'but I'm embarked if you like on a sort of greater mission which is that of understanding' (in Frostrup 2010). Reading Nazi noir offers the audience the possibility of inhabiting a fascist universe by sharing the perspective of a character who is ostensibly not a Nazi but so often so deeply compromised in his views and actions that the distinction between monstrous Nazism and ordinary fascism is hard to maintain. In the crumpled overcoat of Bernie Gunther every reader can be a little fascist without pleading guilty to that charge.

This liminal position of enforced collusion with the regime is the elect framework of the popular Anglo-American imagination vis-à-vis historical fascism. Nazi noir rejects the role of the true subaltern (the Polish emigrant, the blackmailed homosexual, the communist dissident, the persecuted Jew): those positions are too curtailed in agency to hold much noir potential: at best we are allowed 'an awkward glance' at the voluptuously portrayed anguish of these minority constituencies. If, according to Umberto Eco, the serial fictional character has the potential 'to acquire citizenship in the real world' (1994: 126), then the first-person perspective of the serial private eye might enable a narrative bridge between private, experienced history and collective public history (Lee 1990: 34–5). But in Nazi noir we are asked to identify with a deeply problematical bystander position in which spectacular violence can be vicariously experienced, and passivity or acquiescence in the face of fascist aggression is sanctioned as a form of temperate masculinity. While the British pre-war thriller at least problematised the potential for violence in 'ordinary men', contemporary Nazi noir historicises the passive bystander as 'the best man in his world and a good enough man for any world'. This is less a transnational mission to understand fascism than the fictional equivalent of a fascist re-enactment society. But can literary fiction avoid the theme-park treatment of 'experiencing' fascism?

Notes

1. The hardboiled genre's 'realism' undermined intellectuals' simplistic notions about popular culture's ability to offer, and the masses' capability to handle, a more differentiated view of contemporary living than the Manichean one. (The masses and the middle classes may of course have read thrillers precisely because they merely articulated more clearly what they had been familiar with all along, a world that was much more violent and brutal than middle-class mores and bourgeois aesthetics let on.) Christopher Caudwell and Alick West acknowledged that the thriller had the potential to critique bourgeois capitalism. For a detailed analysis of leftist responses to the thriller see Hopkins 2003.
2. The relationship between modernist aesthetics and the 1930s thriller still exercises critics. See, for instance, Chapter 1 of Diemert's *Graham Greene's Thrillers* (1996) and Lisa Fluet's 'Hit-Man Modernism' (2006).
3. In his notes on *Arturo Ui*, Brecht hinted at the political utility of 'average' ('*durchschnittlich*') men, who regularly find themselves in positions of power because they are both popular with the masses and biddable to the ruling classes; they merely create the impression of greatness through the size of their ambition (1973: 132).
4. Paula Rabinowitz makes a very similar argument for American film noir as a negotiation of mass culture and politics in *Black & White & Noir* (2002).
5. Journalists are also popular as professional and independent investigators (Frederick Forsyth's *The Odessa File*, Harris's *Fatherland*, David

Downing's Berlin stations series), not least because the author invests his former profession with such kudos.

6. Kerr continued the series in 2004 with *The One from the Other*, followed by *A Quiet Flame* (2008), *If the Dead Rise Not* (2009), *Field Grey* (2010), and *Prague Fatale* (2012). The end is not in sight.

7. In *Coming Up for Air* (1939) Orwell makes a very similar point about the use of violence being a common denominator between ostensibly very different ideologies. Ordinary man George Bowling attends an anti-fascist lecture at the Left Book Club but only takes in a blur of terms that become curiously synonymous: 'Democracy. . . . Fascism. . . . Democracy. . . . Fascism. . . . Democracy'. At times anti-fascist agitation ('hate, hate, hate') seemed to rest on the same fear of otherness as fascism (Orwell [1939] 1990: 153; 156).

8. 'Heinrich Himmler', Holocaust History Project, available at <http://www.holocaust-history.org/himmler-poznan/speech-text.shtml> (last accessed 17 July 2010). This site also features the full audio recording of this speech and transcriptions in German and English.

9. If online reviews of internet booksellers are anything to go by, the audience of Nazi noir indeed sticks with what they know and recognise, immersing themselves in the universe of Kerr, Downing and Furst.

10. The German spelling is Hildegard, often abbreviated to Hilde. Such anglicised spellings and names are part of a rather strange transliteralisation phenomenon in Kerr's novels that also includes versions of Berlin slang. These are meant to make the setting *feel* more authentically German for the English-language reader. Gunther's first name Bernhard, for instance, would usually be shortened to Bernd rather than Kerr's anglicised Bernie.

11. This is precisely the kind of logic that informs first-person shooter war games like *Medal of Honour* or *Call of Duty* in which excessive violence is sanctioned by the valour of saving Europe and shooting Nazi zombies.

12. Kerr won the *Literary Review*'s Bad Sex Award in 1995, for his science fiction novel *Gridiron*, an honour he shares with Jonathan Littell who won it in 2009 for a passage in *The Kindly Ones*. See <http://www.literaryreview.co.uk/badsex.html> (last accessed 18 July 2010). According to an interview he gave for the *Telegraph* on the occasion of his eighth Bernie Gunther novel, he started out writing with an 'erotic' novel, an homage to Lawrence, entitled *The Duchess and the Daisies*. Toby Clements interviewing Philip Kerr, *The Telegraph*, 23 January 2012, available at <http://www.telegraph.co.uk/culture/books/bookreviews/9025756/Philip-kerr-Interview.htm> (last accessed 4 August 2012). The dramatisation of fascism through outlandish or violent sex seems regularly to result in bad prose.

13. Interview with Mariella Frostrup (who can barely contain her sarcasm), 2010.

14. In *The Quiet Flame*, a young woman is found raped and shot by SA thugs. This is a minor plot event to demonstrate anti-communist violence in the final days of the Republic, but why comments about her shaved genitalia should underscore the point is anyone's guess. In the same volume Gunther and his lover Anna are apprehended by a filthy guard in a derelict warehouse where they are searching for classified documents. The guard forces

Anna to strip and tortures her breasts. The scene only seems to serve as a pretext for another retributive execution, meted out to an expendable character who comes through the door with a gun (Chandler's jocular recipe for flabby moments in the plot): 'The poor man had it coming, if you ask me' (Kerr 2008: 248). Later in the plot Gunther is bundled into a plane and forced to witness the manner in which the Argentine authorities dispose of subjects who know too much (one of them a naked woman). Showing his lover Noreen the body of a Jewish boxer who committed suicide by drinking lye reveals to Gunther his capacity for 'something like sadism' in *If the Dead Rise Not* (Kerr 2009: 197). Postwar Cuba offers a stream of disgusting objectified bodies that includes most of the women in Havana who all look like underage prostitutes; the theatre manager Garcia, whose bald head is compared to that of an ancient Egyptian looted 'from the gully of the slimy-looking satraps'; or the *faygele* Irving Goldstein, the fall guy who can't tell real women from female impersonators (2009: 295; 363; 418).

Chapter 2

The Fascist Corpus in the Age of Holocaust Remembrance: Robert Harris's *Fatherland* and Ian McEwan's *Black Dogs*

In January 2005, Prince Harry, Queen Elizabeth II's second grandson and third in line to the British throne, made headlines as he was photographed attending a friend's birthday party with the theme 'Colonials and Natives' dressed in the shirt of the German Afrika Corps, complete with swastika armband. If his judgment was spectacularly bad, his timing was even worse: two weeks before the 60th anniversary of the liberation of Auschwitz. 'Harry the Nazi' screamed the headline of the *Sun* the following day, the British Jewish community was stunned, and Clarence House swiftly issued a statement that the Prince apologised for any offence and embarrassment caused by his poor choice of costume.[1] What was perhaps most offensive to the British public in this minor royal incident was that this privileged and expensively educated twenty year old, on course for officer training at the elite military academy Sandhurst, showed so little respect for the national values he was expected to embody privately and publicly. The comments this photograph provoked raise a number of important issues about fascist semiotics, national character and the transnational uses of history. On the BBC news website, former armed forces minister Doug Henderson said the incident demonstrated that the prince was 'unfit to train as a British Army officer at Sandhurst'.[2] Arthur Edwards, royal photographer for the *Sun*, commented that veterans would be sickened to see 'the prince behaving like a drunken member of the Hitler Youth'. His remarks were printed alongside a short article that juxtaposed the party snapshot (in which Harry was seen a little the worse for wear, holding a beer and smoking a cigarette) with more dignified archive images of the Royals during the war.[3] And remarkably, the editor of the *Jewish Chronicle* Ned Temko 'misspoke' when venting his anger: 'a swastika armband isn't just a fashion item'. The adverb 'just' in this sentence would really require some explanation since it suggests that swastikas once were, or could now be reduced to, lifestyle symbols as if one could simply separate ideology from its aesthetics: 'luvv the uniform, hate the politics'.[4]

In all of these statements the judgment of inappropriate conduct is founded on assumptions about 'correct' uses of the past, or rather a representation of German history and Nazi semiotics as essentially other from British history and British values. Even the members of Axis re-enactment society insist that they are merely interested in the uniforms and equipment of ordinary German soldiers and will not tolerate the promotion of 'extreme political beliefs'.[5] The re-enactment of 'Naziness', then, must have its limits, but precisely where are these situated? Is one allowed, for the sake of authenticity, to perform a Hitler salute as the ordinary German soldier did whether or not he had extreme political beliefs? The meaning of the Second World War for postwar British identity as a successful test of a morally superior national character has been so naturalised that any deviation from the mythologised narrative in public provokes consternation. Yet re-enactment has provided a safe space in which othering can happen in a ludic form, in the way games platforms have achieved. What I mean by safe here is that for the dura-tion of the experience the participant is in a simulated environment that acts as a disavowal of reprehensible pleasures: this is merely play. The difference between re-enactment or online gaming and attending a fancy dress party is that there is a pre-existing consensus amongst gamers and actors about the purpose of such role-play. At a fancy dress party, no one knows why someone chooses a particular outfit.

In Prince Harry's royal blunder, the appropriateness of the 'Colonials and Natives' theme of the party seemed to have escaped scrutiny, which suggests little public knowledge of, and even less sensitivity to, Britain's violent history of imperialism and its ramifications for modern multicultural society. Prince Harry's social set, in any case, seems to have had few qualms about the political correctness of re-enacting the British Empire. The instantaneous apology issued by Clarence House forestalled the more crucial inquiry into why the prince had chosen the costume in the first place – was this an act of rebellion against royal codes of conduct; an (ignorant? absurd? knowing?) indication of his military aspirations; an allusion to Rommel as an honourable enemy; sheer stupidity? Reportedly their father despatched the two heirs to the throne to the museum and memorial in Auschwitz so they could get an idea of what wearing an Afrika Corps shirt ostensibly endorsed. This is a very interesting punitive or educative measure, since it seems to assume that a visit to a camp memorial site produces certain and predictable results. As I have explained in the introduction, the encounter with violent history is by no means so predictable.

I would like to use this royal blunder to ask two important questions about the function of uniforms and camps within the re-enactment of fascism. Rather than focus on games or historical societies that enable simulation I want to focus on literary forms that enable such fantasy. We have already seen the problematics of such a strategy in Nazi noir. In this chapter, I want to examine two novels that are formally fundamentally different but demonstrate a rather ambivalent response to the Nazi corpus: Robert Harris's allohistorical thriller *Fatherland* and Ian McEwan's novel of ideas *Black Dogs*, both published in 1992. They belong to a spate of novels that re-engage with fascism at the very moment when it appears to fill a vacuum of alterity in a changing European political landscape after the collapse of the Soviet Union, the reunification of Germany, and the signing of the Maastricht Treaty that consolidated the European Union.[6] Was the old fascism the new enemy? I am interested in the way in which both texts embody fascism and frame its cultural legacies. On a literal level, what role do fascist corporeality and iconography play? And figuratively, how do these novels situate the fascist body in the material remnants of fascist ideology (most notably the camps) that feature so prominently in our memorial landscape of fascist crime and genocide? How do these books negotiate the representation of fascism at a politically highly sensitive moment?

Nazi Noir: uniformed men and ghostly women

Robert Harris's bestselling thriller *Fatherland* imagines the nightmare scenario of a Nazi victory in the Second World War. By 1964, the Reich has devoured most of Eastern Europe where it fights a never-ending guerrilla war against American-sponsored Soviets, while Western Europe, including Britain, has been conquered by cultural and economic German hegemony. In Albert Speer's monumental Berlin, preparations for the Führer's birthday pageant form the background to an ostensibly ordinary murder case. On the surface, this is a detective thriller in which 'regular' crime is committed to keep genocide a secret: one brutalised Nazi corpse will lead to eleven million murdered European Jews who have vanished without a trace. For the unknowing detective, the clues eventually reveal the greater 'mystery' of the Shoah. For the informed reader, the suspense consists in the interpretation of a documentary trail that retraces the process of the 'Final Solution' from the Wannsee Conference in early 1942 to the death camps in Poland, and in the question of whether the noir hero will survive to disseminate this illicit body of knowledge. The novel thus sets up two oppositions: the readable, ubiquitous Nazi bodies that populate the plot against an invisible, undetectable mountain of genocidal victims; and a material body of evidence in the form of documents about the Shoah to which the detective's vulnerable body gives access.

The plot of *Fatherland* rests on the investigative zeal and uncompromising integrity of its noir detective, SS-*Sturmbannführer* Xavier March, just as much as it depends on the reader's willingness to suspend disbelief about the plausibility of a secret Shoah. Much is made of March's difference from the police officers around him, not least because Harris has to construct a character in this corrupt Nazi state for whom the reader can root and who constitutes a credible object of desire for a female representative of democratic America, the journalist Charlie Maguire. True to the rules of noir, March must be 'the best man in his world and a good enough man for any world' (Chandler [1950] 1988: 18). Yet in a police state in which security forces proliferate (*Kriminalpolizei, Ordnungspolizei, Sicherheitsdienst* and Heinrich Müller's *Gestapo*) and their remits blur into one another, straightforward crime cannot be sharply separated from ideological transgressions, and vice versa.[7] This is precisely the point of the plot. Pitched against 'real' Nazis like the historic Artur Nebe, Joseph Bühler and Odilo Globocnik (organiser of the Operation Reinhardt death camps), March becomes that oxymoronic figure, the Good Nazi: a cynical cop whose mediocre career and failed marriage to a party faithful reassures the reader of his fundamental decency. Yet his appearance constantly undermines his position on the margins of authority where we might expect the stereotypical noir hero to operate. His menacing and dramatic SS uniform turns him into an official embodiment of the state's power *and* constructs his body as sexually attractive. Even in a capital bustling with uniformed bodies, this is the Nazi outfit that dramatises the hero as less ambivalently 'noir', fully implicated in the social world he polices

> His uniform was laid out in the bedroom: the body-armour of authority. Brown shirt, with black leather buttons. Black tie. Black breeches. Black jackboots (the rich smell of polished leather).
> Black tunic: four silver buttons; three parallel silvered threads on the shoulder tabs; on the left sleeve, a red-white-and-black swastika armband; on the right, a diamond enclosing the gothic letter 'K', for Kriminalpolizei.
> Black Sam Browne belt. Black cap with silver death's head and Party eagle. Black leather gloves.
> March stared at himself in the mirror and a Sturmbannführer of the Waffen-SS stared back. He picked up his service pistol, a 9 mm Luger, from the dressing table, checked the action, and slotted it into his holster. Then he stepped out into the morning. (Harris 1993: 45)

This reads like a more sexed-up version of the picture captions for *SS Regalia*, that odd, fetishistic compendium of paraphernalia which Susan Sontag cites in her essay 'Fascinating Fascism' as 'a breviary of sexual fantasy': 'For fantasy to have depth, it must have detail' ([1975] 1996: 100). Unlike so many of the grotesque bodies of the Nazi leaders, March's body is indeed that of the 'Aryan superman' of Nordic race, yet it is his uniform that visibly certifies his racial superiority (Harris 1993: 96, 192). Encased in that uniform, March turns from an inconspicuous individual into a military rank; as he will tell Maguire, the armoured corporate body 'blots out the man' (208). To himself and to her, March justifies this armour of authority with the same exculpatory reasoning that became a well-worn refrain in postwar German courts of justice: 'either I am an investigator in that uniform, and try to do a little good; or I am something else without that uniform, and do no good at all' (211). Moral agency here seems to be tethered to the semiotics of power: uniformed state-empowered bodies versus an ineffectual civilian non-existence. In order to be 'the best man in his world', March must not just look like a Nazi, he must be part of the very system in which he has such bad faith.

On his path to truth March dismisses his apologia as 'bullshit' but the plot nonetheless depends on the effects of the uniform. Without the dramatisation of power, March is 'barely recognisable' for his lover (1993: 208), which suggests that it is indeed the uniform that stimulates desire rather than the man or the male body inside.[8] The liaison between the American journalist and the Good Nazi in *Fatherland* bluntly literalises the erotic attraction of democratic culture to fascism although it is meant to be read the other way round, as a redeeming feature of the Good Nazi's convertibility to democratic values: having been 'brought up to think of Germans as something from outer space', of the SS as 'murderers . . . . Sadists. Evil personified' (208–9), Maguire nonetheless goes to bed with what she purports to hate 'on sight' and explores – like the reader – the darkest secret of the fascist vision.

To be sure, March's dressing routine is much more important than taking his clothes off: getting into uniform is described three times in the novel, while sex happens, coyly, off-stage. In one of the novel's most potent scenes, when March is finally arrested, interrogated and tortured, he is still in uniform. Indeed he has prepared himself for the final stage of this investigation through the dressing ritual: this 'would be the last time he wore it, one way or the other' (1993: 337). While he is violently beaten, Maguire has become the carrier of incriminating evidence; the longer he can keep his torturers occupied the greater her chances of escaping over the Swiss border with crucial documents. Even before the torture scene, March's knowledge of the corrupt Nazi regime is written all over him: the sleeplessness, the poor diet and alcohol abuse, the deepening loneliness of a failed marriage and the impossibility of friendship mark his body. The torture scene, then, imprints the detective's knowledge on his body only more violently. Maguire's escape depends on March's ability to keep this intensely physical scene entirely homosocial – a punch-up between men in uniform. When the torturers punctuate their blows with the question 'Where's the girl?', the grammar of this sadomasochistic scene is predicated on a woman's absence.[9] As Gill Plain has argued in her analysis of Chandler, the hardboiled genre reserves sensuality for the less familiar corporeality of the male. Its objectified females may in fact be the red herring in a form that, underneath frustrated heterosexual romance, may be much more interested in equally unsatisfiable homosocial dynamics (2001: 62). In Nazi noir, *Fatherland* suggests, relationships between men are constantly betrayed for the sake of that one Big Man, the Führer, whether they are between fathers and sons, colleagues, protégés and protectors, or between war veterans.

If male friendship is unattainable, torture offers its violent, perverse replacement. In enduring pain March assumes an abject, passive position in which violence is framed like a sexual consummation: 'I have waited for this moment as a bridegroom waits for his bride' (1993: 345) whispers Odilo Globocnik before delivering the first blow. The cruelty he metes out in precise knowledge of the pain he inflicts is described with more detailed sensuousness than the coy brevity of off-stage, straight sex: the kidney punches, the hair pulling, the repeated beating and kicking, the grinding of boots into March's ear or on his hands, are foreplay to a debilitating climax in which Globocnik, having tenderly brushed the tip of a baseball bat across March's knuckles, crushes the detective's right hand to pulp. In this sadomasochistic theatre of violence, Harris makes March's body come alive in a fascist apotheosis of suffering and renunciation, superseding the little deaths in anonymous hotel rooms with those in a blood-spattered subterranean prison cell.

While he is violently beaten, March both fantasises about his lover and shouts the names of death camps at his torturer. This confluence of violence, an elusive female body and the death camp is repeated in the novel's final scene in the ruins of Auschwitz, when March gives himself up to die in the fantasised knowledge of his lover's escape. Thus the woman is both with him in her past familiarity and irrevocably gone as a fugitive in disguise; both a spectral object of desire and a real refugee; both a distant memory and a contingent future. Already somewhat chimerical in her threadbare characterisation, the

female object of desire becomes a ghostly woman on the final page of
Fatherland.

The nexus of sacrificial death, spectral and spectacular women, and
unfulfillable desire on Holocaust territory is a now familiar problematic
that perhaps first surfaced in the controversies over Liliana Cavani's *The
Night Porter* and Fassbinder's *Lili Marleen*. Ian McEwan's *Black Dogs*
demonstrates the libidinal shortcomings of non-fascist ideologies vis-à-
vis the continued seductions of violence in postwar Europe – a continent
where the material traces of war and Holocaust elicit an uncannily
sexual response in his English characters. Here too a death camp features, and here too we find the confluence of an eroticised female body,
fascist violence and the material evidence of the Shoah. The narrator
Jeremy first meets his wife-to-be Jenny Tremaine on a tour of Poland
in the early 1980s. On this tour Jeremy is asked to accompany her to
Majdanek:

> Three years before . . . I had been to Belsen and had promised myself that I
> would never look at another camp. One visit was a necessary education, a
> second was morbid. But now this ghostly pale woman was inviting me to
> return . . . she explained that she had never visited a concentration camp
> before and preferred to go with someone she could think of as a friend.
> As she arrived at this last word she brushed the back of my hand with her
> fingers. Her touch was cool. I took her hand and then, because she had taken
> a willing step towards me, I kissed her. It was a long kiss in the gloomy, un-
> peopled emptiness of the hotel corridor. (McEwan 1992: 108)

The camp visit is staged as a thanatic seduction, with a woman as
catalyst and prize for the sexually timid narrator. The ghostly female
only becomes flesh and is only sexually fully available once she's been
in a camp: after the visit to Majdanek, they immediately enter a hotel
and don't leave their room for three days. As in *Fatherland*, the hotel
door closes discretely on the lovers' consummation. In her review of the
novel, Kerry Fried argues that the Majdanek visit as the beginning of
romance 'comes dangerously close to being obtrusive, grotesque, but
McEwan is so deft a writer that again the violence does not, finally, seem
gratuitous' (1993: 37). Yet it is not the deftness of McEwan's prose that
accounts for the lack of gratuitous violence of which we find plenty in
his earlier fiction. While there is, in *Black Dogs*, some interest in real
manifestations of violence (political, sexual and familial), it is the ubiquitous *potential* for violence that is embodied in the central metaphor
of the book. If the camp visit is indeed a literalised Freudian 'morbid'
return, we should perhaps ask precisely what is being repressed that so
uncannily surfaces in Majdanek?

On the other side: fantasy and the perpetrator's premise

During their visit to Majdanek, Jeremy deals with two synecdochal bodies: the material remnants of the victims (masses of shoes displayed in wire cages) and the remainder of the camp as the fascist vision of 'racial cleansing'. In his encounter with this fascist corpus he rejects the moral efficacy that cultural memory of the Shoah is supposed to produce. Instead, he is 'drawn insidiously to the perpetrators' premise':

> We were strolling like tourists. Either you came here and despaired, or you put your hands deeper into your pockets and gripped your warm loose change and found you had taken one step closer to the dreamers of the nightmare. This was our inevitable shame, our share in the misery. We were on the other side, we walked here freely like the commandant once did, or his political master, poking into this or that, knowing the way out, in the full certainty of our next meal. (McEwan 1992: 110)

Note the near-compulsive move, from the tourist's stroll to the commandant's stride within the psychology of identification. Obviously this passage addresses the irrational feelings of guilt in the post-memorial, postwar generation, and it raises important issues about the cultural meanings and psychological effects of memorial sites, which I will address in the next section. It is the shame of the disempowered bystander whose scrutinising gaze seems to fix violated bodies in their victimhood and repeat the violation *ad infinitum* that ultimately makes the narrator cross to 'the other side'. In this moral transgression guilt is converted into a fantasy of domination, from whose vantage point of omnipotence the panorama of the concentrationary universe is surveyed:

> After a while I could no longer bear the victims and I thought only of their persecutors. We were walking among the huts. How well they were constructed, how well they had lasted. Neat paths joined each front door to the track we were on. The huts stretched so far ahead of us, I could not see to the end of the row. And this was only one row, in one part of the camp, and this was only one camp, a smaller one by comparison. I sank into inverted admiration, bleak wonder; to dream of this enterprise, to plan these camps, to build them and take such pains, to furnish, run and maintain them, and to marshal from towns and villages their human fuel. Such energy, such dedication. How could one begin to call it a mistake? (1992: 110–11)

This fantasy seems more in keeping with reports about lower-ranking staff in camps and ghettos who assumed godlike roles in these lawless spaces whenever they believed or knew themselves to be beyond sanction: police officers or individual camp guards (Mallmann 2002). Notwithstanding the evidence of such monstrous conduct, McEwan's

fantasy of omnipotence is of a different calibre to that of 'Evil personified' that is such a staple of the popular imagination – the sadistic torturer Globocnik in Harris's *Fatherland*, the trigger-happy psychopath
Amon Goeth in Keneally's *Schindler's Ark*, or Peter O'Toole's leering
serial killer in *The Night of the Generals*. Here the ordinary Jeremy
fancies himself as Kommandant.

Jeremy's 'bleak wonder' and 'inverted admiration' is kindled by
the dimensions of Majdanek as a (reconstructed) memorial site near
Lublin.[10] The perpetrator's application of ordinary managerial criteria
and industrial processes to the extraordinary phenomenon of exploitative genocide is the only access point to a rationalisation (in both senses
of the word) of the crime: to *understand* the Shoah one might have to
assume the morally untenable position of the perpetrator. Even if the
dreamers are still seen to produce a 'nightmare' rather than a vision,
Jeremy's train of thought demonstrates that the vision is preferable to
the despair of identification or empathy with the suffering it produced. It
counters Sontag's and Friedländer's explanations of 'fascinating fascism'
as a Genettian dramatisation of death and violence. Rather, it implies
that the focus on perpetrators we find in such genres as Nazi noir or
post-Holocaust science fiction precisely *avoids* a confrontation with
death:[11]

> The extravagant numerical scale, the easy-to-say numbers – tens and hun-
> dreds of thousands, millions – denied the imagination its proper sympathies,
> its rightful grasp of the suffering, and one was drawn insidiously to the per-
> petrators' premise, that life was cheap, junk to be inspected in heaps. As we
> walked on, my emotions died. (1992: 110)

The scale of the crime, still visible in its memorialised reconstruction,
is made responsible for the visitor's confounded response. The first
stage of this response echoes the sarcastic prophecy of an SS officer,
cited in Primo Levi's *The Drowned and the Saved*, that the crime is too
fantastic in conception and too monstrous in proportion to be believed.
McEwan's Majdanek scene explains how the move from Holocaust
testimony to Nazi fantasy might be possible: 'one was drawn insidiously
to the perpetrators' premise' because in that move from stunned but
helpless empathy to guilt-laden awed fantasy, identification shifts from a
vulnerable body, doomed to die, to a well-fed uniformed body seemingly
impervious to death in its 'body armour of authority'.

The extent to which comprehension of the perpetrators has to be
qualified and differentiated against unseemly identification becomes
clear when one looks at how historians approach studying mass murder.
I have already commented in the Introduction on Saul Friedländer's

project of mobilising disbelief against objectivity, seamless interpretation and the domestication of genocide. In some of his methodological essays, Friedländer suggests that the historian should even adopt meta-historiographical practices, more familiar in literary studies as metafictional self-reflexivity:

> The voice of the commentator must be clearly heard. The commentary should disrupt the facile linear progression of the narration, introduce alternative interpretations, question the partial conclusion, withstand the need for closure. Because of the necessity of some form of narrative sequence in the writing of history, such commentary may introduce splintered or constantly recurring refractions of a traumatic past by using any number of different vantage points. (1995: 261)

This passage advocates a polyphonic representation of the Shoah and is surely indebted to the postmodern genre of historiographical metafiction. The purpose of such writerly intervention is to enact, in the aesthetics of historiography, the traumatic events it describes. The reader, it seems, must not be given the chance to integrate the Shoah into history but, paradoxically, must be made to understand its occurrence as a rupture of historicity. Such statements of course indicate the impasse of historiography when faced with the doxa of the Shoah's 'ineffability'.

In the preface to *Ordinary Men*, Christopher Browning anticipates objections to his study precisely because of 'the degree of empathy for the perpetrators that is inherent in trying to understand them': 'Clearly the writing of such a history requires the rejection of demonisation . . . Not trying to understand the perpetrators in human terms would make impossible not only this study but any history of Holocaust perpetrators that sought to go beyond one-dimensional caricature' (2001: xx). Jacques Semelin counters 'Holocaust piety' by suggesting that the researcher has a moral 'duty to apply our intellect': 'Refusing to understand would amount to acknowledging [the perpetrators'] posthumous victory. It would amount to admitting that the intelligence of evil-doing was and remains decidedly stronger than that of attempting to untangle its mysteries. From an ethical standpoint such a position is untenable' (2005: 2). Such prefatory justifications for inquiry into the manner and motivation of perpetrators are to a certain extent rhetorical; they underline the scholar's awareness of Holocaust history (and genocide studies) as a sensitive discourse.

Perpetrator texts, such as Rudolf Höß's memoirs (*Meine Psyche: Werden, Leben u. Erleben*) are often published with a critical preface by an editor whose rhetoric is partly defensive and partly appalled. The implication of such 'health warnings' are that the audience requires ethical guidance lest they fail to recognise in whose company they are. Martin Broszat, editor of the German version, repeatedly emphasises Höß's peculiar aesthetics which combine sentimental mannerisms, cliché and Nazi jargon but aspire to elevated expression: rhetoric becomes an expression of psychopathology (an interpretation encouraged by the diary's title). On the one hand, publication underlines the ordinariness of the perpetrators. Höß is merely another obedient, bureaucratic and duty-bound petit bourgeois 'working towards' the Führer for whom a genocidal career entailed professional advancement. On the other hand, the memoirs serve as 'an extreme case' of the perversion of emotion and morality, just one example of a split personality of which there are millions (Broszat 1964: 17; 19). In Broszat's preface we already see that the motivation of mass murderers, whether desk killers or special forces, resists simple explanation and therefore exerts fascination.

Primo Levi's preface to the English translation of Höß's narrative has a different function: he confirms the veracity of Höß's statements. Since he is a survivor of Auschwitz the reader may also feel that this strange endorsement gives her permission to read a perpetrator text. However, in his study on moral life in the camps Tzvetan Todorov offered a counter-confession about reading Höß's memoir, typographically set off by italics in a separate parenthetical paragraph:

> *(Each time I read Höss's book, I am deeply disturbed . . . a kind of nausea washes over me . . . Doubtless because of several factors combined: the enormity of the crime, the absence of sincere regret on his part, and the many ways he elicits my identification with him and manages to make me share his way of seeing things. The first-person-singular point of view is also important, as is the absence of any other voice alongside his own . . . Finally, there is the complicity Höss creates by inviting his reader to take advantage of his singular experiences to observe human beings as if they were laboratory animals at a particularly interesting phase of their lives, the hours before death. When I read Höss's book, I consent to share with him the role of the voyeur who looks on as others die, and it makes me feel unclean.) (1999: 170–1)*

Todorov's self-critical reflection on the paradoxical effect of reading a perpetrator narrative perhaps most usefully explains the reader's dilemma: the sensitive reader should be (and is) appalled at what she reads and the rhetoric in which it is couched. Höß fashions himself as a man of feeling, burdened with an impossible task and struggling to fulfil his duty with too few resources and poorly qualified staff, suffering under the atrocities committed when the mechanised process of killing is not adopted or does not work. He abhors blood baths and lawlessness and prefers order and efficiency. He praises those victims and staff who, like himself, manage calmness and detachment in the face of chaos, filth and cruelty. As Todorov suggests, our outrage should be tempered by a realisation of our 'complicity' and our 'voyeurism' that sharing his perspective involves: how can we be both horrified and curious; sensitive and sympathetic? Our ambivalence is rooted in the fact that understanding even some aspects of Höß's situation and conduct implies a shared humanity and therefore our contingency for perpetration.

As we shall see in the next chapter, tackling the perpetrator perspective is a rare and risky business. In David Albahari's *Götz i Majer* (*Götz and Meyer*, 1998) the Jewish narrator attempts to imagine the daily lives of the two drivers of the Saurer gas vans with which the Jewish inmates of a Belgrade camp are being killed:

> Anyone could have been Götz. Anyone could have been Meyer, and yet Götz and Meyer were only Götz and Meyer, and no-one else could be who they were. It is hardly surprising, therefore, that I constantly had this feeling that I was slipping, even when I was walking on solid ground. The void that was Götz and Meyer so contrasted with the fullness of my relatives, if not of their real beings at least of their deaths, that my every attempt to reach fullness required that first I had to pass through void. For me to truly understand real people like my relatives, I had to first understand unreal people like Götz and Meyer. Not to understand them: to conjure them. Sometimes I simply had to become Götz, or Meyer, so I could figure out what Götz, or Meyer (really I), thought about what Meyer, or Götz (really I), meant to ask. (2004: 65–6)

Rhetorically, this passage is full of 'slippage'. The slippage between the interchangeable drivers and the narrator and between their imagined characters and the parenthetical, impersonating self renders the novel blackly comical. The constant refrain 'Götz, or Meyer', that runs through the novel reminds the reader of 'the void' that is perpetration; how little we know of the ordinary men who participated in mass murder. The victims are 'real' not just because they are the narrator's relatives and can be given a story but because victim testimony by far outnumbers perpetrator texts. The murderers are 'unreal' not just because we know so little about them but because the popular imagination of 'fascism' has routinely rendered them monstrous and pathological in a radical disavowal of the contingency of perpetration. Albahari's narrator vacillates between universalising perpetration ('Anyone could have been Götz. Anyone could have been Meyer') and insisting on individual culpability ('and yet'); between specificity and ordinariness to the point of interchangeability. Note also the correction with which understanding perpetration is replaced by, ostensibly, an act of magic (avoiding the ethically problematic slippage of fantasy, empathy, identification): something or someone conjured remains unreal. This passage rhetorically and typographically enacts the slippage to the other side and back again (identification and alienation) in a tacit dialogue with the discursive rules surrounding the Shoah. Understanding how this mass murder happened is prohibited and declared obscene; as a result such endeavour is constantly qualified, bracketed off, consigned to the space of the unreal, but of course the territory of the (amoral and uncensorable) unreal is precisely fantasy. In a novel that has to 'conjure' the 'fullness' of dying just as much as the void of killing this is a delicate balancing act, and one of which the reader is constantly reminded through metafictional remarks.

Such postmodern devices as well as the cautionary paratextual framing of perpetrator testimony with prefaces, essays, footnotes, etc., suggest a certain suspicion towards the reader (one finds similar 'information' on, say, the DVD sleeves of Leni Riefenstahl's films or documentaries including *Wochenschau* extracts). The seductive force of the perspective must be counteracted with educative warnings and admonishments (like the calorie count on a chocolate bar). This emphasises how little the audience or the reader is trusted with the faculty to read critically. It is of course possible to read these narratives against the grain. Many passages in Höß's memoir are astonishing, if not grotesque, in the way in which he applies ordinary standards of decency to an extermination process, marvelling at the powers of deception evinced by the *Sonderkommando* or blaming fellow inmates' selfish behaviour for the swift deterioration and suffering of prisoners.

By the same token, we can see that Harris's *Fatherland*, ostensibly a horrified vision of a fascist worse case scenario, crucially depends on the fantasy of the perpetrator's premise and pushes this fantasy further since his plot demands a Nazi corpus of gargantuan proportions. Harris provides maps of the enormous expansion of the Nazi Reich and of Albert Speer's new Berlin with its megalomaniac architecture.[12] He grants the Nazis an Orwellian *Reichsarchiv* with six subterranean floors and a furnace for undesirable history at its centre. The narrative is replete with historical Nazi leaders and functionaries whose biographies have been altered, but whose pronouncements are accumulated in citations and epigraphs. Remarkably, when it comes to uncovering the Shoah and turning the detective into a reluctant historian, the documentary evidence Harris marshals barely includes any Jewish testimony, only Nazi correspondence about the Wannsee Conference, rail timetables to death camps, and witness reports from functionaries' visits to camps. The more we learn about the Shoah in *Fatherland*, the more we are pushed to 'the other side', seeing it with the perpetrators' eyes: 'such energy, such dedication'.

However, for Gavriel Rosenfeld, Harris's scenario belongs to a category of counterfactual history that continues to perform an important moral function in underlining the barbarous nature of the Nazi period before books like Martin Amis's *Time's Arrow* (1991), Christoph Ransmayr's *Morbus Kitahara* (1996) and Peter Quinn's *After Dachau* (2001) ring in a more 'normalised' engagement with fascism (Rosenfeld 2005a: 242). Contemporary culture's increasing exhaustion with the cultural memory of the Holocaust manifests itself in the desire for a more 'uninhibited' relationship with the Nazis (Rosenfeld 2005b: 292). Yet is it not precisely the uninhibited imagination of Harris or McEwan that lends such fictitious Nazism its noir aesthetics and thereby reduces its moral impact (only a mind for which the historical horrors of the Nazi regime and its genocide have palled needs a worse case scenario)? Neither critique nor irony change the associations with the Nazi system; nor do they make this representation of fascism less 'fascinating', since the detailed evocation of the fictional Nazi 'background' utilises the same semantics as the historical original. Read thus, we would have to concur with Saul Friedländer's scepticism about the possibility of an ethical representation of Nazism. (That Harris's novel became very popular with continental neo-Nazis once a Swiss publishing house chose to translate it suggests the multivalent grammar of its scenario as well as significantly different cultural responses to 'fascinating fascism' in Europe and Anglo-America: finding this book gripping in Germany betrays right-wing leanings; finding it gripping in the UK is supposedly a reassurance of one's democratic normality.)

This representational impasse seems to have escaped Harris, whose choice of allohistorical form (in a bleak elsewhere, in another time) allows him to suggest a conflation of contemporary continental Europe with Nazi-occupied Europe: 'There are things that Germany would have achieved in 1945 which have come true in 1992, in particular the economic domination, and so on. The collapse of Bolshevism. The strength of Germany in Eastern Europe.'[13] More recently, Harris has emphasised the continued relevance of his book: 'historical fiction ... does not date':

> *Fatherland* in particular – set in an imagined past that is also a conjectured future – is doubly insulated against fashion.
>
> Besides, the 140-year-old 'German question' – how can this great and industrious nation exist in the centre of Europe without dominating it? – still awaits an answer. The current problems in the eurozone have brought all kinds of ghosts out of the shadows. 'Suddenly Europe is speaking German', one of chancellor Merkel's more tactless colleagues boasted recently – thus demonstrating, I suspect, why *Fatherland* continues to attract readers who weren't even born when it was first published. (2012: 6)

The point Harris makes here not so tacitly is that Germany remains a 'problem' even though (or probably because) it has successfully managed the transition to a stable democracy. This transition is merely seen as a convenient masquerade – a 'fashion' perhaps – which is carelessly abandoned in moments of crisis to reveal fascism as merely dormant. John LeCarré made this point with more justification in *A Small Town in Germany* (1968), at a time when there were still palpable personnel continuities between fascist Germany and postwar Germany that made headlines intermittently. To make this point in 2012 for a weekly reading group column in a left-wing broadsheet suggests that this is not an unusual, let alone controversial, view of fascist or contemporary Germany. It chimes with broad scepticism about the European project in the UK and renders traditional Germanophobia respectable for a middle-aged generation.

For Harris, fascism is quite literally undead, a revenant, the most recent manifestation of a 140-year-old unanswered question, but also somehow the essence of the German soul. In this paranoid reading, the Second World War may have been won on the battlefield but was subsequently lost in the corridors of Brussels. McEwan, too, concludes his novel ominously with the prediction that evil 'will return to haunt us, somewhere in Europe, in another time' (1992: 174). Thus their readers are reminded of a fascist Europe at the very moment when Britain's ties to that fateful continent become stronger (through the Maastricht Treaty of 1991), as if the fascist threat had gradually metamorphosed into the spectre of European integration, or in 2012 the spectre of European disintegration. Invoking fascism as a shorthand for German responsibility for the calamities of history remains so suspiciously versatile a rhetoric that I am inclined here to remind the reader of Godwin's Law.[14]

Fatherland's crucial body, then, may not be the fascist corpus or the vanished bodies of the Jews, but the lost integrity of a body of water: the Channel that so fortuitously preserved British independence and democracy from continental fascist contamination. Read through its emphasis on corporeality, the novels betray a deep uncertainty about the boundaries between liberal democracy and fascist otherness. Harris's plot consequently allows the reader to inhabit various conflicting positions all at once: to be the Aryan superman and the lonely noir hero; to engage in straight sex but yearn for male friendship; to watch Nazi sadism and be its victim; to remain a decent police officer when Himmler's secret speech in Poznan in 1943, cited in an epigraph, discredits the very notion of decency; to wear an SS uniform and yet be 'the best man in his world'. If, as George Mosse has argued, the Western imagination principally shares one stereotype of masculinity and Nazism provides merely its most warlike manifestation (1996: 180), then Nazi noir clearly offers the reader a safe and exciting fascist fantasy in which the Aryan protagonist with his inquisitive intelligence, bravery and rugged attractiveness invites identification despite *and* because of the ideology symbolised by the uniform. Even in pain and death March's body still conforms to aestheticised Nazi masculinity. His fate is precisely the glorified death of the Aryan soldier hero in Nazi art and propaganda, who exalts in suffering and renounces sexuality. While his body goes the way of the persecuted Jewish other – classified, hunted, arrested, tortured, forced to die in a camp – his death remains an impeccably honourable thanatic apotheosis either as a redemptive suicide or a violent fusillade that cleanses the Reich of a traitor: a luxury of ambivalence that the inmates of Auschwitz did not have.

Bodies of evidence: cultural memory and fascist representation

Auschwitz and Majdanek are of course memorial sites whose remit is the preservation of a body of evidence relating to industrial genocide and murderous inhumanity. In the 'rhetoric of ruins', as James E. Young has called it, those remnants are presented as synecdoches of historical phenomena. Our encounter with the artefacts of genocide is shaped by the manner of their presentation; indeed the latter may actually perform the task of interpretation (Young 1993: 128). By themselves these artefacts do not necessarily mean anything and consequently, framed in a different context, they are open to alternative appropriations. This is precisely the case with the camp sites in *Fatherland* and *Black Dogs*. In *Fatherland*, the barely recognisable foundations of brick buildings at Auschwitz have no evidentiary status without a documentary trail that gradually explains the purpose of the site. Maguire reports that survivor testimonies of atrocities are often dismissed as anti-German propaganda, hysterical outpourings of deranged people, or simply meet with indifference. In a world that has no ready-made context for industrial genocide, it remains unreadable. And yet, Harris does not seem to trust his own plot of proving the existence of the Holocaust without marshalling further evidence in the form of epigraphs that cite actual perpetrators and survivors, which suggests that *counterfactual* fiction is not really the appropriate medium to represent historical genocide. *Black Dogs* makes an even stronger case for the multivalence of memorial sites by revealing how the victims of genocide were subsumed in an ideological narrative of national suffering and Soviet liberation. Thus they disappear three times: once as a result of the historical crime, then in the manner of commemoration in Communist Poland and finally in Jeremy's refusal to empathise and identify.

The irony of some of the camps' pastoral names (Birkenau, Buchenwald, Gross-Rosen) and the beauty of their settings have often been commented on, precisely because these signifiers cloaked their function. Their nature and size is harder to grasp, either because they are only partly reconstructed or because they were successfully destroyed, such as the Operation Reinhardt camps. Gitta Sereny, on visiting Sobibor in 1972, initially drove past the small monument that marked the site. On Treblinka, long a national memorial, she remarked:

> The Poles have spared no effort to reconstruct the whole of the camp as a national monument which, while adequately portraying the horror, can also leave one with some feeling of human dignity. But it doesn't work. All one can think of is the terrible smallness of the place . . . the main reason why it is so difficult to visualize lies in nature itself: where there used to be huts, barbed wire, tank traps and watch towers, there are now hundreds of bushes, and young pine trees which the Germans planted to camouflage this site when, having accomplished what they set out to do, they obliterated the camp at the end of 1943. (1995: 145)

And so Sereny concludes, 'We know that more than a million human beings were killed and lie buried in these few acres, but it cannot be believed' (1995: 145). We can only see the result of obliteration, and this means to engage unwittingly in the perpetrator's premise: to see the site with the Nazis' eyes post-genocide; to reject what we know even though monuments mark an event and museums offer us its interpretation.

Paradoxically, the material fragment makes remembering redundant and reduces it, at best, to 'a necessary education' tethered to an optional museum visit. That artefacts (like photographs or artworks) need to be framed suggests that visitors' responses are by no means self-evident. The presentation may indeed imply that the perpetrators' perspective is a more instinctual one, and might be unavoidable. As James Young argues, that a murdered people should primarily be recalled through images of their death, and that the memorial institutions utilise the very artefacts of their expropriated belongings, risks 'perpetuating the very figures by which the killers themselves would have memorialized their Jewish victims' (1993: 133). The accumulations of specific artefacts found in the camps (spectacles, suitcases, shoes, clothes, etc.), which are now often displayed as synecdochal exhibits of victims' bodies, are the result of the perpetrators' selections for reuse. Bodily artefacts such as hair remain controversial and profoundly shocking, such as the display cases of human hair in the museum at Auschwitz I (Paris 2000: 312–53; 340–2). With these artefacts, museums simultaneously enshrine the perpetrators' fantasy, the vision of omnipotence and dominance. In visiting and preserving these sites, we might even, according to the Austrian survivor and writer Ruth Klüger, service our superstition about the ghosts of the victims and our own 'necrophilic desires' (1992: 68–70). For Klüger, the memorial landscape of the Holocaust is about the needs of posterity: it actually distances the visitor from the Shoah and sentimentally returns him or her to self-conscious navel-gazing, thus creating a boundary between historic Jewish suffering and what one might cynically call Holocaust tourism. There is a sense here – uncomfortable as it may be – that through different modes of othering, neither Jewish suffering nor Nazi perpetration can be 'safely' represented.

Jeremy's reaction, in *Black Dogs*, of being 'insidiously drawn to the perpetrator's premise', is therefore by no means as outlandish and macabre a response as one might think, but indeed retraces the way in which the material remnants of genocide were originally intended to be seen and treated. The camp is turned from a metonymically preserved site of atrocity to a fascist body beautiful; it moves our engagement from corpses to a corpus, an ever-lasting and indestructible enterprise, a machine eternally fed by the ghosts of its victims. His 'inverted admiration' captures very neatly 'fascinating fascism' as a postwar cultural phenomenon that allows us to transgress into that morally prohibited zone of the Nazi vision that museums and memorial sites consistently deny in their rules of engagement with this body of evidence. As educational and moral spaces, then, museums must disavow the psychological complexity of any encounter with atrocity.

Reflecting on the contradictory positions of liberator or survivor which the Holocaust Museum in Washington DC allows its visitor, Tim Cole questions the museum's practice of assigning the visitor victims' identities in the form of ID cards:

> Why don't they give out the cards of perpetrators and bystanders as well as victims, so that somewhere towards the end of the second floor I come to the shocking understanding that I'm a member of the German battalion which is involved in killing Jews in 1942, or a Hungarian municipal officer involved in drawing up plans for the local ghetto in 1944? (1999: 164; 157)

Cole inscribes a moral response to the unexpected position of perpetrator that is by no means self-evident ('a shocking understanding') and which suggests a view of history as fate rather than the collective product of individual agency (precisely the exculpatory position of many Germans taking recourse in having been the victims of Nazism as a fate beyond their control). Cole's question may be a symptom of the cultural exhaustion with official trauma discourses and ubiquitous commemorative culture that manifests itself in the desire for a more 'uninhibited' engagement with the Shoah and the Nazis alike. In contemporary museum culture, the contingency of victimhood seems to have preferable educative value to the contingency of perpetration, which we still like to confine to popular visions of 'murderers . . . Sadists. Evil personified'. As Omer Bartov has argued, neither individual visitors nor state-funded public institutions wish to contemplate contemporary society's potential for fascism and genocide but prefer a comforting encounter with violence as historically remote and foreign (1996: 182). What would be the explanatory power of putting into practice Cole's suggestion, and say, handing out random *Einsatzgruppen*-IDs? There might be considerable merit in making visible how easy it is to become complicit in the abuse of power or to become habituated to committing atrocities. The unexpected and alarming perpetrator position surely requires a great deal more explanatory investigation than a metaphysical concept such as 'evil' could offer, and would therefore stimulate reflection. Yet we have seen how carefully even historiographers and political scientists have to guard against charges of 'Holocaust impiety' in the study of mass murder. McEwan's novel also shows us that the response to atrocity cannot be easily controlled: are we too susceptible to the Kommandant's fantasy to be encouraged to inhabit it? But if we cannot be trusted, this only confirms that the (ethical) boundary between the liberal 'us' and the Nazi 'other' is one that museum culture must police and maintain.

In recent historiography the very ordinariness of the perpetrators has complemented a discourse that primarily focused on the Nazi elite. Zygmunt Bauman's *Modernity and the Holocaust* or Christopher Browning's *Ordinary Men* are not interested in the psychopathic Butcher of Riga or the fanatical ideologue. Rather, they examine the insidious sliding into opportunistic lawlessness, the gradual brutalisation *process*, or the effects of a modern administrative apparatus on the sense of individual responsibility. They seemed eager to dismiss 'Evil personified' as a predictable historical vicissitude:[15]

> It is not the brutal SS man with his truncheon whom we cannot comprehend; we have seen his likes throughout history. It is the commander of a killing squad with a Ph.D. in law from a distinguished university in charge of organizing mass shootings of naked women and children whose figure frightens us. (Bartov 1996: 67)

This is precisely the premise of Jonathan Littell's novel *The Kindly Ones*, told from the perspective of Dr. jur. Maximilien Aue, who affronts the reader with an avuncular voice and the affirmation, 'I am just like you!' (2009b: 24). The critical furore occasioned by such a daring assumption (discussed in the next chapter) is indicative of how uncertain even the literary and critical establishment is about the reader's ability to control his fantasies and become complicit with the first-person mass murderer. If we understood what moved the professional classes to sanction and participate in mass murder, we would, like McEwan's narrator, be 'on the other side' with him. In fact, there would be no 'other side', only a continuity between him and us. Therefore any encounter with atrocity must disavow the contingency of identification even if this results in a categorical prohibition to comprehend or even to represent (Friedländer 1993b: 111; Rose 1996: 43). In contrast, the brutal SS man with a truncheon is a welcome relief despite his historical commonness, an emotionally satisfying representation of appalling alterity. Extraordinarily other in his psychopathology, the man with the truncheon is not us.

The proliferation and popular success of narratives of perpetration – from the contemporary fascination with serial killers to Nazi noir; from bestsellers of simplistic historiography such as Goldhagen's controversial *Hitler's Willing Executioners* to ubiquitous TV documentaries and films about 'the Nazis'– is a fair indicator of our need for the man with the truncheon in the tight black uniform. As Liliane Kandel suggests, the theatre of cruelty has its risks; not just of complaisance or voyeurism but of identification with the executioner (1997: 53). The man in the SS uniform is of course not an object of desire but a fantasy of dominance, doubly disavowed as a projection and a fascist representation: I am not other. So why is it that what lingers in the reader's mind, after putting *Fatherland* aside, is its excess: the size of the fictional buildings of Speer's Berlin, the expanse of the gigantic Reich, the scale of its undiscovered genocide, the detail of its torture scene. Harris chose his arch-villain well: the historic Odilo Globocnik was not only a convicted anti-Semitic murderer but also a fraudster, embezzler and organizer of 'Operation Reinhardt'. 'A bull in uniform' with enormous hands (1993: 138), Globocnik's size gives him the nickname Globus (globe). Outsized corporeality stands for the outsized Nazi corpus, for the grotesque megalomania of its genocidal vision. Detailed scenes of violence and torture are staple set pieces in Nazi representations on the basis of creative contiguity: because we know of actual Nazi atrocity, fictional Nazi cruelty is presumably not pornographic but merely a plausible fictional illustration of historical fact.

McEwan's response to this strategy is to dramatise it as an eroticised fantasy that complicates the relationship between bystanders and perpetrators. Close to the end of *Black Dogs*, he offers an explanation for the evil the eponymous dogs represent throughout the story. They were trained by the Gestapo to rape their victims, in particular a pretty and independent young woman, Danielle Bertrand, who was unresponsive to some villagers' advances. The story comes several times removed, which highlights its unreliability. The rape was allegedly observed through the window by two brothers. It is then retold by the mayor with many ellipses and periphrases. His account is disputed by Mme Auriac, the female proprietor of the village inn:

> The simple truth is that the Sauvy brothers are a couple of drunks, and that you and your cronies despised Danielle Bertrand because she was pretty and she lived alone and she didn't think she owed any of you an explanation. And when this terrible thing happened to her, did you help her against the Gestapo? No, you took their side. You added to her shame with this story, this evil story. All of you, so willing to believe a couple of drunks. It gave you so much pleasure. More humiliation for Danielle. You couldn't stop talking about it. (1992: 161)

Here McEwan offers us a 'simple truth' about our fascination with fascism: it allies us to those who seem omnipotent and it isolates the victims in their shame. A veritable fictionalisation of the *mise-en-scène* in Freud's essay 'A Child is Being Beaten', this scenario implicates the passive bystander as an active voyeur, and it replaces our fundamental ignorance of the victim's experience of physical cruelty (the nameless 'terrible thing') with a sexualised narrative: a child is being beaten (and I am watching); a woman is raped by Gestapo dogs, and I cannot stop talking about it. For Madame Auriac, the salacious gossip that circulates long after it drove the victim from the community is a vicarious gang rape, endlessly repeatable. 'The shame is on you', she insists to the mayor, but of course her interpretation of the rumour identifies it as a way of deflecting the unbearable shame of the victim from becoming 'our inevitable shame, our share in the misery' (1992: 111). In the Majdanek scene McEwan suggests that our response to Nazism might be impossible to regulate towards the only morally appropriate position. In the Gestapo dogs story he demonstrates how (disavowed) tacit identifications are articulated in voluble tales of contiguous atrocity: identification becomes fantasy becomes projection.

There is an unresolved tension between fascism's pole position in our cultural inventory of evil alterity and its thoroughly disavowed fascination. Whenever our certainty of the clear boundary between fascism's otherness and our democratic respectability is challenged, regulatory mechanisms are called upon in order to police moral landmarks, or as Laura Frost has argued, the trope of sexual perversion is invoked to construct fascism as politically *and* libidinally deviant and reassures 'us' implicitly of 'our' democratic and sexual normality. For Frost, this cliché has its origin in the Germanophobia of the First World War and fully blossoms when German comes to mean fascist. But it is the longevity of this phantasmagoria-as-trope, or as a kind of cultural screen memory, that ought to make us think about why anxieties about sexual and ideological transgression are so habitually conflated. Precisely what does this conflation really obfuscate? One would certainly not want to elevate fascism to the level of the ineffable. However, its ubiquitous referencing should perhaps tell us something about the way in which Western culture has utilised 'Nazism' precisely to avoid looking at it and at itself. In this defence strategy, the representation of fascism more often than not seamlessly slides into or towards what Gillian Rose has called 'the fascism of representation'. Insisting on its absolute alterity, we have created fascism as an alter ego. As the next chapter will demonstrate, if this construct is radically challenged, controversies abound.

Notes

1. 'Harry the Nazi', *Sun*, 13 January 2005, p. 1.
2. 'Harry says sorry for Nazi Costume', *BBC News*, 13 January 2005, available at <http://news.bbc.co.uk/1/hi/4170083.stm> (last accessed 23 December 2010).
3. Arthur Edwards, 'Soldiers will feel disgust', Jamie Pyatt and Duncan Larcombe, 'Prince wears Nazi regalia', *Sun*, 13 January 2005, available at <http://www.thesun.co.uk/sol/homepage/news/article101247.ece> (last accessed 23 December 2010).
4. Glenn Frankel, 'Prince Harry's Nazi blunder burns Old Blighty', *The Washington Post*, p. C01, available at <http://www.washingtonpost.com/wp-dyn/articles/A7286–2005Jan13.html> (last accessed 23 December 2010).
5. See, for example, *Grossdeutschland Aufklärungs* Living History Group at www.gdrecon.co.uk and as an umbrella website: www.panzergrenadier.net.
6. For example, Kazuo Ishiguro's *The Remains of the Day* (1989), Philip Kerr's *Berlin Noir* series (1989–92), and Martin Amis's *Time's Arrow* (1991).
7. All levels of police were implicated in implementing racial laws, ideological reliability and persecution from the very early days of the Third Reich, when political dissidents were spirited away into 'protective custody', and SA thugs could terrorise opponents and abuse Jewish citizens without police interference or legal sanction. See Paul 2002, Hilberg 1993: pp. 36–50, and Browning 2001.
8. In the 1930s, it had been the other way around for British observers of Nazi pageantry. While tourists came to inspect the new Germany, it was the splendidly regenerated German body that validated the new Nazi state

as a success. Among the physical evidence was Germany's strong performance at the 1936 Olympics, the exhibition of the national labour service
at the annual party rallies and the physical fitness and condition of German
youth. See Rau 2009a: 149–83.

9. The same homosocial triangulation of female absence informs the torture
scenes in Philip Kerr's *March Violets* and Robert Wilson's *A Small Death
in Lisbon*.

10. Before the implementation of 'Operation Reinhardt', Majdanek was conceived as the largest camp in the *General-Gouvernement*, accommodating
up to a quarter million of prisoners and PoWs on 500 hectares (at twice
the population density of nearby Lublin's pre-war population), all working
for the German war machine and the SS textile industry. For a map of
the original gargantuan scale of Majdanek see Samek's *In the Middle of
Europe* (2001). The camp was scaled back to less than a quarter of its original conception. For a painstaking analysis of Majdanek's evolution from a
work and prisoner camp to a site of extermination see Schwindt 2005.

11. On the habitual omission of the Holocaust in the Hitler-wins scenario see
Gordon 2002: 207.

12. For a comparison between Harris's map, Hitler's new Berlin and Speer's
model see Spotts 2003: 357. Much of the detail and the anecdotes for
Hitler's architectural vision comes from Speer's bestselling memoirs *Inside
the Third Reich* (1970).

13. Cited in Fassbender 1994: 243. And the cat comes out of the bag in a
long article in *The Sunday Times*: 'One does not have to share the views
of Nicholas Ridley or Margaret Thatcher to note the similarity between
what the Nazis planned for western Europe and what, in economic terms,
has come to pass.' Robert Harris, 'Nightmare landscape of Nazism triumphant', *The Sunday Times*, Section 2: News Review, 10 May 1992, p. 1.
He made the same point, if more subtly, to the *New York Times*: Craig
R. Whitney, 'Inventing a world in which Hitler won', *New York Times*,
Section C: The Arts, 3 June 1992, pp. 17 and 19.

14. *Plus ça change*: John Sutherland reads several bestselling 1970s novels
that imagined Britain invaded (*SS-GB*; *The Eagle Has Landed*) or believed
that despite the Allied victory in 1945 fascism was ineradicable and merely
dormant (*Marathon Man*; *The Odessa File*; *The Fourth Protocol*) as a
response to Britain's entry into the Common Market (1981: 179, 242).

15. See also Hannah Arendt's comment on 'such types of which every city has
more than we would like to believe' ([1955] 2005: 920).

Chapter 3

'Fascism' as Excess and Abjection: Jonathan Littell's *The Kindly Ones*

Jonathan Littell's epic novel *Les Bienveillantes* (*The Kindly Ones*, 2006) consists of the memoirs of the fictitious Franco-German *SS-Obersturmgruppenführer* Dr. jur. Maximilien Aue. It focuses on his deployment as an SD intelligence officer on the Eastern Front, in the Caucasus, at Stalingrad, with the mobile *Einsatzgruppen* in the Ukraine, and at Auschwitz. A Zelig figure of the war in Europe, he meets various historic and imagined characters, talks to French collaborators in occupied Paris, survives the siege of Berlin and an encounter with bands of Nazi Werewolves (roaming teenage guerrilla fighters), before he vanishes into anonymity in the chaos of the early postwar months. His memoirs relay in graphic detail persecution, murder and genocide, war crimes, battle scenes and sexual encounters. Interlaced with these events are revelations about his incestuous relationship with his twin sister Una, many passive homosexual experiences, and (possibly) his murder of his parents. After the war, Aue leads a quiet existence as a family man and director of a lace manufactory in the North of France.

The Kindly Ones was short-listed for six French literary prizes and garnered the two most prestigious ones, *Le Prix Goncourt* and *Le Prix du roman de l'Académie française*. It won praise from filmmaker Claude Lanzman and historian Pierre Nora; the Spanish Holocaust survivor and novelist Jorge Semprun endorsed it with superlatives. Yet there was no shortage of reviewers who denounced the novel as kitsch, pornographic, and exploitative in its attitude towards war and Holocaust. A bestseller in France and cautiously praised in the UK, the book's reception in Germany (2008) and the USA (2009) gave rise to a collective shrillness one rarely finds in august journals and reputable broadsheets (see Theweleit 2009; Golsan 2010). There *The Kindly Ones* was rejected as 'fascism' gone a step too far. As a *succès de scandale*, Littell's novel is reminiscent of an earlier controversy, that of Daniel Jonah Goldhagen's *Hitler's Willing Executioners* (1996), in which he claimed that virulent

German anti-Semitism was solely responsible for the Holocaust. Today, Goldhagen's theory and his methodology are discredited but the impact he had on the historiographical discourse and the public debate about the Holocaust (particularly in Germany) – the so-called 'Goldhagen effect' (Eley 2000) – is perhaps more interesting than the questionable logic he offered. The same, I think, is true for Littell's book: its effect is fascinating because it challenges discursive rules and taboos within Holocaust studies. Goldhagen was criticised for his dramatised accounts of perpetration; for an excessive imagination that fed a narrative ventriloquism (Wood 1999: 97–111). In contrast, Littell was accused of historiographical ventriloquism and a surfeit of intertextuality, that is, a lack of imagination (as well as a lack of sensitivity towards the victims of the Shoah). In addition, critics also censured both the historian and the novelist for their attitude towards the perpetrators in their writing. Goldhagen demonised them, Littell universalised them. What is notable in this heated discourse about perpetration, in the age of 'empathetic history', is a pervasive concern about the excess or lack of critical distance; about how the work steers the reader's affective relationship to what she reads.

I have already discussed some of the effects of specific points-of-view, not least in conjunction with the intended mobilisation of affect and empathy in modern Holocaust education, historiography and museum display. In this chapter I want to focus on the representation of perpetration from a first-person perspective in fictional autobiography because this strikes me as the most subversive choice. Such a perspective is still rare and has previously been accused of encouraging unethical reader identification which is deemed disrespectful to the victims of fascism as well as exploitative, voyeuristic or sensationalist (and we have seen examples of such focalised passages in the previous chapters). This critique is also levelled at Holocaust fiction irrespective of the technical and narratological devices often used to make point-of-view more complex (see Vice 2000; Young 1998). Issues raised by the representation of perpetration (a particularly violent form of 'fascism') cannot easily be divorced from those relating to the representation of the Holocaust, and both are equally divisive.

Joachim Landkammer, in a provocative essay on dealing with the Nazi past, has questioned whether we actually need the illustration of graphic violence through artefacts of torture and sites of atrocity. Is it not sufficient to *know* (as opposed to see, feel, touch and piously remember) how many perpetrators killed how many millions how and where (2006: 61)? Does our culture of excess now require our exposure to visceral graphic images or narratives about historical violence for knowledge (and horror) to sink in? Or does non-representational art continue to be the most effective and ethical approach in a culture of excessive visual consumption of simulated violence? Has the insistence on the non-representability of the Shoah created a problematic 'void' that actually *produces* a prurient fascination with the killers? We certainly seem to have reached an *impasse* between the demands for empathy and respect extended towards the victims of violence, whose suffering is seemingly beyond representation, and our habituation to images of violence (and sex) through embedded reportage, 'militainment' and entertainment in the visual media. In a rather self-reflexive passage in his comparative analysis of genocide in the twentieth century, *Purify and Destroy*, the political scientist Jacques Semelin emphasises the importance of 'an appropriate distance' vis-à-vis 'this hideous object' – atrocity; a distance that negotiates the representational extremes of omission and denial on the one side and centre-stage exhibition and macabre contemplation on the other (2005: 290). For the researcher such distance might be achieved through an appropriate intellectual framework; the novelist, however, might want to test the very notion of 'critical distance'.

The Kindly Ones makes a significant and timely intervention in this debate. It is indicative of the way in which provocative artworks have challenged the rules of engagement with the Shoah. I will focus on three aspects of the novel that exercised critics and that all have to do with excess: the construction of an overdetermined Nazi perpetrator; the surfeit of intertextuality; and the ostensibly pornographic focus on abject bodies. These excesses, I suggest, are textual markers that ask the reader to reflect critically about her position vis-à-vis fascism and its representation, particularly in relation to genocidal violence and sexuality. That many critics should feel it necessary to militate so vehemently against the experience of reading the novel (of encountering an excessive 'fascism', that is) must direct our attention to the position in which Littell places the reader and the mechanisms by which he prevents us from easily disavowing the reprehensible pleasures of consuming sex and violence via 'fascism'.

Consuming perpetration and the culture of excess

In a scathing review of Littell's novel in the German weekly *Die Zeit*, Iris Radisch asked: 'Why, for Heaven's sake, should we read this badly written book by an educated idiot who struggles with his sexual perversions and has abandoned himself to elitist racist ideology and an antiquated belief in fate' (2008; my translation)?' Why indeed? Why has this novel become a bestseller in Europe? Perhaps more importantly, what exactly does a reader expect who picks up the fictional memoirs of an *SS-Obersturmbannführer* deployed on the Eastern Front? The furore surrounding *The Kindly Ones* is not dissimilar to the reaction of the diegetic audience in Brooks's *The Producers* who go to see a play entitled 'Adolf and Eva: A Gay Romp in Berchtesgarden' and are outraged when the play delivers just that. If the novel is replete with horrific and graphic detail about murder and sex, this is neither unusual for bestselling war fiction (indeed it is a pre-requisite since the bestselling war fiction of Sven Hassel and 'Leo Kessler') nor extraordinary in terms of the 'shock and awe' excesses of late capitalist Western consumer culture. Not only are there formidable literary precursors in both the French and the English tradition – de Sade, Bataille, Genet, Houellebecq, Burroughs, Ballard, Bret Easton Ellis; as we shall see Dr Aue can enjoy the company of quite a number of fictional fascist perpetrators.

To the extent that the novel provides an extended insight into the mind of a violent and aberrant perpetrator, it certainly partakes of a cultural trend that has emerged since the late 1980s (roughly corresponding with the post-communist period I am focusing on). Contemporary serial killer fiction and film, which has developed into a highly lucrative subcategory of the crime genre, has not only elevated the psychopathology of perpetration to celebrity status but led to the standard integration of criminal psychology into the narrative in general. Fictional serial killers come two a penny; in real life they are mercifully rare, and yet the combination of their extremity with inconspicuous extraordinariness evokes fascination. The ostensibly aberrant nature of the serial killer provides a convenient reason for crime writers' increasingly outlandish choice of method, the sheer number of mangled and mutilated corpses, and the shrouding of morbid curiosity and prurient voyeurism in scientific babble. Patricia Cornwell's Scarpetta series, Thomas Harris's Hannibal novels, Val McDermid's Tony Hill books, and – most self-conscious and ambiguous of all – Jeff Lindsay's Dexter series assemble key ingredients in this homicidal soup: the female pathologist, the intelligent glamorised psychopath, and the troubled profiler-detective. Crime and horror fiction satisfies our appetite for increasingly graphic and bizarre violence and overdetermined homicide, but we see these elements also in embedded reportage, murder-as-entertainment on TV and in first-person shooter games. This constitutes what Mark Seltzer (1998) has called our 'wound culture', and perhaps it points to a contradiction that is thrown into relief when we are asked to engage with large-scale historical and authentic violence. That young people particularly might struggle to differentiate between simulated and documentary representation has always troubled pedagogues. Another issue is that the perception of violence as remote (geographically removed, culturally other or temporally distant) and simulated allows the audience to disavow the reprehensible pleasures of consuming violence. More crucial is perhaps that *all* such violence is mediated rather than empirical: this gruesome death does not happen to us. We never identify with the victims and their vulnerable bodies but are in the position of the bystander, the saviour-detective or even the perpetrator.

The habitual consumption of violent death seems at odds with a simultaneous cultural focus on victims and trauma, not least in the memory boom of the last decades. However, for John Lennon and Malcolm Foley (2007), unabating interest in historical violence, in particular that relating to the Third Reich and sites of the 'Final Solution', is not just integral to commemorative awareness but forms part of consumer culture. 'Dark tourism', as they call it, has turned genocide monuments and memorials into morbid attractions. As we have seen in the last chapter, what kind of identification happens at a site of atrocity is hard to regulate. If we remember teachers' concern about the 'wrong' identifications and their strenuous endeavours to mobilise empathy in at least a few, we might come to the conclusion that empathy towards a stranger or a historical victim is a truly rare affect. But even such an emotion, according to the historian Amos Goldberg, may have become part of a culture of consumption underpinned by our libidinal economy:

> In a culture addicted to the 'excessive', these voices [of individual victims and witnesses] provide the most expected excess and create the most believable and conventional disbelief. Excess and disbelief have become the most commonplace cultural *topoi*. I contend, therefore, that to a certain extent, in our current culture the excessive voices of the victims have exchanged their epistemological, ontological, and ethical revolutionary function for an aesthetic one. They operate according to the pleasure principle in order to bring us, consumers of Holocaust images, the most expected image of the 'unimaginable', which therefore generates a melancholic pleasure. (2009: 222; 229)

The mention of 'disbelief' refers to Saul Friedländer's method, in *The Years of Extermination* (2007), of integrating Jewish victims' voices as a way of creating a more dialogical narrative without domesticating horror through objectivity and interpretation. Yet Goldberg sees disbelief as a habituated response (an empty affect) rather than an ethical one. Since the Shoah and its iconography are now part of a consumer culture, disbelief is merely an acceptable clichéd reaction to its cultural ubiquity and its pious rhetoric. Note the slippage, in this passage, of 'excess': a culture addicted to excess requires excessive representation (the 'excessive voices of the Jews') as the only appropriate aesthetics to illustrate the excess that is the Shoah. The libidinal gain for the consumer is a 'melancholic pleasure' – alongside presumably some feeling of moral elevation or relief about being alive. For Luc Boltanski (1999), such 'distant suffering' is indicative of a crisis of pity in our modern culture because apprehending temporally or geographically remote suffering through its representation does not necessarily mobilise behaviour or political action but may dull the senses into accepting both historical *and* present violence. Yet if the function of representing violence is now largely aesthetic as opposed to documentary (an excess that demonstrates our *dearth* of empathy and imagination) then this aesthetic must be subject to analysis.

For Jonathan Littell, the perpetrator's perspective was crucial to his project of approaching war and genocide. In an interview with the Hebrew newspaper *Haaretz* he justified his choice of voice:

> In general I am much less interested in victims than I am in perpetrators. That's because they are the ones who are doing something and changing the reality. It's very easy to understand the victim: something terrible happens to him and he reacts accordingly. But in terms of trying to understand something there is nothing to examine. The perpetrator is more complicated to understand, along with the apparatus that activates him. (Uni 2008: n.p.)

This is perhaps a rather careless and muddle-headed statement. Whether it is 'very easy' to understand the victim (should he or she survive) given the nature of trauma is a matter of debate. Many Holocaust testimonies and memoirs are full of survivors' expressions of uncertainty over whether they themselves comprehend what happened to them and whether they will be able to render it even approximately. Our culture's turn towards 'trauma studies' and the proliferation of testimony may be symptomatic precisely of our inability to know the victim's experience. Conversely, the ineffability of suffering may propel us towards the perpetrator (as is the case with the protagonist in McEwan's novel). In our imagination (an imagination also shaped by 'fascism'), suffering is contingent and perpetration deliberate; it requires agency and volition. The victim is often cast as feminised, passive, while the murderer acts out and 'chang[es] the reality'.[1] Notable in the passage above is Littell's emphasis on comprehension (the verb 'understand' is repeated three times): disbelief or piety do not feature here. We have seen in the last chapter how museum culture and historiography attempt to police the boundary between empathy for the victims and identification with the perpetrators, straining against the intellectual cul-de-sac of 'Holocaust piety' while making every effort to remain sensitive to the topic of mass murder. Littell is not hampered by such considerations.

Unlike many of his readers and critics, Littell has had long experience of conflict zones as a humanitarian aid worker. From 1994 to 2001 he travelled to Bosnia-Herzegovina for *Action Against Hunger*. His work also took him to Chechnya, the Republic of Congo, Rwanda, Afghanistan and Sierra Leone where he 'had hung out with the killers' (in Blumenfeld 2006). He could, in other words, have chosen a more contemporary setting and a different state-ordained mass murderer.[2] That he contributes to the discourse on 'fascism' with what he has called a 'phantasmagoria' (rejecting the term historical novel) suggests that contemporary excesses of mass violence ought to be brought into dialogue with the most extreme case of ideologically driven extermination policy in the twentieth century: 'By means of the attempt to give a voice to the perpetrator, lessons can be learned that will affect the way we look at the world today' (Uni 2008). As Richard Golsan rightly points out, in *The Kindly Ones* Littell is interested in those aspects of genocide that are not unique, if he does not actually wish to challenge the doxa of the uniqueness of the Shoah as obstructive to a proper study of our genocidal potential in contemporary politics.[3]

In a culture of excess and consumption, then, a novel such as Littell's is symptomatic in its graphic violence and sex. Its reception is also indicative of a certain schizophrenia, not to say hypocrisy, in our consumer ethos that manifests itself in a rejection of responsibility for both excessive consumption and the consumption of excess: we can habitually disavow reprehensible pleasures because we enjoy them through simulation or we blame the producers of such material. The Western consumer indulges freely in fictitious brutality to satisfy all manner of desires, mildly titillated by the frisson of proximate horrors, but largely insulated from whatever real-life catastrophes and wars embedded reportage might broadcast on the TV screen (Boltanski's 'distant suffering'). This excess of vicariously satisfied bloodlust and terror has to be reconciled with respect for and empathy with the victims of historical violence. However, as I demonstrated in the previous chapters, the division between phantasmagoria and (historical) reality, between violence as aesthetics and violence as catastrophe cannot be strictly policed, particularly in our affective responses to them. In fact historical violence is often instrumentalised for an aesthetics of violence, for instance to justify the specific psychopathology of fictional perpetrators, as in Thomas Harris's prequel *Hannibal Rising*, Tom Rob Smith's *Child 44*, or Bryan Singer's film *X-Men*.

What is at stake in the critical debate Littell has given rise to is precisely our mode of consumption: the way in which the reader relates (or is invited to submit) to the first-person voice and the arguments it marshals and the experiences it relays, and the degree to which this relationship produces unseemly pleasure (or even entertainment) and unethical identification. Let us remember here Lukács's dictum that the reader of the historical novel 'should re-experience the social and human motives which led men to think, feel and act just as they did in historical reality'. Do we dare imagine and 're-experience' mass murder? Dominick LaCapra has accused Littell's narrative of 'a rather manipulative, pseudo-dialogic relation aimed at generating complicity and even subordination rather than critical exchange', because the novel does not establish sufficient 'critical distance' between reader and narrative voice, via any 'focalisers', 'textual markers' or 'procedures' that would allow resistance to such complicity (2011: 73; 76). In her lecture on *The Kindly Ones*, Julia Kristeva (2007) voiced a certain alarm at the novel's monological strategy: 'le volume agit comme un colossal *virus* propre à contaminer peu à peu le naïf lecteur, ce "semblable, [ce] frère", pour en fait un *otage*: de Jonathan Littell ou de Max Aue?' The naive reader is contaminated and taken hostage; a victim of – and this is deliberately left unclear – the fascist narrator or the book's author. That the reader should be thought of as a naive person without any agency, responsibility or judgment let alone the ability to be an attentive close reader seems a rather Catholic pronouncement to me, highly suspicious of the audience (and its indecent submission to intoxication voices). Kristeva's patronising rhetoric here reminds me of Susan Sontag's similar phrasing, in her essay 'Fascinating Fascism', of the mass audience's susceptibility to fascism (and therefore of the reprehensibility of 'fascism' in mass culture). Such critique only comments on technique in order to subject aesthetics to higher moral and ideological considerations. Paradoxically, this rejection ignores precisely the literariness of *The Kindly Ones*, its use of the imagination to plumb what for most readers is entirely beyond their everyday consciousness (Bohrer 2011: 136). To obtain the reader's reluctant consent for this exposure requires a great deal of rhetorical skill. Indeed, the reader's putative moral rejection of Dr Aue's memoirs is the focus of the novel's first section, 'Toccata'.

Brother Aue: contractual reading and mass murder

'Toccata' offers us a provocative meta-discursive engagement with war and Holocaust before the historical part of the novel begins. Four times in this prologue does Aue offer a statement about why he writes:

If after all these years I've made up my mind to write, it's to set the record straight for myself, not for you.[4]

No, if I have finally decided to write, it really is probably just to pass the time, and also, possibly, to clear up one or two obscure points, for you perhaps and for myself.

And in the end, even though I'm addressing you, it's not for you that I'm writing.

Maybe that's why I am writing these memoirs: to get my blood flowing, to see if I can still feel anything, if I can still suffer a little. (2009b: 3; 5; 8; 12)

None of these 'reasons' are in themselves sufficient to account for what follows nor do they adhere to the conventions of the confessional. According to Theodor Reik confession is equivalent to an acceptance of being deserving of punishment, that is, it becomes an act that guarantees reintegration into the community of men (1959: 7). Aue freely concedes culpability but he does not offer contrition or shame. In this he resembles another fictional perpetrator, Otto Dietrich zur Linde in Jorge Luis Borges story 'Deutsches Requiem' (1958). Borges presents us with a camp subdirector's monologue on the eve of his execution:

> I do not seek pardon, because I feel no guilt; but I would like to be understood. Those who care to listen to me will understand the history of Germany and the future history of the world. I know that cases like mine, which are now exceptional and astonishing, will shortly be commonplace. Tomorrow I will die, but I am the symbol of future generations. (Borges [1958] 1972: 173–4)

We endure zur Linde's 'confession' over a mere six pages (in contrast to Aue's loquacious 975, or 1390 in the original French), but it is all the more shocking for the prediction of the future 'commonplace' nature of what we reassure ourselves must remain an 'exceptional' life. What is at stake here – and in Aue's curriculum vitae – is precisely to convince the reader or listener of the ordinariness of the perpetrator and therefore of the possibly representative or symbolic nature of the narrative and the sentiments it expresses. Carl Lovitt argues that the ultimate purpose of the confessional narrative is not repentance but to 'attenuate the stigma of the crime and to dispel the ignominy surrounding the writer before he is silenced' (1992: 33). For this to happen, the relationship between reader and narrator is crucial. Perpetrators divulge their deeds for a whole host of reasons, and often in an idiosyncratic idiom that is part of the very apparatus that enabled mass murder. Rudolf Höß, Kommandant of Auschwitz, co-operated freely with his Allied interrogators out of a sense of duty to a higher authority. In his memoirs, entitled *Meine Psyche* (my soul) he fashions himself as a man of feeling, troubled by the managerial difficulties of staff shortages, disciplinary failures and overcrowding. Yet, as Littell commented about his research, 'the more I read the perpetrators' texts, the more I realized they were empty' (in Blumenfeld 2006). They might be sickening but they are often rationalised accounts rather than visceral narratives about 'obscure points'. Given that Aue suffers from vomiting and constipation, his narrative is a (literally) sanguine talking cure for a psychosomatic metabolic disturbance. The memoirs are meant to animate the writer-narrator, not the reader, to combat an affective emptiness.

To open his memoirs with an inclusive formula that stipulates a common bond between narrator and reader is not unusual. In his essay 'Bruder Hitler' (Brother Hitler, 1939) Thomas Mann pointed to the commonalities between Hitler and his detractors (including himself), suggesting that Hitler could not be dismissed as a political aberration but was a logical consequence of already and broadly existing traits and thoughts in German culture and politics. Aue, too, provocatively challenges the gulf between himself and the ostensibly morally superior reader. He anticipates the novel's reception in the opening sentences: 'Oh my human brothers, let me tell you how it happened. I am not your brother, you'll retort, and I don't want to know.' In this first address the reader is certainly credited with agency and the ability to judge. The imagined retort rejects the suggestion of the mass murderer's ordinariness and humanity, as opposed to his sociopathic monstrosity, as well as the need to see graphic details or listen to an account of, let alone a rationale for, mass murder. In his insistence that 'this concerns you' (2009b: 1), Aue underlines that this is not just a narrative about a specific perpetrator (his memoir or confession) but also a story about perpetration and the smug disavowal of its contingency: in wartime the male citizen loses his right to live as well as his right not to kill (2009b: 17). The possibility of participating in, and the coercion to commit, state-sanctioned murder has haunted Littell since his childhood experience of mediated war:

> I am from a generation that was very marked by Vietnam. I was a very small boy but it was in the living room every goddamned day – much more than the Holocaust and Israel or anything else. We saw it on TV every day for my entire childhood. My childhood terror was that I would be drafted and sent to Vietnam and made to kill women and children who hadn't done anything to me. (Uni 2008: n.p.)

The perpetrator changes the reality of his victims but in turn his world has been changed by the state (or some authority) which compels him into perpetration, or into a series of minor decisions that culminate in mass murder. Motivation is here taken out of the equation through conscription, but it remains of course the unresolved question of much historiographical inquiry into the Shoah. That we might kill because we can (and not just because someone tells us that it is our patriotic duty) and because we will subscribe to ideological rationales for killing affronts most Western readers who deem themselves miraculously immunised against fascism merely because they fortuitously live in a democratic country. Therefore Aue provocatively constructs his reader as male and from a Western democracy that prefers to be oblivious to the fascist traits in its imperialist foreign policy: in French he is reminded of 'votre petite aventure Algérienne' (2006a: 23) while the English (and German) translation imagine an American forgetful of 'your little Vietnam adventure' (2009b: 16).[5]

In a mock-dialogical structure, Aue (trained jurist that he is) anticipates his reluctant male reader's responses to the arguments he marshals ('you will object', 'I know', 'I can guess what you're thinking'). He was merely following orders ('I did my work'; 2009b: 5); he defends the killing of unarmed civilians invoking the conditions of total war in which these distinctions are no longer valid; compares the deaths of the Shoah to those of carpet bombing ('the only difference between the Jewish child gassed or shot and the German child burned alive in an air raid is one of method', 18); rejects the 'sloppy' verdicts of the Nuremberg Trials since 'the laws [were] written after the fact' (20); suggests that mass killing is less the action of psychopaths and sociopaths than of a Marxist modernity in which the worker (professional or labourer) is alienated from the product of his labour (death); indicates a vulgar-neurotic obsession with bodily fluids but maintains a bourgeois, even learned register; dismisses war writers (and the fascists and collaborators among them in particular) as 'confused' or cliché-ridden, but forewarns us of the incoherence of the final section ('by that point I was no longer entirely myself', 5) and of the opaqueness of his memoir ('of no use', 24); emphasises that violence is part of human existence but also resorts to metaphysical notions ('all this evil entered my own life', 24). For those who insist on the uniqueness of the Shoah and its incomprehensibility such rhetoric is a relativising and universalising gesture through which historical events and subjects-in-history become interchangeable or are at least integrated into a continuum of violence. The incompatibility of these arguments, however, ought to indicate the various discourses on which Aue draws: how we read fascism and assess the means of the struggle to vanquish it are by no means uncontentious issues even among historians and philosophers. We have not yet answered the crucial questions.

For the reader to continue, the narrator has to forge a contract with the reader in which his agency (to resist, to recoil, to abandon the book) is either converted into interest and curiosity or at least suspended into the contemplation of Aue's arguments. The provocative and crucial passage that forms this contract is offered before a single shot is fired:

> I am guilty, you're not, fine. But you should be able to admit to yourselves that you might also have done what I did. With less zeal perhaps, but perhaps also with less despair, in any case one way or another. I think I am allowed to conclude, as a fact established by modern history, that everyone, or nearly everyone, in a given set of circumstances, does what he is told to do; and pardon me, there's not much chance that you're the exception, any more than I was. If you were born in a country or at a time not only when nobody comes to kill your wife and your children, but also nobody comes to ask you to kill the wives and children of others, then render thanks to God and go in peace. But always keep this thought in mind: you might be luckier than I, but you're not a better person. (2009b: 20)

This passage begins with an absolute dichotomy between the criminal narrator and the innocent or at least morally superior reader, yet by the end of Aue's rhetorical manoeuvres the difference between being guilty and not being a better person has been eroded. Every statement is followed by a qualifying or modifying phrase that makes it easier to subscribe to the overall assumption. As a result, the passage slides, seamlessly, from the contingency of perpetration ('you might have done what I did') to an assertion of its near-universality ('you're not a better person'). Agency is reduced to fortuitousness rather than acknowledged as the use of a moral compass. Note how cleverly the subjunctive, the conditional and the adverb 'perhaps' disintegrate the reader's disinterest and moral superiority without removing agency and resistance from him. Indeed for the contract with the reader to work, the rhetoric of this passage requires no more than that the reader remain resistant but merely suspend this resistance into a repeatedly contemplated 'perhaps'. If the reader continues he has presumably consented to consider the provocative premise of Aue's plea: 'I am just like you!' 'The real danger for mankind is me, is you. And if you're not convinced of this, don't bother to read any further. You'll understand nothing and you'll get angry, with little profit for you or for me' (2009b: 24; 21–2).

Such passages, in which the reader is reminded of his moral stance and his agency, are dotted throughout the narrative. Our complacently imagined bubble of moral exceptionality finally bursts, very late in the book, when our agency is both reinvoked and mocked:

But perhaps you really don't care about any of this. Maybe, instead of my unwholesome abstruse reflections, you would rather have anecdotes, spicy little stories . . . You see, I'm thinking of you too, not just of me, a little bit in any case, there are limits of course, if I'm putting myself to so much trouble, it's not to make you happy, I will willingly admit, it's above all for my own mental hygiene, like when you've eaten too much, at some point you have to evacuate the waste, whether or not it smells nice, you don't always have a choice; but here, you have an irrevocable power, that of closing this book and throwing it in the rubbish, a final recourse against which I am powerless. (2009b: 783)

If the reader has stayed the course of 783 pages, he is not likely to suddenly exercise this 'irrevocable power' and abandon the novel. In fact, by then the reader has long become habituated, like the protagonist, to graphic accounts of sex and atrocity, consumed as so many 'spicy little stories', and has been fully complicit in observing war crimes and listening to their rationale. The purpose of this rhetoric of continual reader address throughout the novel is to reassure the reader of the ostensible moral gap between himself and the narrator but to make the reader bridge that gap at the same time through the act of reading. Every time we continue reading, we subscribe to the contingency of perpetration and renew the contract with the narrator that allows him to exercise his 'mental hygiene' over our moral hygiene. Therein lies the subversive effect of the novel; this is the lesson we do not wish to draw.

Aue's somatic response to perpetration (vomiting and diarrhoea) is now provocatively equated with his confession while in 'Toccata' he had interrupted his narrative to 'go and vomit' (2009b: 18). From Zhitomir to Auschwitz and beyond, Aue cannot digest, hold in, keep inside what he has seen and done; his bowels, tightly encased in uniform, need this body armour since they actually begin to dissolve into the waste to which the East is being laid. In the next section, 'Air', this gesture will be taken one step further, mirroring Pasolini's *Salò* in its coprophagic and sexual excesses. For Liran Razinsky, the novel drifts from an excess of facticity to an excess of corporeal fantasy; the perspective on the war becomes literally 'embodied' (2010: 188; 190). Confession as evacuation, as emetic or diarrhoeic narrative, adds another flavour to our consumption of 'spicy little stories': we read this 'shit'. Yet rather than rail against the author and his unethical project that makes us so complicit with the narrator's perspective, the attentive and self-critical reader should ask herself why she has not exercised her irrevocable power. The vitriol that literary criticism poured so liberally over this book seems a retrospective disavowal of the reader's submission to the desire for 'fascism' as 'spicy little stories' of violence and sexual perversion (as opposed to the tedium of sober, lengthy historiographical accounts).

And voice is crucial in this project as it is in most controversial texts charged with pornography or voyeurism since it is expressive not just of what is being observed but also of the attitude of the observer – a differentiation that often escapes the outraged reader.[6] The reader may recognise in the first sentence the final line from Baudelaire's 'Au Lecteur' ('hypocrite lecteur, – mon semblable, – mon frère') or the first line from François Villon's 'Ballade des pendus': 'Frères humains, qui après nous viviez'. The former suggests precisely the unacknowledged boredom that an excess of violence and sex may produce in a reader who may be unwilling to concede his readerly voyeurism or his shared humanity. The latter refers to the posthumous, ghostly voice of the executed criminal, pleading for pity and forgiveness. Max Aue is of course not dead, but the tone of his narration suggests an emotional emptiness, or what Littell has called 'froideur' and even 'a sort of transparency to the real, an extinction behind what is said or described, perhaps what Blanchot calls the neutral'.[7] More precisely, in an interview with Pierre Nora: 'He is not so much a character than a voice, a tone, a point-of-view. There is a distance, a cleft between what Max describes (and he sees everyone else with extreme clarity) and himself, as if he weren't the narrator, in a manner of speaking.'[8] If Aue is indeed 'manufacturing memories' the way he now manufactures lace, the void around which the narrative is woven is as important as the thread of his narrative and the tone of his voice. Indeed the story is a process of voiding and evacuating that which has proven indigestible, clumsily called 'mental hygiene'. He pleads an inner life precisely because he now has none: 'But why couldn't an *SS-Obersturmbannführer* have an inner life, desires, passions, just like any other man?' (2009b: 23).

We may suspect that a perpetrator's account may not be reliable, merely a biased articulation of the executioner's truth, as Julia Kristeva (2007) has claimed. We may well have qualms about listening to perpetrators unless we can justify our interest as part of a juridical process (as in the documentation of the Nuremberg trials) or the scientific inquiry of say, a historiographer (Browning), a documentary filmmaker (Ophuls; Lanzman) or a psychiatrist (Gilbert; Lifton). Yet one might also argue that the logical contortions and rhetorical manœuvers of these statements are in themselves revealing. Let us recall here once more Rudolf Höß's managerial treatment of Auschwitz, so telling of an authoritarian character; or the cabinet maker and *SS-Hauptscharführer* Felix Landau's diary of his work with an *Einsatzkommando*, voicing romantic anxieties about his lover's faithfulness in the matter-of-fact reports of his genocidal 'work' (Klee, Dreeßen, Riess 2000: 185–203). Our suspicions, I would argue, are rooted precisely in the tone of these accounts which in their ordinariness do not match our notion of the monstrous. Our moral rejection of these narratives is a refusal to contemplate the humanity of the perpetrators. To reject their proximity to us avoids any sense of common human responsibility for these crimes.

The tonal cleft Littell insists on between Max and what he narrates points to a range of subject positions the protagonist inhabits – perpetrator, witness, retrospective commentator, author. That he can step back from his historical self and comment on (or even contextualise) his actions and thoughts, often through long passages culled *post factum* from historiographical study, may make this character implausibly self-reflexive. Susan Rubin Suleiman, however, sees the effect of this anachronistic narration or disguised retrospection as the novel's postmodern and highly original element: it turns the perpetrator into a reliable historical witness (2009: 8–9). Aue's well-researched retrospection adds another perspective to the story (or another voice), namely that of historians' interpretations. The effect is perhaps a greater degree of dissociation in his manner (what Littell calls 'froideur' or 'disjonction') precisely because he has to ventriloquise historians. Even for Aue his own perspective as witness and perpetrator, his being present in the historical moment, remains insufficient to explain the precise nature of his actions and motivations:

> I was curious: I was trying to see what effect all this would have on me. I was always observing myself: it was as if a film camera was fixed just above me, and I was at once this camera, the man it was filming, and the man who was then studying the film . . . But the answer to my question kept slipping through my fingers. (2009b: 107)

These different subject positions are of course mirrored in the polyphonic voices *within* the first-person perspective (witness/camera; perpetrator/man being filmed; writer/man studying the film). The visual metaphor is important not just because many scenes are narrativisations of authentic documentary or trophy photographs, and thus can provide a critical gloss on the perpetrator perspective,[9] but because they also problematise watching and, implicitly, reading about atrocity. Aue's hybridised style, sliding from subjective facticity into appropriated extradiegetic historical interpretation, suggests that the explanation for his experience may have to come from outside (as if he were not the narrator). Indeed his ongoing non-metabolised somatic responses and his frequent headaches are an indication that war and genocide have not been forgotten – note his insistence on 'manufacturing memories' – but continue to haunt him to the point where he consults historiographical material to try to make sense of what he did.[10] On a technical level, this hybrid voice should alert the reader to Aue as a construct (rather than a realistic character): what he presents to us is not just empirical but also the product of reading, and therefore his voice is less an individual one than an intertextual chorus.

The fascist perpetrator as narrative construct

To collapse fascist perpetrator and narrator is not a new device. In both Martin Amis's *Time's Arrow* (1991) and Edgar Hilsenrath's *Der Nazi und der Friseur* (*The Nazi and the Barber*, 1977) the narrator is a Nazi mass murderer, while Maurice Blanchot's *Le Très-Haut* (*The Most High*, 1948) tells of a bureaucrat in a totalitarian regime. In Robert Merle's *La Mort est mon métier* (*Death is my Trade*, 1952) and Jorge Luis Borges's 'Deutsches Requiem' (1958), the camp commandant is the central character. These fictional perpetrators are given fantastical voices or made unreal, grotesque, spectral – devices that prevent the reader's identification with the perpetrator, and it is useful to compare these strategies to Littell's riskier venture. Amis reverses narrative time and offers a doubled narration in which the perpetrator's conscience or soul is split off from his body until the two aspects of the protagonist are fused again in Auschwitz. There, where 'there is no why' but where anything is possible, everything makes sense again to the narrative voice because the split into corporeal actant and disembodied spectator is overcome. Temporal (and semantic) reversal and irony challenge the reader to reflect on her interpretive framework for making sense of reality long before she encounters the place that defies conventional reasoning: the camp where we 'dream a race. To make people from the weather. From thunder and from lightning. With gas, with electricity, with shit, with fire' (Amis 1991: 128). This is not just a reversal of the extermination process but also a comment on the absurdity of Nazi racial policy to dream an Aryan race. 'Arriving' in Auschwitz in the latter part of the novel 'explains' the peculiar numbness of the protagonist (that is, how 'Tod Friendly' evolved from Odilo Unverdorben), but this seems mere readerly wish-fulfilment: if a mass murderer gets to live out his days amongst us, he must at least be emotionally undead. Making us see Tod from the point of view of his lost soul crucially distances us from this character. By the time we find out that he has a genocidal career – quite late in the novel – we resist the fusion of body and soul since we know now that the soon-to-be 'unspoilt' (unverdorben) Odilo has committed horrific crimes.

Hilsenrath's *The Nazi and the Barber* revolves around the mass murderer Max Schulz who in the course of his genocidal career (estimating his death toll at roughly 10,000) also killed his former neighbour, the barber Itzig Finkelstein. In order to escape punishment after the war he takes on his victim's identity and emigrates to Palestine where he opens a salon himself. Schulz's narration is a monologue directed at Finkelstein. Hilsenrath offers us a conventional temporal sequence of events but his narrator frequently reminds us of his culpability and his Jewish impersonation with the formula 'I, Itzig Finkelstein, formerly Max Schulz' or 'I, Max Schulz, mass murderer' similar to Albahari's metafictional formula 'Götz, or Meyer (really I)'. Max is a grotesque character and his narrative a picaresque story with mythological elements, both outrageous and blackly comical in its radical dismantling of perpetrator and victim positions. As a trope, Max embodies the moral distortions of the fascist world. The effect is similar to Grass's opening of *The Tin Drum* (1969), where the diminutive Oskar Matzerath tells his story in retrospect from the cell of a lunatic asylum. We can neither trust any of these narrators nor identify with them but gawp at a universe utterly out of joint.

In his new life in Palestine, Max Schulz eventually confesses to mass murder but no one believes him. As in *The Kindly Ones*, Michel Tournier's *Le Roi des aulnes* (*The Ogre*, 1970), and *Götz and Meyer*, the final part of *The Nazi and the Barber* becomes surreal and phantasmagorical, leaving the reader in doubt over the main character's sanity. Maximilien Aue believes himself pursued by the Eumenides ('the kindly ones') for the putative murder of his parents, which he can't remember; Tournier's Abel Tiffauges turns into legend (St Christopher and the 'steed of Israel') and wades into a swamp with a young Jewish boy on his shoulders. Max Schulz, continually talking to Finkelstein, mentally wanders of into the 'Forest of the Six Million' to have conversations with 'the trees'. Perpetrator fiction, then, seems to answer two questions: how anyone could commit such crimes and how one can live with oneself afterwards. If the perpetrator 'changes the reality' of the victim, that altered reality may effect a change in the perpetrator, too. As both Raul Hilberg (2003: 1080–3) and Jacques Semelin (2005: 305) have argued, the transgressive nature of mass murder traumatises the perpetrator – certainly in different ways than violence traumatises victims – but perpetration, too, subjects killers to an intense act of psychological degradation. Fictional perpetrator-narrators seem haunted precisely because they *know* they are guilty but do not *feel* remorse. The speech act of their narrative fills the moral void left by cognitive dissonance:

Die meisten Massenmörder leben auf freiem Fuß. Manche im Ausland. Die meisten wieder in der alten Heimat. Habt ihr keine Zeitung gelesen? Es geht ihnen gut, den Massenmördern! Die sind Friseure. Oder was anderes. Viele haben eigene Geschäfte. Viele besitzen Fabriken. Sind Industrielle. Viele machen wieder Politik, sitzen in der Regierung. Haben Rang und Ansehen. Und Familie. . . . Das ist die volle Wahrheit! Sie leben auf freiem Fuß und machen sich über Gott und die Welt lustig. Und auch über das Wort 'Gerechtigkeit!' (Hilsenrath [1977] 2007: 459–60)

[Most mass murderers are at large. Some abroad. Most of them have returned home. Don't you read any newspapers? They are fine, the mass murderers. They are barbers. Or something else. Many run their own business. Many own factories. Are industrialists. Many are in politics again, even in government. Got status and reputation. Are family men . . . It's the whole truth! They are at large and laugh at the world and his wife. And at the word 'justice'. (My translation)]

Hilsenrath's point here is more politically loaded than Amis's who had split his Nazi doctor from his soul. Littell too mentions the postwar life of perpetrators who live as a quasi-masonic secret community only in exculpatory discourse with itself. All three writers I think play with the reader's naive notion of 'justice' rather than attempt to discuss the moral dimensions of guilt. Putative insanity as phantasmagoria and moral deformity as grotesque are narrative strategies for converting the psychological consequences of transgression. In real life, perpetrators have a range of processes available to enable a form of cognitive dissonance. The most harrowing moment in Marcel Ophuls's *Hôtel Terminus* is Klaus Barbie's puzzled incomprehension, on his way to stand trial for the persecution, deportation and murder of the Jewish population of Lyon, of why the world remembers what he certainly has long forgotten.

Max Aue clearly has not forgotten, but keeps on 'manufacturing memories' from a variety of sources so that the educated reader identifies a certain ventriloquised polyphony, a rich fabric of intertexts. Sue Vice has argued that the successes and failures of intertextuality are key to the methods of Holocaust fiction (2000: 2). Historiographical or testimonial intertexts often serve the purpose of anchoring the fiction in authenticity, giving it credibility and documentary character. One finds them cited in afterwords or prefaces.[11] In historiographical metafiction, such as Laurent Binet's *HHhH* (2009), many of the sources are overtly discussed and assessed in their usefulness. The writer-narrator's reflections about the difficulties of writing a historical novel about the Heydrich assassination constantly disrupt the flow of the narrative and prevent the reader from 'consuming' history. Yet such postmodern intervention can also be rather tedious and patronising because it seems to assume a reader who does not know the difference between historiography and historical fiction and who is more interested in the process of writing rather than the story.

Since the publication of *The Kindly Ones*, German and French publishers have issued companion volumes that index and explain some of its sources (Lemonier 2007; Littell 2008).[12] The intertextual over-determination of 'history' and of character, I would argue, is crucial to the representation of fascism in the novel. For an attentive reader, this strategy acts like a textual marker that condenses what might look like realism[13] into a compact metaphor. In other words, this is not just a novel that purports to be about fascist perpetration but also a reflection on how we have tried to explain fascist perpetration to ourselves in historiography, fiction and testimony. *The Kindly Ones*, then, is about fascism and 'fascism' as a now hybrid phenomenon. Documentary facticity, testimony and historiography are interwoven with more imaginative treatments and suggest indeed that mere facts are not enough to grasp the historical phenomenon of war and Holocaust. Littell counters the emptiness of perpetrator texts (what Albahari called the 'void' of such 'unreal' people) not with the fullness of victim testimony and their histories but with the fullness of both our knowledge *and* our imagination (Bohrer 2011: 132). This is not a new device either but was already a conspicuous and transgressive feature of Goldhagen's *Hitler's Willing Executioners*, a book Littell has rejected as too simplistic (Littell and Nora 2007: 32). Omer Bartov suggested that elements in Goldhagen's narrative 'seem to reflect his own fantasies – themselves most probably the product of (over)exposure to media representations of the Holocaust and other massacres'. As a result the reader is asked to 'fantasize atrocity and be morally outraged by the horrors conjured up in our minds' (2000: 77). Goldhagen's dramatising style, then, is already the kind of hybrid history-cum-fantasy characteristic of the society of the spectacle. Unlike the many (drier) historiographical accounts of the Third Reich and the Holocaust, this prurient 'drama' (like the soapy 1978 TV series *Holocaust*) became an international bestseller.

The Kindly Ones grafts itself onto an entire archive of 'fascism'. The musical structure in which sections of the novel are titled according to parts of a baroque dance suite, is reminiscent of *Rigadon* (1965), the final novel of Céline's war trilogy. The leitmotivish structuring principle is already apparent in Curzio Malaparte's Proustian account of the Eastern Front in *Kaputt* (1944), where sections are given the names of animals whose corpses then feature prominently. Incest and parricide point to Sophocles and Aeschylus, but the former is also part of Thomas Bernhard's most-performed play *Vor dem Ruhestand* (*The Eve of Retirement*, 1979) in which a former camp commandant quietly celebrates Himmler's birthday by donning his old SS uniform, sleeping with one sister and dressing the other in striped prison garb. He too has a legal profession; his remarkable genocidal career is also narrativised in trophy photographs. The fascist as sexually aberrant constitutes a predominantly Italian cinematic trope, running from Fellini's *Rome, Open City* through to Pasolini's *Salò*, Visconti's *The Damned*, Cavani's *The Night Porter* and Brass's *Salon Kitty* until it finally degenerates into Holocaust porn. By the 1970s it is already a tired cliché.

Max Aue shares his name with Max Schulz, Edgar Hilsenrath's war criminal who also has a rather peculiar phantasmagorical sex life involving abject and grotesque bodies, and a 'difficult' relationship to his parents. Like Céline's *D'un chateau l'autre* (*Castle to Castle*, 1957), Littell marshals a whole host of historic characters and a protagonist obsessed with waste and shit (also a feature of Tournier's *The Ogre* and the coprocentric observations in Amis's *Time's Arrow*). The surreal nature of the final section, when the regime veers towards its collapse, borrows its conceit from Céline's sequel *Nord* (*North*, 1960) and John Hawkes's *The Cannibal* (1949), both set in a fantastical vanquished Germany. The thanatic excess is strongly indebted to Léon Degrelle's *La Campagne de Russie* (1949), the memoir of a Belgian collaborator Littell read during his work on *The Kindly Ones* and which he analysed in his essay *Le sec et l'humide* (2008), a Theweleit-inspired interpretation of the soldierly self. The passages on the Eastern Front and Stalingrad owe a debt to Elem Klimov's film *Come and See* (1985), Theodor Plievier's novel of the same name, to Gerd Ledig's *Die Stalinorgel* (*The Stalin Organ*, 1955), to Vasily Grossman's epic *Life and Fate* and to Curzio Malaparte's *Il Volga nasce in Europa*. One could add, for good measure, the enormous number of historiographical voices that echo through, from Raul Hilberg to Saul Friedländer, Hannah Arendt, Ian Kershaw and Ulrich Herbert. Their accumulation is not merely excessive but representative, in the rhetorical manner of Dostoyevsky's *Notes from Underground* in which the 'editor' confirms the fictionality of the work while maintaining its veracity:

> I have tried to present to the public in a more striking form than is usual a character belonging to the very recent past, a representative figure from a generation still surviving. In the chapter entitled 'The Underground' this personage introduces himself and his outlook on life, and tries, as it were, to elucidate the causes that brought about, inevitably brought about, his appearance in our midst. (1972: 13)

This epitaph might have sat just as appropriately at the beginning of *The Kindly Ones* whose narrative strategy also brings before the reader 'in a more striking form than is usual' 'a representative figure' and attempts in this hyperbolic fashion to elucidate the fateful inevitability of his existence and actions.

As Jochen Hörisch has pointed out, Bernhard Schlink's Hanna Schmitz is not a realistic character but overdetermined (2010: 596). Similarly Maximilien Aue is a perpetrator as *Kunstfigur* (Dostoyevsky's 'personage'), an atrocious composite as polyphonic voice or genocidal career – precisely the compacted accumulation of research with all its polarised discourses. Like Schmitz, he asks us 'what would you have done'? Emerging from all this accumulated knowledge the key question still requires an individual's answer. Samuel Moyn (2009) rightly called Aue a 'Nazi Zelig', implausible in his presence at Babi Yar, Sobibor, Auschwitz, Stalingrad, the siege of Berlin and occupied Paris but emblematically a mirror of Nazism with all its contradictions, and only in that sense 'representative'. Aue's very implausibility, ubiquity and excess ought to alert the reader to the protagonist's artificiality and lead us to question our peculiar readerly desire for 'fascism': to read about perpetration in novelistic form, and on an epic scale; to seek out the perpetrator's voice is perhaps, as in Stephen King's 'Apt Pupil', the consequence of elevating the Holocaust to the unrepresentable. Aue is a product of reading – Littell's research, our reading process of his 'confession', the character's own study of historiographical and testimonial texts as well as his visually consumed interpretation of the war, his actions and his psyche, not to speak of the rich visual archive of cinematic 'fascism' alongside war film or photography. We too have been 'manufacturing memories' of 'fascism' as fascism, so what we are presented with in *The Kindly Ones* is recognisably familiar. Aue emphasises that 'What I did, I did with my eyes open' (2009b: 18) – a phrase that runs through the book like a refrain. In this context one might do well to recall the Wehrmacht exhibition of 1996/97. Its photographic documentation of war on the Eastern Front did not just debunk the myth of the clean Wehrmacht, leading to renewed inquiries into family history. It also demonstrated the habituation and indifference of ordinary soldiers to what they did or witnessed. What the visitor saw was a twofold horror: that of atrocities committed and how they had been framed by the perpetrator's or the bystander's touristic gaze. How problematic that gaze is we have seen in the previous chapters, particularly in relation to the depiction of sexualised violence. How Littell handles Aue's gaze on abject female bodies tells us a lot about how his novel differs from, say, Kerr's and McEwan's 'fascisms'.

The pleasure of flinching: abjection and the fascist gaze

In *Regarding the Pain of Others*, Susan Sontag emphasised the *inevitable* voyeurism that pertains to the act of looking at suffering. She traced the iconography of such images back to classical antiquity, pagan myths and Christian martyrology, plastic and visual representations of which abound in Western culture without any moral charges attaching to them. The flaying of Marsias, the tortures of Tantalus, the martyrdom of St Sebastian or the slaying of the virgins, Christ's crucifixion and Goya's *Disasters of War*, are all part of our (educated) archive of the body-in-pain. As Sontag pointed out, 'There is the satisfaction of being able to look at the image without flinching. There is the pleasure of flinching' (2003: 36–8). Literature, too, has offered us graphic depictions of corporeal horrors, from Homer's and Livy's battle scenes to Dante's Inferno; from biblical scenes of slaughter to the *Chanson de Roland*, from Flaubert's *Salammbô* to Kafka's penal colony. Readerly flinching (and the moral elevation it carries) is precisely what is at stake in *The Kindly Ones*. Unlike the books we have discussed in Chapters 1 and 2, Littell problematises the visualisation and visual consumption of violence on the level of character, writer and reader.

Aue's reflections on why he can't stop looking although what he sees physically and mentally troubles him returns us once again to his initial and repeated claim on common human traits. He recalls a passage from Plato's *The Republic* in which he cites Leontius' ambivalent reaction of fascination and horror vis-à-vis a pile of corpses: '*he struggled with himself and covered his eyes, till at length, overcome by the desire, he forced his eyes wide open with his fingers, and, running up to the bodies, exclaimed: "There! you devils! gaze your fill at the beautiful spectacle!"*' (2009b: 98). Given how often Aue and the reader look at 'the beautiful spectacle' of atrocity (rendered as 'spicy little stories') such passages give the reader permission to gaze upon horror through Aue's eyes precisely because we may feel the same ambivalence. The graphic depiction of killing and dying follows on from, and offers an important contrast to, the circumlocutions, abstractions and euphemisms of fascist jargon which obfuscated the truth of mass murder through syntax and lexis.[14] Yet what we are presented with is no glamorisation of the suffering heroic man-in-uniform, nor pruriently displayed abject female bodies, and certainly no aestheticised Proustian passages about horses artistically frozen into a lake, strong hands gliding through wicker baskets full of human eyes, corpses gracefully tumbling out of carriages as in Malaparte's *Kaputt*. This genocidal war, in contrast, is full of bureaucracy and cynical power machinations. Mostly in the company of men he dislikes, Aue does without the homosocial camaraderie or the sexual opportunism that is such a staple of war writing. Long before his head injury during the battle of Stalingrad, Aue is assaulted by what war means to his sense of self, the threat of losing himself in chaos, lawlessness, brutality and mess.

Let me return, then, to Aue's emphasis on 'mental hygiene', as if his confession were a ritual of purification (he admits to postwar constipation). Already in 'Toccata' we sense his aversion to disorder, dirt, filth and excreta in a narrative that will be saturated by these effusions. He has ritualised vomiting ('I brush my teeth, down a little shot of alcohol, and continue what I was doing'; 2009b: 8), and he never goes near the looms in his factory lest he gets dirty. In *Male Fantasies*, Klaus Theweleit identified the construction of 'hard' or 'dry' fascist masculinity as a defence against feminised 'liquid' states that threaten the boundaries of fascist masculinity: 'dirty' Jews, 'filthy' Slavs, the 'swamp' of democracy, and bolshevist red floods are fended off through the orderly rows of marching soldiers in their racialised struggle for political renewal (1977: 492–519). Fascism takes over the role of art or religion, to cleanse and purify, but in that, according to Aue, it mimics Judaism, which – provocatively – makes victims and executioners 'interchangeable':

> The Jews too had this strong feeling of community, of *Volk*: they mourned their dead, buried them if they could and said Kaddish; but as long as one single Jew remained alive, Israel lived. That no doubt, was the reason they were our privileged enemies, they resembled us too much. (2009b: 102)

This reads less like a plausible retrospective reflection on the psychological motivation of Nazi racial policy than a Kristevaen commentary on the pathology of abjection, that is, turning a phantasm of what is abjected into an object of hatred (Kristeva 1984: 10). In fact, much of Aue's reporting on war and genocide is about abjection, and his self-reflexive interventions could be read as that peripheral consciousness in which abjection remains present. 'Toccata' offers us a fantasy of the purest return to narcissistic pleasure, boundless unity with the maternal body in the image of the conceiving woman:

> I probably would rather have been a woman. Not necessarily a woman living and functioning in this world as a wife or a mother; no, a woman naked, on her back, her legs spread wide open, crushed beneath the weight of a man, clinging to him and pierced by him, drowning in him as she becomes the limitless sea in which he himself is drowned, pleasure that's endless, and beginningless too. (2009b: 23)

This is not a transgender phantasy, I would argue, but a yearning for an earlier, oceanic state of being, a plenitude with which women are identified. Amis's reverse temporal trajectory also returns the perpetrator to the mother's womb. Aue's incestuous love for his twin sister, stated in the subsequent paragraph, is a pleasurable attempt at such unity through dissolution in an other. War, like sex, also offers longed-for and dreaded dissolution, and this ambivalence is of course reflected in the *narrative* disintegration from a realist representation of physical dissolution to a phantasmagoria about sexual and physical dissolution, the merging of real and symbolic.

The desire for limitlessness finds fulfilment in the sense of absolute power that gradually takes hold of officers and soldiers, who 'thought they were allowed to do all sorts of things, unimaginable things' (2009b: 88) in the early 'amateurish' phase of the mass shootings. Haunted by 'a passion for the absolute', Aue experiences war as an opportunity 'for the overcoming of all limits' (96). This unboundedness is also subject to a concomitant dread. In a commentary reminiscent of Léon Degrelle's account of local conditions, Aue describes how the fertile Ukrainian loess soil turns in late summer into a primeval morass: 'a sticky mud, thick and black, that the soldiers called *buna*. Endless stretches of swamp formed then, where the corpses and carcasses of horses scattered by the fighting slowly decomposed. Men were succumbing to endless diarrhoea' (79–80). Men and earth dissolve into brown matter, liquefy in fecundity and fetidness, a revolting union of beginnings and endings, life and death. As Kristeva argues about the relationship between the self and the corpse-as-waste:

> refuse and corpses *show me* what I permanently thrust aside in order to live. These body fluids, this defilement, this shit are what life withstands, hardly and with difficulty on the part of death. There, I am at the border of my condition as a living being. My body extricates itself, as being alive, from that border. Such wastes drop, so that I might live, until, from loss to loss, nothing remains in me and my entire body falls beyond the limit – *cadere*, cadaver. If dung signifies the other side of the border, the place where I am not and which permits me to be, the corpse, the most sickening of wastes, is a border that has encroached upon everything. (1984: 3)

The war, and the novel, is precisely an attempt as extrication from that encroaching border. Even in his dreams Aue cannot hold in excreta, he fills toilet bowls to overflowing and gradually sinks in his own faecal matter until its stench fills his mouth (2009b: 114). In Auschwitz, he observes how prisoners defecate while walking (Amis recounts, in reverse, how a prisoner is drowned in a latrine), their emaciated bodies dissolving more and more. One could read Aue's account as the auto-biographical equivalent of the work of the '*Scheisskommando*' (the unit of intellectuals ordered to work in the camps' latrine blocks). In evacuating his story, Aue voids himself and hopes for rebirth, or at least for the re-establishing of borders. At the same time the reader drowns in the effluence of fascism, in floods of violence and tedious officialese, typographically condensed into interminable paragraphs (Littell 2006b).

In 'Allemandes I and II', the section covering the invasion of the Soviet Union and the work of the *Einsatzgruppen*, Aue is assaulted by a sense of chaos and dissolution. In Lutsk Castle he observes how an arm comes loose when Wehrmacht soldiers try to clear a pile of putrefying corpses. 'The smell was vile; and this smell, I knew, was the beginning and end of everything, the very signification of our existence' (2009b: 33–4). The lawless chaos in Lemberg, where Ukrainian nationalists and locals unleash a pogrom on the Jewish population, fills him with 'anguish', accelerates his heart beat and makes him 'feel oppressed' (48–9). The dead and dying contribute to this alarming threat of liquefaction for the fascists as the victims' blood and excreta make bodies slippery, turn mass executions into a gory mess that splatters all over the perpetrators. This is a literalisation of liquidation: dying reduces the solid body to the body-as-fluid, which is paradoxically the moment when the killers' live bodies (consuming vast amounts of alcohol, suffering from loose bowels, disgorging machine gun salvos like fountains) most resemble their victims' corpses. Mass murder, of course, is anything but orderly or clean: 'Seen close up, things were proceeding much less calmly' (128), Aue comments in the ravine of Babi Yar.[15] As we know from Rudolf Höß's autobiography, calm orderliness was one of the main goals of the industrialised killing process, not only to make it more efficient but also to reduce the psychological and physical impact on the killers. For this reason, eye contact and any physical contact have to be avoided (Semelin 2005: 273).

In the ravine of Babi Yar, however, where Aue kills for the first time, his anguish is projected outwards. The fear of liquefaction and liquidation is transformed into a phantasmagorical aggression against the prone body of a young woman still breathing. The more hardened the killer, the less he resembles the soft flesh of the corpses he produces. Note the breathlessly long, paratactical passage:

> She stared at me with her large surprised incredulous eyes, the eyes of a wounded bird, and that look stuck into me, split open my stomach and let a flood of sawdust pour out, I was a ragdoll and didn't feel anything, and at the same time I wanted with all my heart to bend over and brush the dirt and sweat off her forehead, caress her cheek and tell her that it was going to be all

right, that everything would be fine, but instead I convulsively shot a bullet into her head, which after all came down to the same thing, for her in any case if not for me, since at the thought of this senseless human waste I was filled with an immense boundless rage, I kept shooting at her and her head exploded like a fruit, then my arm detached itself from me and went off all by itself down the ravine, shooting left and right, I ran after it, waving at it to wait with my other arm, but it didn't want to, it mocked me and shot at the wounded all by itself, without me . . . (2009b: 130)

The catalyst for Aue's rage is the woman's gaze and what it harbours, her ineffable knowledge of her imminent death. At her most vulnerable she is at her most powerful, opening up his armoured body into 'a flood' that 'pour[s] out' of him. Yet in this instance of disembowelling he turns out to have been already dead or, more precisely, merely a simulacrum of something living: an unfeeling 'ragdoll'. Knowledge, in this passage, excludes feeling. The *coup de grace* is not an act of mercy but a pathological symptom of abjection in which the 'ragdoll' turns the knowing woman into 'fruit': no one is allowed to know since knowledge requires feeling and feeling requires vulnerable flesh. Only the victim can know but for this reason she is resented. The moment of realisation that the woman-about-to-die possesses the knowledge of dying is also the moment in which the narrative enacts a disintegration from visceral realism to phantasmagoria. This is a vignette of what will happen to the narrative as a whole, notably in the section 'Air'. The convulsively, madly shooting anthropomorphised arm is all that is left of the hard, armoured body rescuing itself from the pulpy mess around it. Just as Leontius treated his eyes as if they were separate wilful entities, Aue writes of his independent shooting arm.

A similar scene follows later on, after Blobel has begun experimenting with Saurer gas vans in Kharkov. Aue inflicts on himself 'this piteous spectacle' of witnessing executions but by then he is beyond the existential 'rupture' that is killing and is – tellingly – 'sinking into mud while searching for light' (2009b: 178–9). His next spectacle is the execution of a female partisan. This scene initially gives the impression of a sexualised scene of ritual humiliation, as soldiers and officers file past the bound and condemned woman, kissing her before she is hanged (reminiscent of the female hanging at the end of Pasolini's *Salò*). Aue's encounter with her, however, again disintegrates into phantasm:

When my turn came, she looked at me, a clear luminous look, washed of everything, and I saw that she understood everything, knew everything, and faced with this pure knowledge I burst into flames. My clothes crackled, the skin of my belly melted, the fat sizzled, fire roared in my eye sockets and my mouth, and cleaned out the inside of my skull. The blaze was so intense she had to turn her head away. I burned to a cinder, my remains were transformed into a salt statue; soon it cooled down, pieces broke off, first a shoulder, then a hand, then half the head. Finally, I finished collapsing at her feet and the wind swept away the pile of salt and scattered it. (2009b: 179)

The catalyst is the same as in the scene at Babi Yar: the woman-about-to-die returns Aue's gaze with, apparently, superior knowledge (of her death, her dissolution). This 'pure' knowledge occasions a phantasmagorical double dying of spontaneous combustion and biblical punishment. Again, the narrative enacts disintegration by shifting from visceral realism to a consummate fantasy of cremation. This scene could be a dramatisation of the fainting fit that Kristeva describes as a response to the perception of a borderless state: 'On the edge of non-existence and hallucination, of a reality that, if I acknowledge it, annihilates me ... I behold the breaking down of a world that has erased its borders: fainting away.' 'Deprived of world ... *I fall in a faint*' (1984: 2; 4). The disintegration of the narrative – the 'hallucination' or combustion Aue describes – is precisely a retrospective acknowledgment of the reality his 'work'. As Jacques Semelin argues, 'the killers' representations continually evolve in line with what they do in the field. It is not just the framework of meaning that precipitates the act itself [i.e. the euphemistic jargon, the ideological justification]; it is the very act of massacring that recreates the contextual meaning of such an action' (Semelin 2005: 250). The repeated insistence by senior staff on discipline and 'decency' in the face of such 'dirty work' as executions of 'partisans' betrays not just an awareness of the lawless vortex of impunity and the swoon of omnipotence that might engulf perpetrators. Such exhortations warn of the dangers of swooning *towards* rather than away from lifeless states; of manufacturing corpses *and* becoming one.

Women carry the mysterious knowledge of dying as both dreaded and desired dissolution. Walking past the partisan's corpse for weeks, Aue recalls:

> The body of this girl was also a mirror for me. The rope had broken or they had cut it, and she lay in the snow in the Trade Unions Park, her neck broken, her lips swollen, one bare breast gnawed by dogs. Her rough hair formed a Medusa crest around her head and she seemed fabulously beautiful to me, inhabiting death like an idol, Our-Lady-of-the-Snows. Whatever path I took ... I always found her lying in my way, a stubborn, single-minded question that threw me into a labyrinth of vain speculation and made me lose my footing. (2009b: 179–80)

This scene is once again the story of an authentic photograph, of the abandoned body of Zoya Kosmodemyanskaya, hanged for arson.[16] For

Aue, her abject body, like that of Jesus or a Catholic saint, becomes sanctified, legendary, fabulous. Precisely because she 'inhabits' death she holds pure knowledge from which he is nonetheless excluded. If her body becomes a mirror its reflection is precisely that: 'vain speculation' rather than insight. What women know remains ineffable for Aue, he can merely attempt to inhabit a female position. Passive sex with men is the closest he can come to such pure (female) knowledge of the limitless sea of endlessness and beginninglessness. Sex, in this novel, is both a way of fending off war *and* of wallowing in it; of hardening the body against disintegration *and* making it permeable to invasion; it is the ultimate abjection.

In 'Sarabande' when he meets his sister Una again, there is a passage in which she appears to let him sleep with her ('I leaned over her and she didn't resist'; 2009b: 491) which is followed by a memory of a visit to a torture museum where he anally rapes his sister on a guillotine. 'But this memory is dubious', comments the narrator:

> after our childhood we had seen each other only once, that time in Zurich, and in Zurich there was no guillotine, I don't know, it was probably a dream, an old dream perhaps that, in my confusion, alone in my dark room at the Eden Hotel, I had remembered, or even a dream dreamt that night, during a brief moment of sleep, almost unnoticed. I was angry, for the day, despite all my distress, had remained shot through with purity for me, and now these foul images were coming and soiling it. It repelled me but at the same time troubled me, since I knew that, memory or image or fantasy or dream, this also lived inside me, and that my love must have been made of this too. (2009b: 492)

At the end we cannot be sure, nor can the narrator, of what is real and what is dream, what is memory and what fantasy but its precise status on the periphery of Aue's consciousness hardly matters. He realises that his sexual encounters with Una constitute an abject narrative of love in which 'foul images' soil the purity of unity. He may well desire a return to a previous state of plenitude, loving her 'more than I had loved her in our mother's womb' (2009b: 491), but at the same time this return can only take on the state of transgressive incest that threatens to undermine his subjectivity. Later in 'Air' his 'sordid anguish' is even described as 'startling fantasies, the demented vision of a coprophagic autarky' (886), in which he and his twin sister live entirely off their excreta in a self-sufficient libidinal economy. Such passages are many in a novel that offers precise descriptions of sex but never clarifies whether it happens or whether it remains a fantasy or a dream, and in this way suggests that our mental sex life is just as real as our empirical one. More importantly, both sex and killing produce 'foul images' and are abject experiences.

Female readers and reviewers were particularly offended by the novel's anal eroticism and its gaze at abject female bodies. We should note here that both war and the camps are part of a coprocentric universe in Hilsenrath's, Amis's and Céline's novels as well. Aue's gaze at female abjection certainly echoes the gender politics of these novels[17] and the cinema of 'fascinating fascism' whose female bodies are both seductive and repellent. One might perhaps ask how one could represent the perpetrator's perspective (amply captured in the hundreds of thousands of trophy photographs and the tons of documents relating to war and genocide) *without* such a pathology of abjection since it is an integral part of war and genocide. In the previous two chapters we have seen that the representation of fascism often relied on female abjection: remember the observed rape of Grete Six in Kerr's *March Violets* or the reported rape in McEwan's *Black Dogs*. Ostensibly these voyeuristic acts of witnessing illustrated the sadistic cruelty of Nazism and created bystander positions for the protagonists. Yet the authors of these texts seemed to believe in the moral neutrality of this position, whereas Littell certainly does not acquit Aue: 'I consider that watching involves my responsibility as much as doing' (2009b: 482), he says repeatedly – an insight that Kerr's Bernie Gunther completely lacks. Watching, for Aue, is a matter of agency, and so is reading. When the 'spicy little stories' finally morph into a flood of masturbatory and coprophiliac fantasy, like Céline's central metaphor of the overflowing toilet in *Castle to Castle*, the reader should see this as an extension of the phantasmagorical sections that accompanied earlier passages of abjection. In the final paragraph, having killed his friend Dr Hauser in the ruins of Berlin Zoo, his mind 'was coming apart'. We leave Aue at the moment he has freed himself from incriminating evidence or witnesses in the middle of an image that could have been painted by Hieronymus Bosch: in contemplation of two bodies, alone with a dying hippopotamus, a few ostriches, 'alone with time and grief and the sorrow of remembering, the cruelty of my existence and of my death still to come' (2009b: 975). He has learnt nothing since he is still alive looking into the open eyes of his dead friend who so teasingly withholds all knowledge.

We read about killing in order to find out what dying might be like (but to own and disavow such curiosity at the same time). *The Kindly Ones* is an excessive book: it presents a veritable database narrative of historiographical, testimonial, photographic and fictional fascism. Its perpetrator is a *compositum* of all manner of psychosexual and sociological explicatory paradigms. Littell's way of making us witness perpetration confronts us with our morbid curiosity for 'spicy little stories' of illicit knowledge. This strategy emphasises that ultimately such knowledge cannot provide insight, only hallucinations or mirror images. *The Kindly Ones*, then, is an abject book about abjection, its 'fascism' is about what we have made fascism mean and what we insist it remain: shocking and banal; inscrutably other and discursively familiar; but above all a projection of all that we disavow: our excess, our waste, our disgusting selves. To pull us along over nearly a thousand pages of an impossible epistemological quest that implicates us as reader-witnesses, reader-bystanders, reader-perpetrators, reader-analysts is no mean feat. That many reviewers responded to this immersing experience with vitriol ('sinking into the mud while searching for light') surely mirrors Aue's response to the gaze of the dying bodies he encounters. Rather than succumb to such soft dying flesh, to such illicit knowledge of one's own weakness, a hard and harsh response is required to cleanse and purify. Accusing *The Kindly Ones* of being an unethical book amounts to the pathology of abjection. It is precisely why the book is a necessary response to 'fascism'. Given how crucial projection is to 'fascism' and to abjection, it is time to see how these phenomena work in our cinematic archive.

Notes

1. Littell offers a more differentiated approach to perpetration in his Theweleit-inspired essay *Le Sec et l'humide* (2008), on the Belgian fascist and Waffen-SS officer Léon Degrelle's memoirs *Le campagne de Russie* (1949), a source for *The Kindly Ones*. In the essay's postscript he distinguishes between, on the one hand, the millions of conscripts and the thousands of career civil servants and bureaucrats who are swept into global wars; and on the other, men whose psychological needs make them volunteer for groups subscribing to extreme violence (the *Freikorps*, South American paramilitaries, Russian and US special forces, or Al Qaida – all tendentiously lumped together). Littell 2009a: 135.
2. On perpetrators in the Yugoslavian civil war see, for instance, Slavenka Drakulić's *They Would Never Hurt A Fly* (2004), Nicol Ljubić's *Meeresstille* (2010) or Alexsandar Hemon's *The Lazarus Project* (2008).
3. Golsan 2010: 182. In several interviews, Littell has rejected the uniqueness of the Shoah and argued for the exceptionality of 'every genocide'. See for instance the interview with Blumenfeld (2008) or with Frank Browning for NPR radio, 'Fictionalized "kindly" Nazi creates a stir', 8 March 2009, available at <http://www.npr.org/templates/story/story.php?storyId=101392286> (last accessed 10 June 2012). Given the frequency of state-sanctioned mass murder in the twentieth century, a comparative approach seems increasingly necessary. Manus Midlarsky's *The Killing Trap* (2005), Michael Mann's *The Dark Side of Democracy* (2005) and Jacques Semelin's *Purify and Destroy* (2005) make a strong case for the merits of *comparing* the social, political and psychological aspects of the

collective and individual dynamics of various twentieth-century massacres, genocides and forms of 'ethnic cleansing'. In their analyses they demonstrate the interplay between ideological state-sanctioned violence and individual 'genocidal careers' thus made possible in a range of social strata, but most remarkably within the professional middle classes: civil servants, officers, managers, lawyers, technicians, engineers, teachers, whose perception of reality has been brought into line with authority.

4. For the sake of convenience I shall cite from the English translation unless the French original yields a different interpretation.

5. A continental European reader may be more willing to contemplate the contingency of perpetration, not least because of the continent's experience of occupation and collaboration. In contrast, readers from formerly Allied nations may feel much more morally and geographically removed from fascism. Such complacency is also challenged through the narrator's comparisons between fascism and (neo-)imperialist policy. For a reading of Littell's comparisons between fascist and non-fascist imperialism see Sanyal 2010.

6. Similar controversies over the perpetrator's voice and the reader's complicity arose over Bret Easton Ellis' *American Psycho*; the point of the book is of course precisely to demonstrate to the reader how we have come to consume sex and murder. D.M. Thomas's *The White Hotel* also had a problematic reception, not least because of a bayonet-rape scene at Babi Yar coupled with the charge of plagiarism. Sue Vice has argued convincingly that a close analysis of the relevant passages reveals changes in voice and point of view that explain voyeurism since it is the perpetrator who becomes focaliser (2000: Chapter 2).

7. In the original: 'une sorte de transparence au réel, un effacement derrière ce qui est dit ou décrit, ce que Blanchot, peut-être, appelait le neutre' (Littell 2006b).

8. 'Ce n'est pas tant un personage qu'une voix, un ton, un regard. Il y a une distance, une disjonction entre ce que Max décrit, puisqu'il voit tous les autres de manière extrêmement lucide, et lui-même, comme s'il n'était pas le narrateur, en quelque sorte' (Littell and Nora 2007: 29).

9. For instance the photographs of the public execution of Mosche Kogan and Wolf Kieper in Zhitomir (Washington Holocaust Memorial Museum #18454) available at <http:resources.ushmm.org/inquery/uia_doc.php/query/8?uf=uia_VAOLOu> (last accessed 14 October 2012), or the beating and terrorising of a near-naked woman being chased through Lemberg by Ukrainian nationalists (photograph available at <http://www.HolocaustResearchProject.org>).

10. Note how different this perspective is to the prurient project in Stephen King's novella 'Apt Pupil' where the adolescent protagonist asks the camp commandant in hiding: 'what did it feel like?' ('it' meaning having power over life and death). The protagonist's sexual fantasies, stimulated by the commandant's reports, are relayed to the reader in graphic, misogynistic and anti-Semitic detail fully congruent with classic 1970s Holocaust porn.

11. Martin Amis, for instance, cites Robert Lifton's *The Nazi Doctors* as crucial to *Time's Arrow*; D.M. Thomas acknowledges Anatoly Kuznetsov's *Babi Yar* and the testimony of survivor Dina Pronicheva for a chapter in *The White Hotel*.

12. See also the German publisher's official website that offers plenty of flow-charts for Nazi organisations, maps of the Eastern front and concentration camps, as well as transcribed interviews, external links and further essays: <www.diewohlgesinnten.de>

13. The French original particularly models itself on the linguistic markers of classic realism in the verb tenses. See Littell 2006a.

14. This jargon literally contaminates the novel's vocabulary through 'barbarisms' of foreign words, according to Martin von Koppenfels (2010). It is the main reason why the German translation is so markedly different from the French original and the English version, because it can never reproduce this effect.

15. For an excellent collection of documents, soldier's letters and photographs of the war of extermination including the massacre of Babi Yar see Klee and Dreßen's '*Gott mit uns*' (1989).

16. The photographs of her execution and her corpse are easily available on the internet but the provenance and source of the photographs are harder to ascertain. Kosmodemyanskaya's case became controversial in the 1990s after it was revealed that she might have been betrayed by villagers who feared their own property might be damaged in her arson attacks: the unity of Soviet resistance to Nazi occupation was at stake. Kosmodemyanskaya is said to have resisted giving away the names of fellow partisans under torture. What is most disturbing about this story of a 'Hero of the Soviet Union' are the prurient conditions of the post-Soviet publication of her martyrdom. Even well-meaning sites that publish Kosmodemyanskaya's story of suffering dwell graphically on the manner of her torture, with widely varying detailed descriptions of methods, instruments and duration.

17. For Anne Fuchs (1999), Hilsenrath's abject and grotesque female bodies are part of a tradition that begins long before the war and the Holocaust.

Chapter 4

The Good German: The Stauffenberg Plot and its Discontents

In 1998 Piotr Uklański mounted his installation *Untitled (The Nazis)* at the Photographers Gallery in London. It consisted of 166 captionless stills, publicity posters and photographs showing well-known actors in Nazi roles, mostly from Hollywood productions with some shots from European arthouse films. Cinema, more than any other art form let alone history education, has shaped our visual inventory of 'fascism'. This seemed an obvious point to make but it was not a welcome one. There were protests outside the gallery accusing the artist of glamorising fascism. When Uklański's photo frieze was mounted at the Zachęta Gallery in Warsaw two years later, the actor Daniel Olbrychski, whose photo was part of the installation, slashed some of the images with a sword. Subsequently the Polish minister for culture demanded that Uklański provide captions that clarified his condemnation of Nazism or the exhibition would close. Close it did. Another two years later, Norman Kleeblatt curated a group exhibition at the Jewish Museum in New York under the title *Mirroring Evil: Nazi Imagery/Recent Art*. It included Uklański's frieze and a number of artworks that pointed at the commercialisation of the Holocaust such as Zbigniew Libera's *Lego Concentration Camp Set*, Tom Sachs's *Prada Deathcamp* and Roee Rosen's *Live and Die as Eva Braun*. This exhibition too drew protests for aestheticising fascism.[1] Such controversies indicate that a new generation of artists has begun to challenge the doxas of Holocaust piety, pointing to the fact that Western culture has merely paid lip service to it while commodifying fascism and Holocaust as entertainment. At the same time the protests themselves suggest that artists' critique of the commodification of 'fascism' is almost consistently misread and their art interpreted as straightforward fascism. Hence the demand for explanatory captions and the return to intentionality.[2] The iconography of 'fascism' seems to have made it harder to distinguish between documentary and pastiche, between provocation and glorification, and between the real thing and its imitation.

This is a crucial issue when it comes to the representation of more differentiated treatments of fascism, for instance films in which characters have doubts about their ideological affiliation or films about the German resistance, such as Bryan Singer's recent *Valkyrie*, which focuses on the failed plot to assassinate Hitler in July 1944, starring Tom Cruise as Colonel Claus Graf Schenk von Stauffenberg. How does the audience distinguish between the good guys and the villains if all of them look like versions of Uklański's stills? In this chapter I want to trace the cinematic history of the figure of Good German to contextualise the representational difficulties faced by a story like *Valkyrie*. What strategies are available to filmmakers in terms of casting, accent, cinematography or production design to construct the Good German? What are the ideological uses of such a figure and how do they change from the postwar to the post-Cold War period? For this purpose I'm going to read the Stauffenberg figure in *Valkyrie* alongside earlier representations of Good Germans, notably James Mason's Rommel and Marlon Brando's Christian Diestl. Despite a star-studded cast of American, German and British actors, *Valkyrie* was a commercial and critical failure, grossing merely $200 million worldwide (£6.3m in the UK, $83m in the USA).[3] Why did this film fail to capture the audience's interest? Is our notion of fascism so ossified through decades of cinematic 'fascism' that resistance or opposition become visually unrepresentable? And how do fascist aesthetics – clearly part of the historical backdrop, of 'periodisation' – function in stories that are ostensibly anti-fascist? Is any of Nazism's power to enthral and fascinate diminished by the protagonists' opposition?

Valkyrie is part of a more recent trend towards a pluralistic representation of the Second World War that hopes to eschew the tired clichés of cardboard villains in SS uniforms. Many German film scholars see the boom in post-unification films about the Third Reich as a conservative phenomenon that helps normalise the position of the present Berlin Republic within a post-Cold War European landscape: high production values create visual spectacles that reduce even the darkest history to heritage.[4] The increasing remoteness of wartime permits an inevitably uneven creative re-engagement with the war in Germany and in many European countries. This is fed by melodrama and sentiment as much as by a desire for a treatment of previously neglected aspects or unrepresented material even if it is part of difficult history: carpet bombing, occupation, or collaboration.[5] The German opposition to Nazism, long dismissed as a disparate and negligible minority, has had a difficult discursive history even in Germany.[6] However, it has recently received attention in a number of films such as Margarethe von Trotta's

Rosenstraße (2003), Marc Rothemund's *Sophie Scholl: Die letzten Tage* (2005) and Jo Baier's *Stauffenberg: Der 20. Juli 1944* (2004).[7] In fact, the story of Stauffenberg's failed assassination plot has been told many times. Three German films – G.W. Pabst's *Es geschah am 20. Juli* (*Aufstand gegen Adolf Hitler!*), Falk Harnack's *Der 20. Juli: Das Attentat auf Hitler* (both 1955), and Jo Baier's TV drama – specifically focus on the assassination attempt, while both Alfred Weidenmann's *Canaris* (1955) and Anatol Litvak's *The Night of the Generals* (1966) reference it. Alongside Lawrence Schiller's TV dramatisation *The Plot to Kill Hitler* (1990), there are also two documentaries produced for US television: the academy-award nominated *The Restless Conscience* (1991), directed by Hava Kohav Beller, and Jean-Pierre Isbouts's *Operation Valkyrie* (2008). Peter Hoffmann acted as historical advisor to both *The Restless Conscience* and *Valkyrie*, and both emphasise not the complex ideological or psychological journey to killing Hitler but the bravery of the men and women involved.

In addition to an impressive corpus of biographies, memoirs and historical accounts of the resistance and previous individual plots, there are also several fictionalisations: Christian von Dithfurth's alternative history *Der 21. Juli* (2003), Stephen Marlowe's *The Valkyrie Encounter* (1978), Steve Erickson's *Tours of the Black Clock* (1989) and Paul West's *The Very Rich Hours of Count von Stauffenberg* (1989). More recently, Justin Cartwright has approached the plot laterally, through the conflicted friendship of one of the plotters, the lawyer and civil servant Adam von Trott zu Solz, with the philosopher and Oxford don Isaiah Berlin. *The Song Before It Is Sung* (2007) asks whether the plotters' deeply nationalist motivation could ever have found any understanding in Britain, where both a tragic conception of destiny and life under a fascist dictatorship seem to have been beyond the imagination of even the brightest minds. In Cartwright's novel, a former student is asked to write the story of this friendship and to look for two films, the public *Wochenschau* newsreel made of the trial of the plotters and the one of their execution, shot for Hitler's private delectation, and presumably lost. In its failure and aftermath, then, the plot immediately became a vindictive cinematic spectacle, used for propaganda and morbid satisfaction. Reading the postmemorial narrative treatment of watching these films in Cartwright's *The Song Before It Is Sung* against their cinematic period-drama recreation in *Valkyrie* will help us explore the potential and limitations of visualising fascism through the trope of the Good German.

Compensatory pleasures: constructing the Good German in the 1950s

The Good German is largely a product of the 1950s. For the home market, West German films dealing with the Second World War showed ordinary conscripted soldiers ('*Lanzers*'). These Everyman figures served as a foil for the 'real' carriers of ideologically motivated crimes, SS, SA, Gestapo, Nazi leadership. Plots spoke eloquently of the absurdity of war but did little to address questions of culpability, complicity or genocide. At best, the Everyman had been following orders under duress. Cinemagoers could see themselves on the screen as victims of a criminal regime. Apart from Wolfgang Staudte's *The Murderers are Amongst Us* (1946), those films addressing German crimes or culpability were by émigré directors (Robert Siodmak's *Nachts wenn der Teufel kam* [1957]; Peter Lorre's *Der Verlorene* [1951]). Casting became part of an exculpatory representational strategy. Fresh acting talent also broke any personnel continuities with UFA: Joachim Fuchsberger in the *08/15* trilogy, Walter Giller in *Rosen für den Staatsanwalt*, Günter Pfitzmann in the Stalingrad film *Hunde, wollt ihr ewig leben*, *Nacht fiel über Gotenhafen* (about the sinking of the Wilhelm Gustloff) and Bernhard Wicki's pacifist drama *The Bridge*. West German war films employed a casting strategy in which the star quality of the actor guaranteed the decency of the protagonist, particularly when that actor had attracted the attention of screen writers or playwrights highly critical of the Nazi regime such as Carl Zuckmayer or Rolf Hochhuth. As Jennifer Kapczynski (2007: 137–51) has argued, stars such as O.E. Hasse could bend ambivalences towards the Nazi past from a muted acknowledgement of responsibility towards atonement through noble suffering (under a criminal regime, wartime conditions, flight and bombardment). In Weidenmann's *Canaris* (1955), Hasse's talents domesticated the shady and highly ambiguous Abwehr Admiral (pitched against Martin Held's Heydrich) into a jolly cardigan-wearing fellow who looked after his employees to the extent of ensuring full bellies and happy romance. Often the script pitched professional integrity against ideological coercion. Hasse would play decent officers in British and German films, be it the fair-minded Colonel von Ecker in *Decision Before Dawn* (1951), the Captain of the Tirpitz in *Above us the Waves* (1955), von Plönnies in the tremendously successful *08/15* trilogy in the same year, or the saintly medical officer in *The Doctor of Stalingrad* (1958).[8] Traditionally *Canaris* has been read as part of a larger legitimising narrative in the ill-reputed repressive 1950s West German cinema to remilitarise the country through the formation of the Bundeswehr and NATO entry.[9]

The two films about the Stauffenberg plot to kill Hitler also belong to this exculpatory narrative of a clean Wehrmacht.

Yet the Good German did not just fulfil psychological and political needs in German cinema. The portrayal of Germans in 1950s Hollywood and British war films was by no means uniformly hostile. In fact, a considerable number showed them as outstanding professionals or were at least neutral about the former enemy.[10] The lead actors performed the task of 'selling' combat against a noble enemy as an honourable craft that tests masculinity and integrity. Different masculinities were mapped onto different national identities and became metonymies of ideology, but the characterisation often foregrounded commonality of purpose or naval tradition. In such moments the war film resembles a professional contest conducted by gentleman heroes as in the naval combat between Captain Langsdorff of the Graf Admiral Spee (Peter Finch) and Captain Dove (Bernard Lee) in *The Battle of the River Plate* (1956) or Curd Jürgens and Robert Mitchum in *The Enemy Below* (1957). Such German characters become interesting (and potentially 'good') when professional integrity comes into conflict with ideological demands and political scheming (Rayner 2007: 66–8; 98–9). This view of naval combat as a chivalric and professional form of heroic combat is partly the result of a retrospective rehabilitation of the *Kriegsmarine* under the umbrella of Cold War cultural politics; Jonathan Rayner calls this 'a displacement of national politics by naval nobility' (2007: 196–7). The effect of this displacement is to reinforce, within popular cultural perceptions of the war in Britain, the memory of a long institutional history of naval supremacy.

Perhaps the first candidate for the Good German was General Erwin Rommel whose soldierly competence was much admired in Britain, not least because in beating back the Desert Fox General Montgomery's soldiers had earned themselves the soubriquet Desert Rats. Both got their Hollywood response: Henry Hathaway's *The Desert Fox* (1951) with James Mason in the lead role which he should reprise briefly in Robert Wise's *The Desert Rats* two years later. Even during the war, Rommel came to embody glamour and the romance of the desert in a similar fashion to the way in which T.E. Lawrence had in an earlier conflict. In addition, the war in North Africa in films such as *The Desert Fox*, *The Desert Rats* or *Ice Cold in Alex* (1958) was presented as an entirely Anglo-German affair and therefore particularly apt in shoring up narratives of British heroism: the more venerable the enemy the greater the victory. The cinematic British Rommel became the paradigm for the decent German officer, and this image survived later revelations of the German military's complicity in the genocidal practices of the regime. Much of this was due to Desmond Young's bestselling hagiography in 1950, which had been serialised in the *Sunday Express* complete with swastika-rimmed advertisements. Young's book divided both public opinion and British historians (a sceptical Hugh Trevor-Roper versus a sympathetic Basil Liddell Hart). Rommel became a test case for the problem of assessing the German military's culpability. As Richard Crossman, former psychological warfare officer and later Labour MP put it succinctly:

> During the war we adopted Rommel, along with Lili Marlene, and made him an honorary Englishman by picturing him as the one German who played war according to the rules of cricket. Of course, this is a myth; many other German generals felt a keen distaste for S.S. methods, and Rommel was by no stretch of the imagination a gentleman . . . As a nation, we deceive ourselves into believing that there are two sorts of Germans – Good Germans and Bad Germans. The 'Bad Germans' are militarists, Nazis, anti-democratic, and perpetrators of atrocities. The 'Good Germans' are peace-loving democrats and real gentlemen. *Ergo*, since Rommel was a clean fighter, he must have been anti-Nazi, and men like him would make good allies of democracy against the Russians. (1950: 41)

For Crossman, the Good German–Evil Nazi dichotomy is merely a British projection of Anglo-Saxon virtues onto (select) German soldiers that follows the laws of postwar political expediency. In his analysis of this postwar British debate about the Rommel 'myth' and its manifestation in popular culture, Patrick Maior (2008) has argued that the international film industry in Britain and the USA contributed as much to the Rommel myth as its West German counterpart which was busy constructing a 'clean' Wehrmacht. War films, of course, are made for an international market, and if British and American productions were to succeed at the German and European box offices they could not constantly offend German sensibilities but must present similar redemptive strategies to those applied to the home markets. The odd Good German, then, was not just a postwar gesture of rapprochement but a lucrative strategy to exploit foreign cinema markets.

In 1943 Billy Wilder had cast Erich von Strohheim as Rommel in *Five Graves to Cairo*. Strohheim brought his pre-war roles to his wartime version of Rommel and turned him into a Wilhelmine officer complete with duelling scar and unbending authority. In *The Desert Fox* Mason's Rommel had proved himself on the North African battlefield but failed to convince a ranting Hitler that the war was lost. Mason brought a brooding darkness to the role. His screen presence evoked the trapped characters from his noir roles in *Odd Man Out* and *The Reckless Moment* which had evolved from the malevolence of his Gainsborough costume-drama villains in *The Man in Grey* and *Fanny by Gaslight*. In the 1950s his Hollywood roles shifted his type from the demonic or doomed lover to the dissenter and the loser (see Evans 2001). His ability to portray doubt and inner conflict helped to lend complexity to screen Germans throughout his career in *The Man Between*, *The Blue Max*, *Dare I Weep, Dare I Mourn*, *Cross of Iron*, *The Boys from Brazil* and *The Passage*.

Mason's Rommel was not an uncontroversial success at the time and gleaned reluctant praise although audiences flocked to the cinema. Many British reviewers resented the glamorisation of a German officer so soon after the war.[11] Mason's biographer, Sheridan Morley, noted that there were angry protests abroad from Jewish ex-servicemen about such a glorified portrayal of a Nazi general (1989: 93). *The Desert Rats* meant to redress the balance in favour of the British army and its commonwealth forces and gave Richard Burton the chance to be a plucky Tommy at Tobruk. Mason was worried: 'I felt that if I failed to play Rommel again they might hire a real German actor, and then my original performance would have been held up to question' Hirschhorn 1975: 99; Morley 1989: 99). *The Desert Rats* returns a stereotypical Teutonic arrogance to a German-accented Rommel in the crucial scene in the medical tent where Burton and Mason can verbally spar. But it is difficult to tell what in the script is meant to account for the tension, a difference in national character or the classic chaffing between different ranks. More important is Mason's claim on his version of Rommel somehow having to be protected from the authenticity effect produced by a 'real' German actor. Mason's Rommel is a British Rommel,[12] and a German general the British 'could take' (just about): an officer whose suicide in the wake of Hitler's post-July 20th purge granted him a merciful exit from the historical stage and whose defeat augmented Montgomery's glory. Perhaps unwittingly, the *Daily Mirror* captured the point of *The Desert Rats*: 'A first rate war film that does Britain proud. I have only one complaint. This film is so good it should have been British' (in Hirschhorn 1975: 114–15).

The cultural function of postwar British war films (and war films about the British experience such as *The Desert Rats*) was not primarily to represent violent history accurately but to make that history tolerable for an increasingly complex audience of war veterans and ordinary movie goers. And in that translation process the (predominantly male) audience of the 1950s might require greater realism but would also trade veracity for catharsis, and accept partial representation as long as some of their experiences were presented in a redemptive fashion. As Sue Harper has argued, popular memory was not necessarily shaped by the commercially most successful films (particularly not in the 1950s, when the film industry faced competition from television). Rather, it was those films that presented a recuperative version of the past for male veterans; that offered an articulate collective mythology as compensation for the unspeakable individual elements of male experience (Harper 1997: 163–77). On the international big-budget level this mythology would culminate and peak in the epic war films of the 1960s.

The success of Mason in *The Desert Fox*, or indeed of German acting import Hardy Krüger, are indicative of shifting audience attitudes while critics remained ambivalent and directors defensive about the screen presence of the Good German. Krüger, who had worked with Alfred Weidenmann in one of his last wartime productions, *Junge Adler* (1944), and later starred alongside O.E. Hasse in *Alibi* (1957), started his international career with three British productions (Williams 2006). In the first of these, *The One That Got Away* (1957), he played the German PoW Franz von Werra who repeatedly attempted to escape his captors. The British audience took to Krüger's rugged good looks and cheered the plucky underdog in the same way in which it would respond to *The Great Escape* a few years later. As with Mason's 'British' Rommel, what made such characters appealing to a British audience (irrespective of the actors' nationalities or the characters' ideological affiliations) was that they embodied what the audience understood to be Anglo-Saxon virtues. This turned them into exceptional Germans; at least it de-politicised them. Increasingly this also meant that non-German actors would play Germans.

Mason's British Rommel would soon have competition from a giant of mid-century American screen, Marlon Brando, who starred in both Dmytryk's *The Young Lions* (1958) and Bernhard Wicki's leaden *Morituri* (1965) as a self-professed 'apolitical' German who has to take sides as a result of the war. Brando stars alongside the other two lions, Dean Martin as the boozy, non-heroic writer Michael Whiteacre and Montgomery Clift, who plays the Jewish GI Noah Ackerman. Dmytryk's star-studded film, loosely adapted from Irwin Shaw's eponymous novel, was a box-office hit and Brando's last success for a number of years. It earned him a nomination for the BAFTA, and the film a Golden Globe nomination in the category Best Film Promoting International Understanding, the latter suggesting that stereotypes had been avoided for the sake of a more rounded portrayal or a differentiated plot. The script does not shy away from controversial themes such as home-grown anti-Semitism and non-heroic masculinity. Yet the sceptical view of war and violence as merely politically expedient is voiced by rather compromised characters, notably Dean Martin's cynical writer.

Like Mason's Rommel, Brando's version of the German officer Christian Diestl attracted adverse reviews for portraying a decent German. Brando's impact on Edward Anhalt's script turned Shaw's brutalised Diestl into a ponderous, softly spoken and implausibly naive officer who can't shoot wounded British soldiers as he is ordered to do: Brando would not play a Nazi.[13] In Shaw's novel Diestl kills the Jewish Ackerman at the moment of the latter's triumph, a murder avenged by Whiteacre. In the film, Ackerman survives the war to return to wife and child, and Whiteacre shoots the unarmed Diestl while on patrol. This encounter, *fin de combat*, may be symbolically satisfying particularly since it follows the liberation of a concentration camp, but it hardly edifies the two remaining young lions. Brando suggested to Dmytryk that his character should die entangled in barbed wire as if crucified. This alteration so infuriated Clift that he threatened to walk off the set (Kanfer 2008: 157). Brando's tumbling off a hill and gradual toppling into a stream still manages to make Diestl's demise look sacrificial and redemptive (Fig. 4.1), not least because this ending portrays Brando's character as the actual and unjust victim of the war. Brando's insistence on playing a Good German was not just a testament to his power over writers and directors as a box-office star. As Patrick Maior has noted, his suggestions received backing from the chief executive of Twentieth Century Fox, Buddy Adler: 'This would be the perfect spot in the script to show that there were *good* Germans too, and that they were not all Nazis even though they are in the German army. If you do not do this, I am sure that even in Western Germany today they will not want to run this picture ... A good picture today can take *a million dollars* out of Germany' (Maior 2008: 534). For good picture read lucrative film. *The Young Lions* had a $3 million dollar budget, and if a foreign market could cover a third of that in revenue its audience could not be neglected. Such economic and political considerations are hardly aired or integrated into the plot before *Judgment in Nuremberg*.

Brando's peroxide Aryan was much commented on at the time. The romance scenes with his superior officer's wife Gretchen Hardenberg (May Britt) now look like a chamber version of a scene from *Siegfried*, and the score indeed offers a Wagnerian prelude to emphasise such clunky Teutonic bliss. There is no little irony in the fact that it took a Swedish blonde and an American method actor to impersonate the master race. The 'real' Germans and Austrians that had so disconcerted James Mason were confined to act 'real' baddies, such as Maximilian Schell's Hauptmann von Hardenberg who kept excoriating Diestl about duty, discipline and the Fatherland. One of the most powerful scenes of the film pitches Brando's Good German against Schell's Nazi on a long

Figure 4.1   Brando's terminal and puzzled Christian Diestl in *The Young Lions*

Figure 4.2   'I schudd haff schot ju.' Maximilian Schell bullying Brando in *The Young Lions*

bike ride. The war weary Diestl thinks the war is pointless and is close to giving up; the Nazi, on his back like a Gothic spectre, torments his subaltern with threats in case of desertion.

The internal logic of the tracking shot of the bike ride is not dissimilar to a crucial scene in Hitchcock's earlier *I Confess* (1953). This film also placed great emphasis on the visualisation of guilt, inner torment and conflicted loyalties and pitched a saintly character (Montgomery Clift's Father Logan) against a 'real' German, O.E. Hasse's desperate refugee Keller.[14] The refugee Keller is a much more complex character than Schell's officer: a terrified murderer, both cunning and craven, deeply caring about his wife as well as determined to survive at whatever cost. Keller's German origin may be incidental to the plot, scripted by the Austro-Hungarian Jewish writer Gyorgy Tabori (himself a former exile from Nazi Germany), and it may serve primarily to explain Hasse's

Figure 4.3   'You sink I am scared after vot I haff dun?' O.E. Hasse's tempting of Clift's saintly priest in *I Confess*

accent, but in 1953 a German accent in a movie that has little to do with the war carries certain connotations.[15] The persecution scene in *I Confess* also happens in close physical proximity between two men, captured through a long tracking shot in the corridor of the rectory where Hasse's Keller both tempts and taunts Father Logan (Fig. 4.3). Both scenes are about the regulation of speech acts, about the character in the foreground conforming to the desires of the one behind him who wishes to control him. Both films share a structural use of Germanic evil: they show a flawed and saintly protagonist who literally has a German on his back, tormenting him about his professional responsibilities while failing to address his own culpability. The two characters are cast as opposites (voluble murderer versus reticent priest; idealistic German versus authoritarian Nazi), but one might also want to see the darker one as a projection of a demonic other.

In both films, this demonic other must be extinguished for the protagonist to redeem himself. Schell's gravely wounded Hardenberg kills himself with a bayonet Diestl unwittingly provided. In *I Confess* Keller is shot by the police but receives absolution in Logan's arms. This doesn't turn Keller or Hardenberg into Good Germans but it suggests that the best ending for a German, good or otherwise, might be terminal. Both Brando's Diestl and Mason's Rommel can be Good Germans because they are flawed, tormented by fascism and do not survive. In fact their status as Good Germans is confirmed as a posthumous mythical rewriting of an original script and crucially depends on their status as exceptions: they require real Nazis as counterparts.

Mission Impossible V: Cruise's Stauffenberg

Brando's efforts at the Good German in *The Young Lions* (and later the largely unknown *Morituri*) had few imitators. The turn to epic war films in the 1960s shifted the focus onto the representation of professional soldiers often played by 'real' Germans and Austrians for added authenticity. In the late '60s and '70s, 'Nazis' made a comeback even if (or precisely because) arthouse films camped them up or glamorised them.[16] The steady global impact of Holocaust memory also can't have helped to lend credulity to this trope. If we want to look for casting that compares to Brando's stature, reputation and salary at the time, we have to leap forward to Tom Cruise's role as Claus Graf von Stauffenberg in *Valkyrie*. One of the world's most highly paid actors in the past twenty years, Cruise has predominantly starred in blockbuster action films such as the *Mission: Impossible* series. Like the pre-Godfather Brando, Cruise has never played a villain.[17] Brando caused problems on set by interfering in scripts and sending budgets sky-high; Cruise became controversial in his avowed and very public turn from Catholicism to Scientology and his odd behaviour on Oprah Winfrey's chat show. *Valkyrie*, it was widely supposed, was meant to re-ignite his career and rectify his bruised star image.

In Germany the casting was controversial. With Cruise as protagonist an important aspect of German history would once again be instrumentalised for cheap entertainment (Beier et al. 2008: 128–31). Stauffenberg's family also voiced doubts, as did those who found the role required an actor with more gravitas and a more substantial acting portfolio. The historical advisor for the script, the renowned historian of the German resistance and Stauffenberg's biographer, McGill University's Peter Hoffmann, took no exception to *Valkyrie*'s presentation of the plot. He underlined that the main aim of the film was to achieve what previous films, particularly American productions, had failed to do: to disseminate knowledge about 'the Other Germany' (Rättig 2010: 135). *Valkyrie*, in other words, was a PR project for Cruise and for Germany, vociferously supported by the director Florian Henkel von Donnersmarck (*Der Untergang*) and the chief editor of the *Frankfurter Allgemeine Zeitung*, Frank Schirrmacher.[18] Other historians felt it was impossible for Hollywood cinema to achieve a faithful rendition of the plot or the plotters because the genre and pace of the Hollywood thriller could not accommodate the complexity of the plotters' motivations let alone the complicated character of Stauffenberg, whom it reduced to an action hero.[19] Peter Hoffmann, of course, is right: however well-intentioned, documentaries do not reach mass audiences. The real concern for both British and German historians critical of the film was that the heroic elevation of 'the Other Germany' might become too popular a compensatory narrative for the descendants of the regular Germany. Resistance and opposition should be put in their proper marginal and 'authentic' place.

The historic Stauffenberg was a complex character – aristocratic, Catholic and deeply rooted in a conservative and nationalistic ideology. Like many in the military, Stauffenberg had supported Nazi policies and Nazi ideas for the sake of national renewal. He shared with his Führer a romantic love for Wagner's operas and their mythical narratives. In letters to his wife Nina sent from Poland (and cited verbatim in Jo Baier's 2004 TV drama) he supported the war in a logistical role, and he spoke of the Poles as a 'rabble, consisting of many Jews and mixed races – a people only happy under the yoke'. Unlike *Valkyrie*, Jo Baier's *Stauffenberg* does not gloss over the quotidian racism of the German elite onto which fascism had grafted itself. Stauffenberg came to the resistance very late when all hope of victory had long gone and when the Allies' demand of unconditional surrender conjured up the humiliations of yet another Versailles. The heterogeneous group of resisters around General Beck envisioned a nationalistic Germany with a military regime and with its territorial gains at least restoring pre-First World War borders. They squabbled over precise aims and were hampered by grave doubts about the ethics of killing a dictator and contravening a military oath of personal loyalty. Stauffenberg's determination to act cut through this dithering. Would the general populace support a coup? Hans Mommsen gives a very clear answer:

> It is not easy to admit that Nazism, or some of the goals for which it stood, had become so deeply ingrained in the thinking and behaviour of the German masses that the forces of resistance could only be mobilized through deeply religious and ultimately utopian thinking ... at no point could the circle of plotters count on finding wide support among the population. (2003: 36)

By then, the plot had a symbolic meaning that overwrote its slim chance of success: even if it failed it was to demonstrate to the outside world the existence of an 'Other Germany'. When it did fail and news of it and the subsequent purge reached the Allies, their leaders played it down. In Parliament, Churchill dismissed the 'tremendous events' of the plot as a treasonous, internecine quarrel, 'manifestations of internal disease' (1974: 6985). It was too little too late.

Cruise's Stauffenberg suggests that we ought to read the film as a thrilling action movie rather than a psychological drama. The psychological and historical factors that contribute to characterisation in *The Desert Fox* and *The Young Lions* – Rommel's conflicted loyalties or Diestl's growing disillusionment with the Fatherland – are simply not part of the story or the characters' motivations. In fact, the means of the plotters' strategy (killing Hitler) becomes their sole aim and thereby replaces precisely what had deferred the plot for so long – disagreement over the kind of future individuals envisioned for Germany post-Hitler. *Valkyrie* offers barely any glimpse of this complex and problematic back story, and when it does it remains incomprehensible. Henning von Treskow's invocation of an 'Other Germany' before he kills himself with a hand grenade on the Eastern front becomes reminiscent of Brando's victim status at the end of *The Young Lions* or Rommel's suicide in *The Desert Fox:* it fails to address the characters' complicity with, and collusion in, as members of the officer class, the crimes committed in the name of the Fatherland. Similarly, when Stauffenberg is executed by a trumped-up firing squad and pronounces his dying words 'Long live sacred Germany', any Anglo-Saxon viewer must wonder what might justify such pathos. What links von Stauffenberg's 'sacred Germany' to von Treskow's 'Other Germany'? Are they the same or different, and does it matter? Instead, the film's script offers a largely linear storyline that begins in 1943 and leads us to von Treskow's assassination attempt before the blow-by-blow reconstruction of the failed coup on 20 July 1944 and its bungled aftermath. Despite the truncated script or because of it, many critics found the story confusing. Some failed to grasp the difference between the assassination attempt (which had no name) and 'operation Valkyrie', the government's contingency plan in case of a military coup to seize power in the Reich with the help of the police and the reserve battalions of the Wehrmacht. The plotters planned to use this existing contingency measure to prevent the SS from taking Berlin and the government quarter.

Valkyrie failed at the box office: this Good German – much better than the real Stauffenberg – excited no one. British film critics too remained underwhelmed despite a stellar cast of British thesps: Bill Nighy as General Olbricht, Kenneth Branagh (Henning von Treskow), Terence Stamp (Ludwig Beck), Edie Izzard (Fellgiebel), Kevin McNally (Goerdeler), Tom Hollander (Brandt) and Tom Wilkinson as the craven Fromm.[20] Casting was only one of the problems with *Valkyrie* but its effect tells us a great deal about the clash between past movie conventions and the contemporary historical war film.

In the UK, the recognisable British co-stars mercifully helped distinguish between individuals in a sea of Wehrmacht uniforms since the script did not overly trouble itself with introducing characters. Attention thus remained focused on Cruise's American-accented Stauffenberg, conspicuous throughout with longer hair, eye patch, and the mutilations sustained in the Libyan desert. Indeed the cast suggested a team of dithering middle-aged British desk sergeants compelled into action by a dashing American full of determination. The British made for implausible Nazis: with the exception of Branagh (who had played Heydrich in *Conspiracy*), most reviewers found they were not Teutonic enough. What this verdict really meant was that their renditions of German Generals did not conform to the traditional screen iconography of Nazism or even the German military; it was too fey, too nervous, and often too wordy: how could Izzard or Nighy have possibly made it to the rank of General? At times *Valkyrie* felt like an extended scene from one of the many earlier war movies in which Allied soldiers had (implausibly) *impersonated* Nazis to sabotage some installation with a few German extras dotted around for added 'authenticity'.[21] Even Uklański's photo frieze had some oddities such as Tom Selleck, Michael Palin, or Leonard Nimoy whose incongruity in Nazi roles merely confirmed the ruling trope of what a proper screen Nazi had to look like. For the *Guardian*'s Peter Bradshaw the problem lay in Singer's use of outdated conventions: British actors playing Germans 'had now become ridiculous'.[22] In contrast, Manohla Dargis (2008b), writing for the *New York Times*, argued that Tom Cruise was 'too modern, too American and way too Tom Cruise' – Cruise emptied Stauffenberg of ambiguity the way Hasse had sanitised Canaris. Both make a similar point, namely that extra-diegetic information hampers the construction of some essential period-specific Germanness; that it either takes exceptional acting to inhabit it or that only a German could do it. This particular Good German, then, is somehow too German; or paradoxically, not fascist enough to be convincingly impersonated. Genre and casting can have positive extra-diegetic effects on the audience. In *The Eagle Has Landed*, the audience roots for Michael Caine (irrespective of his Nazi character) because of his screen history as lovable rogue and the caper genre with which he is associated, in the manner in which we root for Frank Sinatra in *Von Ryan's Express* and Burt Lancaster in *The Train*. In *Valkyrie* we root for Tom Cruise largely because otherwise we would be siding with Hitler. Strictly speaking, it is not the plot that guides us but mostly extra-diegetic information: genre structures, the conventions of 'fascism', historical hindsight, and the star's action-man portfolio. Paradoxically, we can only make sense of the film *in spite of* the plot rather than because of it.

Figure 4.4 © Tom Batchell, illustration for *The New Yorker*

Killing Hitler: Hollywood realities and the Third Reich

Tom Batchell's cartoon that prefaces Anthony Lane's scathing review of *Valkyrie* in *The New Yorker* captures the central problem of the film: how to dramatise an officer in Nazi uniform before ample swastika bunting and yet communicate that he is an anti-fascist hero? The caricature of the dashing Cruise suggests conventional semiotics in which, at best, the eye patch has replaced von Strohheim's Wilhelminian monocle.

The question really is a larger one and has been asked before, notably by Saul Friedländer in *Reflections on Nazism*, and Alvin Rosenfeld in *Imagining Hitler*: does the representation of fascism in its specific theatricality not automatically reproduce its seductive force? Does the effort at authenticity that we expect from period drama not also run the risk of invoking the spectacular power of Nazi semiotics? The 'miscasting' in *Valkyrie* is indicative of how powerful 'fascism' has become in overwriting the semiotics of historical Nazism; if actors did not conform to the cinematic register of German militarism they had not performed fascism credibly, never mind that they were actually meant to be non-Nazis, former-Nazis or no-longer-Nazis, not-quite-Nazis, or whatever ideological gradation their conscience now suggested. Yet as we have seen in the discussion of Harris's *Fatherland*, these ethical developments are hard to perform or communicate visually while wearing a Nazi uniform.

In many ways, the special features on the DVD, such as the 'making-of' documentary *The Journey to Valkyrie*, are a rich source of extra-diegetic information about why the quest for authenticity must fail after decades of 'fascism'. Unlike Anna B. Sheppard, who invented dress uniforms for *Inglourious Basterds*, Joanna Johnston had Wehrmacht uniforms meticulously made according to historic sources – they were so authentically fascist that Tom Cruise felt compelled to emphasise that he had 'at first, actually, . . . repelled' the uniform. Kenneth Branagh similarly commented in this feature:

> Many of the German military had a *very* strong sense of how important their look was; how important the uniform was. Aside from pride in the uniform [there] was as sense of how good they looked and what an impact it made. You start to feel that once you put those boots on, and once you see the detail[ed attention] that they took with how they presented themselves.

What happens when a famous actor puts on a Nazi uniform? For Tom Cruise and Kenneth Branagh, the clothes that are merely necessary props for the impersonation of a particular character acquire near magical qualities in their performances. Actors who normally pride themselves in their craft here credit the tailoring of the uniform and the fit of the boots as if the clothes wore them rather than the other way around. Note the rhetorical manoeuvring that initially insists on the foreignness of the attire ('at first, actually'; 'the German military') before elaborating enthusiastically on its effect. That the actors should feel the need to explain to the audience the wearing of the uniform in a film set in Nazi Germany is astonishing in the first place, as if we needed reassuring that *they* were not real Nazis irrespective of how convincingly they managed to inhabit their characters. The skill of the costume department is explicitly acknowledged although all it does is replicate the original design.[23] It is supposedly the quest for authenticity that legitimises the Riefenstahlesque cinematography of some of *Valkyrie*'s scenes and that accounts for the fetishistic display of bunting, swastikas and uniforms. Faithful reproduction cannot gloss over the fact that what purports to be dramatic history ('based on the incredible true story') is perhaps primarily a fantasy about being a 'good Nazi', and for fantasy to have depth, as Susan Sontag said in 'Fascinating Fascism', it must have detail ([1975] 1996: 100). In fact the camera lingers lovingly on Cruise's shape, not just in those scenes involving mirrors as a conventional shorthand for self-scrutiny or doubt. The duration of these shots is a semantic device, like the eye-patch and the American accent. The camera must dwell on the maimed protagonist in order to build him up as a man-of-action, distinguish him from the prevaricators around him and ultimately remind the audience that *this* man in uniform is the hero. The effect, as the reviewers emphasise time and again, is merely a prestigious albeit lame addition to Uklański's photo frieze.

'To do this story justice was to try and be as authentic as possible' said Patrick Lumb, in charge of production design. Cruise confirmed: 'We're all going for the same thing: that authenticity.' In earlier productions, such as *Canaris* or *Der 20. Juli*, 'authenticity' meant splicing in documentary footage, which often manipulated a character's subjective point of view to coincide with historical objectivity. Cinematographer Newton Thomas Sigel stated that *Valkyrie* was 'fuelled' by shooting on location; at sites which conjured 'immediacy' or invoked the 'ghost' of the past, 'infusing everything that people do'.[24] These statements all amount to the same discrepancy: the topic demands a sincere, documentary effort yet somehow striving for 'authenticity' develops a magical dynamic of its own. Friedländer called this the 'dissonance' between 'the declared moral and ideological position of the author or the filmmaker, the condemnation of Nazism and the will to understand' on the one hand and 'the aesthetic effect, be it literary or cinematographic' on the other (1993a: 20).[25] *Valkyrie*'s production comments indicate that if the costume department gets it right, if the casting produces fortuitous facial similarities and if the location shoots work, everything else will fall into place, as if the reality effect depended on makeup, tailoring and architecture. (The reviewers of course demanded 'fascism' as acting-according-to-trope rather than mimesis.) This naiveté on the side of the director is all the more peculiar since one of his previous films, *Apt Pupil*, had explored precisely the seductive impact of an authentic voice of fascism.

The kind of authenticity *Valkyrie* subscribes to is also rather selective. The scenes at Tempelhof airport and the Bendlerblock (the army high command headquarters in Wilhelmstrasse) offer us a city ostensibly untouched by carpet bombing. The aborted assassination attempt on the 15th is set in a bunker rather than in the conference hut where it originally took place because the filmmakers wanted to avoid repetition. In the overwhelming greenish-greyish palette of the film, however, it is the swastika that stands out prominently. Patrick Lumb again in *The Journey to Valkyrie*: 'There are certain parts where we have lots of flags, for example the Messe[gelände] Berlin where we actually had 120 swastikas flying.' In fact, there are two exterior scenes in which large swastikas are used (outside the Bendlerblock and a mass display of flags at the Messegelände) and two interior scenes (inside the People's Court either

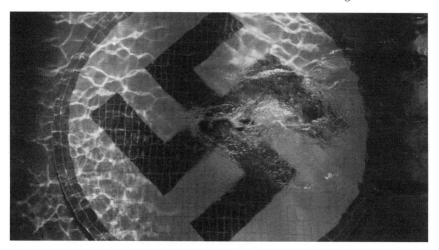

Figure 4.5   Swastika free style in Bryan Singer's *Valkyrie*

side of the judge; and in one interior scene inside a swimming pool). In a film in which everyone wears the signifiers of evil – the Wehrmacht uniform – the swastika becomes an *additional* ideological sign to distinguish between the plotters and those faithful to the regime. It becomes a crucial element of staging fascism. So on the few occasions when the spectator encounters the swastika, it is either displayed en masse or very large so that this signposting is clear. The officer's mess hall is full of loyal soldiers so that the two plotters literally have to escape this fascist space. There's a brief (unwitting?) reference to Fassbinder's *Lili Marleen* in a dance hall scene when in a high-angle shot the swastika grows out of a singer's head like a contorted halo. Remer runs up a flight of stairs overlooked by a tall vertical stained glass swastika window in Goebbels's ministry of propaganda. The Wehrmacht soldiers sent to seize the plotters rather than cooperate with them run awkwardly through a square pitted with swastika flagpoles. The judge at the people's Court is of course not beyond ideology but one of its tools. And the muscular German who swims freestyle through a swimming pool whose tiled floor displays a swastika is Major Remer, who will come to arrest Stauffenberg and his allies (Fig. 4.5).

The high-angle and low-angle shots in those scenes underline the force of fascism: the swastika is always huge, dwarfing any people on the screen. The spectacular top-down shot in the swimming pool might remind us of the identical point of view on the Busby Berkeley dance number in *The Producers*, or the long shots for the concert hall decoration in Fassbinder's *Lili Marleen*, but Singer's use of the symbol is not ironic but pragmatic and hyperbolic. We are never encouraged to think of Major Remer, immediately identified as a Nazi in a scene in which he can't possibly be wearing a uniform, as a ridiculous figure. In fact the few swastika scenes are so conspicuous because their strategic signification *requires* theatrical cinematography, and this specularity is of course modelled on fascist propaganda tools. As Singer naively concedes on the audio commentary these 'shwastikas' (sic) are a nod to the marble ambition of the Third Reich to last a thousand years.

This specularity begins with the opening credit sequence with partial giant swastika arms reaching into the frame to bursts of percussion. The flourish of this display references Litvak's opening of *The Night of the Generals*, a film whose crime plot demands attention to the details of uniforms and therefore courts an element of voyeurism in its fetishistic visual entree. Perhaps more important here is *Judgment in Nuremberg*. Stanley Kramer used a swastika for his opening credits (to well-known German *Marschmusik*) because it prepared the first frame of the film in which we see the giant swastika above the *Reichsparteitaggelände* in Nuremberg being blown up. Kramer's first frame underlines the link fascism forged between cultural tradition and ideology, and the remainder of the film will retroactively ironise as facile such naive gestures as removing ideological signifiers just as much as it suggests that justice is always hostage to political expediency. *Judgment* is about the difficulty of eradicating fascism from people's minds (about the insufficiency of both dynamite and court rooms as political and educative tools); in contrast, *Valkyrie* places tremendous confidence in both dynamite and court rooms.

But it is not only fascist semiotics that *Valkyrie* cannot resist; paradoxically a film about the plot to assassinate the Führer manages to mythologise him. Ironically David Bamber was one of the few British actors in the film to receive laudable mention by the critics just as Bruno Ganz had before him, irrespective of the critics' opinion of *Der Untergang*. The daunting task of impersonating this overdetermined historical figure always predestines critics to kindness. On the DVD's audio commentary Cruise comments on the first Hitler scene: 'A lot of work went into Hitler.' Prompted thus, Singer elaborates:

> After looking at hundreds of hours of films of Hitler, it's basically his eyes ... something in Hitler's eyes. And I knew I could build the makeup around him, but finding the essence of Hitler in his eyes and having an actor who isn't aping Hitler with just a moustache and hair but actually is *playing* Hitler was very important.

Singer's distinction between evoking – aping – Hitler through the recognisable features and playing some Hitlerian essence raises the issue of whether the audience should get a taste of Hitler's eyes/essence in a full-frontal shot. Singer and Cruise intended to show the depressed, withdrawn and laconic Hitler rather than 'the carpet eater' of maniacal rages. Later in the commentary Singer concedes that Hitler needed to be shown as a dictator yet Bamber could not really do anything that Hitler had not done in reality. Indeed the only 'dictatorial' moment Bamber is allowed is hitting a map table with his fist before the bomb goes off in the wrong place. As we shall see, there is a great deal of ambivalence in Singer's approach to Hitler.

Hitler only appears in those four scenes to do with assassination attempts, and here the narrative pace slows markedly; the shots last longer; the soundtrack offers the kind of score that builds up suspense with staccato horn blasts or string vibratos. This speed is subjective: it suggests that this durée is what the plotter feels in anticipation of the momentousness of his deed, and it is meant to create identification and suspense. Yet audience direction through pace is at variance with audience direction through framing. We are never entirely sure whether Henning von Treskow (Branagh) and Stauffenberg (Cruise) are nervous and tense because they are placing a bomb, or whether they are in awe of Hitler, or both, since the shots on Hitler and reverse shots on their faces do not make this clear.

In the first failed assassination attempt on 13 March 1943 we see von Treskow await Hitler's arrival on an airfield. When Hitler descends from his plane the camera uses an over-the-shoulder position so his leather-coated figure is seen from the rear and dominates the frame. As he walks past the row of officers on the runway we see him from the side, followed by a shot of Treskow breathing in deeply and stepping forward. The cinematography builds Hitler up as an auratic lugubrious Führer. Every camera angle takes up the perspective of those around him, looking at him but fearing to meet his eye. As we follow the officers to lunch in a nearby tent the camera gives us a brief full frontal shot on Hitler seating himself at table but his figure is almost immediately cast in shadow and his face bent in concentration on a dish of rice and boiled carrots ('and the whole vegetarian [eating] that's again for those historians that follow Hitler and his idiosyncrasies'). The phrasing here is interesting: detail and idiosyncrasy become synecdoches for wholesale historical authenticity; boiled vegetables will satisfy the fan-historian who 'follows' Hitler. Singer's comment perhaps unwittingly captures the Hitler myth and its legacy: this subject of study fascinates to the extent that historians would be turned into 'followers' whose very work pays tribute to and prolongs the myth and Führerkult that built him up in the popular imagination during his lifetime. Despite the earlier talk about essences, Singer's cinematography suggests that one cannot look at this Medusa-like Hitler, one cannot face the man and must therefore circle around him in awe, synecdochally, fixed precisely on the little idiosyncrasies, the moustache, the vegetarianism, and so forth. Singer offers an oblique reference to the media construction of this myth by showing a cameraman descend from a second plane: this descent of the leader from Heaven to his corps too will be documented on film, perhaps for a *Wochenschau* clip, but it is merely a mediated, widely distributed image in which the Führer does not face the camera and therefore the audience never faces the Führer.

A similar effect is achieved through the low-key drum roll that accompanies the scene at the Berghof, where Stauffenberg travels to have Hitler sign the amended Valkyrie contingency plan. Before we enter the stateroom with the panorama window, three close-ups on decorative features set up the incongruous aesthetics of the oversized interior: two tapestry details of a warrior queen and a lion, and a small onyx statue of a bacchant. Hitler is in the presence of Goebbels, Goering, Speer and Keitel (and, another 'authentic' idiosyncrasy: Blondie, his German shepherd). Yet what we see looks less like a cabinet meeting and more like an intimate *Altherrenrunde*, some alumni or veterans' gathering. Again the camera approaches Hitler laterally and indirectly: through a long shot that establishes the incongruity of the room, pitching its outsized proportions against the kitschy 'Altdeutsch' domestic decorations, the significance of the personnel gathered here against the avuncular tone of their chit chat (Fig. 4.6). The scene cuts to a top-down shot on the back of Hitler's head when seated in a chair with the back to the audience. This is followed by a lateral low-angle shot in which he greets the arriving officers by placing his hand on Stauffenberg's remaining hand holding his briefcase: such a touch confers trust in an exemplary, sacrificial vassal. The next shot shows Hitler once more from the rear, facing the officers, then turning to face the room again but without looking directly at the camera and with the left side of his face obscured by shadow. The interior shots in the Berghof scene cannot help but reproduce the stage setting of the hall that, like much of Speer's architecture, dwarfs the people inside. Hitler's familiar demeanour, like the living room aspects of the stateroom, and his non-statesmanlike behaviour are precisely part of his mystique and enable the projection of a paternalistic attitude (he is a man of and for the people). David Bamber's Hitler captures this beautifully – at the cost of reproducing this auratic mystique.

In close-up shots the camera often slices through Hitler's shape or, focusing on Stauffenberg in the mid-screen, un-focuses Hitler in the foreground. Yet such re-direction on Stauffenberg is again undermined

Figure 4.6 Cosy chit chat at the Berghof in Singer's *Valkyrie*

by the over-the-shoulder shots on the document Hitler is to sign, accompanied by musings on valkyries and Wagnerian myth. When the officers leave, Hitler is again obscured from view, a powerful shadowy presence. Hard to see how one could assassinate an aura.

On 15 July Hitler arrives in the conference room where his staff are assembled and stand to attention around a gigantic map table. Again he does not look up at the camera. We see him laterally from an angle behind those standing around the table while we also perceive the effect his presence has on the people in the room: silence, deference, obsequiousness. Small wonder the man can only die from his own hand, the cinematography seems to say: no one would even meet his eye. On 22 July he is already in the map room and Stauffenberg joins his staff there, an occasion which gives the filmmakers the opportunity to have Hitler and his would-be assassin exchange glances in shot reverse-shot fashion. This is the only time the camera allows for a close-up of Hitler's face, but only in half-profile and largely in shadow. We see a tired dictator who in the second close-up turns away a distracted eye. This squaring up precedes Hitler's loss of temper which the camera only captures from the rear and which does not affect Stauffenberg who has already left the room. The purpose of this ocular focus is to elevate Stauffenberg to the only man who literally faces up to Hitler. After the assassination attempt we do not see Hitler (and the uneducated spectator must wait to figure out that the body carried out of the conference hut under Hitler's coat is not the Führer). What is left after the failed assassination attempt is pure Hitler myth, pure aura: Hitler's disembodied voice on the phone to

Goebbels and Remer and finally on a radio broadcast defying the plotters – precisely because we don't see him he's alive.

These scenes and their editing and cinematography demonstrate a rather ambivalent attitude to representing Hitler. Much here is synecdochal. As if terrified of some Medusa effect, the camera avoids facing Hitler or putting him fully in the frame: like his vassals we don't see much of those eyes. The editing suggests that Hitler's effect on others is discursive and tells us more about his power than any direct shot. In contrast, Cruise's Stauffenberg benefits from low-angle shots that aggrandise him to a soldierly hero with nerves of steel. His bravery is the focus of the film, not Hitler's dictatorship, yet both have to be augmented cinematographically. Without the semiotics of fascism – the swastikas, the staging of troops, the Hitler myth – it is impossible to communicate the meaning of Stauffenberg's act. Since Singer chooses to 'follow' Hitler we always see too much of 'fascism' – an excess of clarity that overwrites the complexity of anti-fascism. Precisely because 'fascism' is so simplistic, anti-fascist opposition and resistance have such a hard time getting their story told.

An 'Appalling Death': fascism as blissful void

Singer relies on recreating the events on 20 July and the aftermath of the failed plot (suicides, the purge, the trial at the People's Court, the plotters' executions) in order to underline the importance of this late act of resistance. The final frame with its extra-diegetic statistics about how many people died in the nine months following 20 July lifts the plot into the 'what if' of alternative history. This juxtaposes the one death that was meant to excite us but that did not happen (Hitler's) with nameless millions that did and for which we are asked to mobilise empathy; it positions the deaths we witness on screen with the ones we cannot apprehend. In terms of the resistance this strategy also privileges action over motivation so that the manner of the plotters' deaths sanctions their courage. It is therefore crucial that *these* deaths be seen in their progressive brutality, from Stauffenberg's swift court martial to von Treskow's lonely suicide to the torturously slow strangulations with piano wire at Plötzensee prison. The scenes of dying, then, carry a moral weight at the end of the narrative that effectively replaces and renders irrelevant a perhaps unromantic or ponderous back story about them.

Given that these executions were filmed on Hitler's orders, however, we might want to ask ourselves whether this particular perspective is not problematical. To look at the commission of prolonged suffering and torture runs the risk of replicating the regime's sadistic gaze on its victims in a film that does not offer us the non-realist techniques that problematised and defamiliarised the perception of perpetration and witnessing in Littell's *The Kindly Ones*. Singer spares the audience the full force of historical reality as it is described in Peter Hoffmann's account of the plotter's last days (1996: 528–9). The hanged men are neither naked nor can they be shown in their full corporeal agony. Yet neither does Singer's script go to the lengths of explaining the running camera in the centre-right of this frame. The fact that someone is filming this agony is perturbing to the condemned man about to be strung up and the audience follows his frowning gaze past the hanged bodies in the centre to the running camera before the blinding spotlight. Someone will be consuming the footage of this execution, but what makes them different from us?

The final question I want to raise in this context is why fascism is so hard to visualise beyond the trappings of form (such as the hardboiled template in Kerr's books). To this purpose I want to briefly compare Singer's cinematic representational strategy for the Good German (heroic action and violent death) with Justin Cartwright's more oblique mode in his novel *The Song Before It Is Sung*. Cartwright's novel is the story of a scholarly inquiry into the nature of a doomed friendship between the Anglo-Jewish philosopher and Oxford don Elya Mendel (a fictionalised Isaiah Berlin) and a diplomat on the margins of the plotters' circle, Axel von Gottberg (modelled on Adam von Trott zu Solz). Mendel has tasked his former student Conrad Senior with undertaking this inquiry, partly out of a sense of guilt over his possible contribution to the failure of von Gottberg's attempts at garnering Allied support for the German resistance abroad: '*it may have been that Axel would have been spared his appalling death. Did you know that a film was made not only of the trial – there's a copy of it in the Imperial War Museum – but also of the hangings? This film was made expressly for Hitler's benefit. It is believed to be lost*' (Cartwright 2007: 6). Senior will find and watch both these films, and indeed the book describes his inquiry as an effort of visualisation through Senior as the focaliser. How we can approach someone else's history and what looking at it will do to us, is the central question of Cartwright's book, and I wish to take this question literally by focusing precisely on the way in which the novel self-consciously foregrounds the problems of transgenerational historical inquiry (or re-imagining the past and giving it narrative shape) and the ethics of cinematic spectatorship. In the course of the narrative both Senior and the reader will make the transition from a surfeit of ignorance to an excess of information; from imagining too little to having seen too much.

The historical von Trott became a rather controversial figure in postwar Britain and – unusual for a German civil servant – the subject of two British biographies: Christopher Sykes's sceptical *Troubled Loyalty* (1968) and Giles MacDonogh's sympathetic *A Good German* (1989). Cartwright's novel is the third instalment in this long debate. What is at stake in the assessment of von Trott's activities is not just the moral compass of the German opposition and the July plotters but, more importantly, the failure of the British intellectual and political establishment to offer this opposition the slightest encouragement.[26] To represent von Trott (or any other plotter) as a Good German, as his contemporary David Astor argued, 'involves the possible admission of some British share of responsibility, even if only passive responsibility, for terrible events' (1969: 12–13). Mendel's culpability is merely the starting point for the inquiry in Cartwright's novel in which fascism remains incomprehensible from outside Germany and inaccessible through hindsight. What frames the narrative is the attempt at retrieving, and the act of watching, the film of the executions. Here, too, the 'appalling death' of the plotters validates their efforts, pitched against the hothouse atmosphere of Oxford colleges, busy with personal rivalries and malicious gossip. In this environment, a German with a sense of urgency and haunted by the possibility of failure comes across as risibly melodramatic. Stephen Spender lampooned von Trott's last night at Oxford in *Horizon* magazine: 'it was impossible to escape from his drama' (in MacDonagh 1989: 135). Von Trott came across as someone who acted a part in Schiller's *Wallenstein* or Kleist's *Prinz von Homburg*, who saw history as a stage and his life pre-scripted by a tragic destiny rather than determined by individual agency.

There are two failures of vision in Cartwright's novel, Mendel's and Senior's, but they are linked, and they explain why 'the Good German' is so hard to accommodate in the archive of 'fascism' (although this one, too, has an obligatory terminal ending). Von Gottberg fails in his mission, like the historical von Trott, because fascism was literally inconceivable to his Oxford friends – ridiculous in its mythologising and unimaginable in its quotidian oppression: 'He talked with . . . those who had been his friends in Oxford days, all blissfully void of the faintest notion of the perils and intricacies which were part of life under Hitler's dictatorship' (Bielenberg 1988: 46–7). What von Trott's close English friend Christabel Bielenberg calls a blissful void is given a more clichéd metaphor in Cartwright's rendition: 'I think it was difficult from Oxford to understand – in fact it was hard to understand from wherever you were – what the atmosphere was like in Germany. It was terrifying. Kafkaesque' (1988: 94). Fascism can only be approximated through comparison with a particular continental imagination. Indeed it seems born from imagination, argues Mendel's friend Lionel (a version of Maurice Bowra): 'They all created the Third Reich with their fucking forests and Wagner and their silly green clothes and their hunting horns and their Teutonic knights and their turgid poets like Stefan George' (Cartwright 2007: 138). Fascism is read, from abroad, as grafting itself onto national mythology and therefore it can only be understood as a logical continuation of such indigenous narratives: foreign, unreal, dark, hyperbolic; less a political reality than the Grand Guignol of nocturnal torch-lit processions, party rallies and dreams of *Weltherrschaft*. The novelist Joseph Roth, observing from his exile in Paris, noted that such logic satisfied 'a romantic need' manufactured for the home audience but equally expected by a foreign one:

> People have gotten used to viewing the shameful theatrical scenes that are produced in Germany from time to time through the same opera glasses they take to Wagner productions. In fact the Western diplomat and observer goes to Germany in very much the same frame of mind as the theatregoer gets into a taxi that will take him to see the Ring. This sloppy and snobbish laziness is sustained by mythology. Western politicians, diplomats and journalists seem to be there in their capacity as Germanists rather than as politicians, etc. ([1938] 2004: 234)

For Roth, the perception of German history and politics is always already mediated by the template of myth (and its literary or operatic versions). To elevate this 'interpretation' to some sort of manifest destiny was an achievement of fascist propaganda, but it is also a reading that is deeply popular abroad because it reduces fascism to a risible Central European spectacle. And it is from this perspective that the real danger of such 'sloppy and snobbish laziness' becomes clear: fascism invented itself as 'fascism' (that is, as a particular aesthetic) and therefore it is passively watched as a spectacle when its aggressive politics would require an active response.

Conrad Senior's research, then, is an effort at visualisation and empathy based on letters, conversations and film footage as if this were a proper perspective, as opposed to a set of 'opera glasses'. Having read von Gottberg's wife's short account of their last evening on their Mecklenburg estate before the assassination attempt, he is assaulted by a surfeit of images:

> Conrad cannot sleep. He sees Axel von Gottberg desperate to hold his wife and his children for the last time. He sees the tall romantic figure striding through the fading light for home; he sees the intensity of that evening, the startled children in their nightdresses, the poignant journey behind the horses

back to the station and on to ruined Berlin, where the twilight of the gods has descended. He sees Axel von Gottberg exactly as he is in the trial footage, tall, hollow-eyed, agonisingly thin, but resolved. (Cartwright 2007: 189)

Amongst all the things that he 'sees' there is no image of von Gottberg that is unmediated. His 'desperate' state is an evocation of the wife's memoir; the adjectives are selected to fit the occasion, which is, in true Teutonic manner, cast in Wagnerian terms or in the glow of German idealism. The landscape and weather speak in pathetic fallacy as if primed for the occasion. (We remember here the 'fucking forests and Wagner' that so irritated Lionel). The taste for drama, myth even, is projected into this scene with hindsight but also informed by a suspicion of *folie de grandeur* which emanates from von Gottberg and the plotters. Conrad's insomniac vision of von Gottberg is, like Elizabeth's of Nazi Germany ('Kafkaesque'), very literary. Time and again, fascism slides into 'fascism'. What Conrad 'sees' is what he has read and what he has seen on the screen, notably in the two films, both of which are scripted: the film of the show trial before Roland Freisler's People's Court for the *Wochenschau* newsreel and the film of the executions ordered by Hitler.

Bryan Singer takes the existence of these films as licence to show both the trial and the executions in Plötzensee. Cartwright never describes the film of the executions. At the start of the novel Conrad is on his way to Berlin to meet the Jew Fritsch whose survival in wartime Berlin depended on cooperation in such odious tasks. Fritsch offers scant information on the technically and psychologically difficult conditions of filming the condemned men's dying that make it clear that his presence at such atrocity has deeply damaged him, not least because it was a condition of his survival. At the end of the novel, Conrad has seen both the trial footage and 'the poisoned film' of the execution (2007: 230), and must decide what to do with it. Should it be preserved for posterity? Can one bear to look at it? Should such sights be seen? Conrad makes an appointment with the Imperial War Museum to watch the film of the trial once more but clandestinely substitutes it for the execution footage, 'afraid of what he is to see' (231). In the subsequent Chapter 24 the perspective changes to von Gottberg whose last moments are relayed in free indirect discourse until he is released into the noose.[27] Here, too, the German's appalling death renders him a Good German whether or not his conception of historical agency chimes with Anglo-Saxon sensibilities. Indeed, as in previous cinematic versions of terminal German Goodness, it is only through this terminal force of fascist oppression that these sensibilities seem to be shaken at all. By implication the Good

German then implicates his surviving fellow countrymen as fascists. Cartwright's narration sympathises with the victim precisely at the moment when he becomes the object of the regime's gaze: the executions are staged to be filmed and watched. In the first sentence of the next chapter Senior exits the Museum, is violently sick and drops the reel into the Thames on Westminster Bridge. Both the act of watching and the process of dying have mercifully fallen into the interstices of a chapter break; in the remaining pages we only see the effect that watching the film has had on Senior.

Cartwright's decision to locate the footage and its consumption in a narrative gap is in itself a verdict on what this film portrays and how watching it duplicates a sadistic gaze, intent on deriving pleasure from another's agony. (According to Hoffmann [1996: 528], photographs of such 'appalling death' were still on Hitler's map table ten days later.) Senior's response to such complicity is physical and moral revulsion – he is violently sick – and he also comes to revaluate Mendel's 'insufficient imagination' (2007: 240) within the sheltered life of an Oxford college. Haunted by the memory of these images, Senior chooses to write a book (rather than the more stagy renditions he had initially planned, a play, or a documentary, 'the sort of thing television will go for' [2007: 7]). This suggests that film, whether fiction or documentary, now fills the gap of our insufficient imagination but that this substitution has ethical implications: it does not make us more empathetic or knowledgeable but reduces us to voyeurs even when we intend to watch against the grain; it does not debunk fascism as 'fascism' but elevates fascism to 'fascism'. Our appetite for representations of fascism, then, places us behind the camera or in the executioner's room, as it did in the torture scenes in Harris's *Fatherland*, Kerr's hardboiled novels or McEwan's *Black Dogs*. How, then, can we approach fascism if documentary forms or realist renditions are problematical? Are we not doomed to remain 'blissfully void of the faintest notion' of fascism, like those Oxford intellectuals, if cinematic versions of 'fascism' are radically rejected? Is there a way of problematising both our voyeuristic gaze at, and therefore our desire for, 'fascism' as well as conveying that there is a crucial difference between historical Nazism and its aesthetic on the one hand and our creative rendition of, or response to, such ideology on the other? Such a project would require dense intertextual layering and a knowing cinephile audience, along the lines of Quentin Tarantino's *Inglourious Basterds*.

Notes

1. More recently, Art Spiegelman, himself a graphic artist who has used the comic strip form to tell his father's story of the Holocaust in the Pulitzer Prize-winning *Maus*, criticised this trend towards 'Holokitsch' (2011: 70–1; 73).
2. Such explanations are hardly necessary in the case of art that merely recycles clichés of evil Nazis versus superior Allies, as in Amir Chasson's *Nazis and Astronauts* (2011), a painting that juxtaposes nine portraits, four black-and-white mug shots of Nazi war criminals and five smiling US astronauts before the star-spangled banner. Available at <http://www.amirchasson.com/health6.html> (accessed 5 August 2012).
3. The film cost $75 million to make. See box office/business for *Valkyrie* at <www.imdb.com/title/tt0985699/business> (last accessed 7 February 2012).
4. See, for instance, Hake 2002; Koepnick 2002b; Kuhlbrodt 2006; Frölich, Schneider, Visarius 2007; Fuchs 2008.
5. See, for instance Florian Gallenberger's *City of War: The Story of John Rabe* (2009); Roland Suso Richter's *Dresden* (2006); Kaspar Heidelbach's *Berlin '36* (2009); Max Färberböck's adaptations *Aimee and Jaguar* (1999) and *The Downfall of Berlin: Anonyma* (2008); Andrzej Wajda's *Katyn* (2009); Rose Bosch's *La Rafle* (2010); Ole Christian Madsen's *Flammen & Citronen* (2008) and Paul Verhoeven's *Black Book* (2006).
6. See, for instance, Large 1991; Peukert 1989; Kershaw 1983; Housden 1997; Hoffmann 1996.
7. For a detailed discussion of these films see Fuchs 2008: 143–60.
8. Curd Jürgens carried similar cachet since *The Devil's General* (1955) and went on to play professional soldiers in international productions such as *The Enemy Below*, *The Longest Day*, *The Battle of Britain* and *Breakthrough*.
9. See Kreimener 1973; Westermann 1990; Kodalle 1981. For Erica Carter (2007: 220–1), however, Hasse's performance style did not just contribute to rehabilitating the ambiguous historical figure and align him with the conservative-nationalist resistance; it also supported an interpretation of the officer (both in the Nazi military and in the Bundeswehr with its citizen soldiers) as capable of individual sovereignty. As a result, Hasse's Canaris helped to displace the many personnel continuities between the Third Reich and the postwar Bundeswehr.
10. For studies of representations of the enemy in 1950s British cinema see for instance: Chapman 1998; Murphy 2000, Chapters 7–9; Ramsden 1998.
11. 'This film does as much to revive the discredited legend of an efficient, wise and above all gentlemanly military caste as if it had been made by the Propaganda Department of the Wehrmacht itself', moaned the *Evening Standard*. The *Daily Mail* dismissed Rommel's reputation with the British army as 'romantic legend' and 'silly fiction' which this Twentieth Century Fox production merely buffeted. And, most grudgingly, Leonard Mosley in the *Daily Express*: 'brilliantly made, fiendishly well-acted, tremendously exciting, but there were moments when I wanted to stand up and throw hand grenades at the screen. It made me *that* angry.' All reviews cited Hirschhorn 1975: 98–9.

12. In later years, Rommel would be played by notable German actors in international productions: Werner Hinz in *The Longest Day*; Karl Michael Vogler in *Patton*; Wolfgang Preiss in *Raid on Rommel*. TV dramas also used German actors: Hardy Krüger in *War and Remembrance*, and Helmut Griem in *The Plot to Kill Hitler*). Canadian Christopher Plummer took over the baton from Mason in *The Night of the Generals* while Michael York made a hatchet job of it in the TV drama *Night of the Fox* (1990).

13. Already involved in civil rights politics, Brando offered Dmytryk speeches on human rights violations against black African-Americans and Native Americans that would not have been out of place in Maximilian Schell's final defence council in *Judgment at Nuremberg*. Publicly he defended his version of Diestl at a press conference during the shooting and in sparring matches with the writer in post-production TV interviews. Cited Kanfer 2008: 155–6.

14. Hasse and Clift had a screen history, having worked together in *The Big Lift* (1950) in which Hasse played a jovial double agent to Clift's GI during the Berlin air lift. More important for Hitchcock's casting in the claustrophobic *I Confess* and its emphasis on the torment of blackmail is perhaps the fact that both actors were closeted gay men acting in a plot that advertises heterosexual romance as a dead end for all involved. For a very persuasive reading of the gay subtext in both *The Big Lift* and *I Confess* see Lawrence 2010: 115–38.

15. According to Lawrence, Tabori's script version of 9 August 1952 casts Keller in the role of a fascist whose wife is aroused by her husband's murderous deed (2010: 125).

16. Klaus Kinski, for instance, played a string of psychopathic characters in Edgar Wallace productions for film and TV in his native country, and imported those infernal types in the Italian productions in which he played German officers, SS-Colonel Müller in *5 per l'inferno* (1969) and General Kauffman in *Eroi all'Inferno* (1974) – and admittedly any other role he ever touched. Wolfgang Preiss was hardly ever seen out of uniform in German or international productions from the 1950s to the '70s, except when he played Dr Mabuse. Gerd Fröbe's penchant for grotesque baddies that made him such fun in *Goldfinger* (1964) and *Chitty Chitty Bang Bang* (1968) also imbued his German officers with an air of pompousness and absurdity in *The Longest Day* (1962), *Is Paris Burning?* and *Triple Cross* (both 1966). An attentive audience can even spot casting continuities: red-haired Aldo Valletti, who plays the President in Pasolini's *Salò*, reappears as a punter in *Salon Kitty*. The latter features Helmut Berger as a demonic Nazi in a performance so camp that one is tempted to read it as a hysterical accumulation of his entire Italian acting portfolio from *The Damned*, *Dorian Gray*, *The Garden of the Finzi-Continis*, *Ludwig* to *Conversation Piece*. More than any other actor, Berger has shaped the perception of cinematic 'fascism' as glamorous and glamorised. Hannes Messemer's short career in international cinema took the opposite turn, from baddie in home productions to decent chap: from *SS-Gruppenführer* Rossdorf in Siodmak's Oscar-nominated *Nachts, wenn der Teufel kam* (1957), the vindictive Russian Captain Markow in Geza von Radvanyi's *Der Arzt von Stalingrad* (1958), SS Colonel Müller in Rossellini's *Il Generale della Rovere* (1959),

to the anodyne Camp Kommandant von Luger in *The Great Escape* (1963). Maximilian Schell's Germans tended to be more ambiguous, beginning with a role as a member of the Kreisau Circle resistance group in *Der 20. Juli* (1955). His Captain von Hardenberg in *The Young Lions* (1958) provided a more fanatical counterpart to Marlon Brando's ponderous Christian Diestl. As the lawyer for the defence in *Judgment at Nuremberg* (1961) he beat Spencer Tracy to an Academy Award. After *The Odessa File* (1974) and *The Man in the Glass Booth* (1975), his Hauptmann Stransky in *Cross of Iron* is perhaps the most polished performance of unbridled military ambition in the history of war film.

17. The top-grossing films of the 1980s in which he starred included the jingoistic *Top Gun* alongside the Vietnam-critique *Born on the Fourth of July*. Even in Kubrick's *Eyes Wide Shut*, Crowe's *Vanilla Sky* or Spielberg's *Minority Report*, he played a confused character, befuddled by the world around him and unsure about where reality ends and dreams or nightmares begin.

18. See Florian Henckel von Donnersmarck, 'Deutschlands Hoffnung heißt Tom Cruise', *Frankfurter Allgemeine Zeitung*, Feuilleton, 3 July 2007, p. 33, available at <http://www.faz.net/aktuell/feuilleton/debatten/stauffen-berg-verfilmung-deutschlands-hoffnung-heisst-tom-cruise-1465934.html> (last accessed 4 March 2012). Frank Schirrmacher, 'Wir in ihren Augen', *Frankfurter Allgemeine Zeitung*, Feuilleton, 2 September 2007, available at <http://www.faz-net/aktuell/feuilleton/kino/stauffenberg-film-wir-in-ihren-augen-1465966.html> (last accessed 4 March 2012).

19. Richard J. Evans, 'Sein wahres Gesicht', trans. Stephan Klapdor, *Süddeutsche Zeitung*, 31 January 2009, Magazin 4, available at <http://sz-magazin.sueddeutsche.de/texte/anzeigen/27972> (last accessed 17 March 2012). Philipp Gassert, 'Thriller "Operation Walküre": Geschichte für Anfänger', *Spiegel online*, 20 January 2009, available at <http://www.spiegel.de/kultur/kino/0,1518, druck-602006.html> (last accessed 4 February 2012).

20. East coast critics agreed with their British counterparts about wholesale miscasting, lack of characterisation and back story as well as a distracting melange of accents. See for instance Anthony Lane, 'Private Wars', *The New Yorker*, 5 January 2009, available at <http://www.newyorker.com/arts/critics/cinema/2009/01/05/090105crci_cinema_lane?currentPage=all>; Stephanie Zacharek, 'Valkyrie', *salon.com*, 25 January 2008, available at <http://www.salon.com/2008/12/25/valkyrie/>; Manohla Dargis, 'Mission Imperative: Assassinate the Fuhrer', *New York Times*, movie review, 24 December 2008, available at <http://www. movies.nytimes.com/2008/12/25/movies/25valk.html>; Philip Kennicott, 'Review of *Valkyrie*', *Washington Post*, 25 December 2008, available at <http://www.washingtonpost.com/gog/movies/valkyrie,1145216.html>. Robert Wilonsky, '*Valkyrie* is Tom Cruise's Latest Impossible Mission', *Village Voice*, 24 December 2008, available at <http://www.villagevoice.com/2008–12–24/film/valkyrie-is-tom-cruise-s-latest-impossible-mission/>; Mick LaSalle (2008), 'Movie review: *Valkyrie*', 25 December 2008, *SFGate.com*, available at <http://www.sfgate.com/cgi-bin/article.cgi?f=/c/a/2008/12/25/DDLO14U652.DTL &type>. (All last accessed 5 February 2012).

21. Related to the casting and the script problems was the discrepancy between

a monoglot storyline and an international assembly of actors. As a result, we have an all-English script in an all-German setting spoken in American, British and German accented English. As in *Morituri*, the effect is rather odd, and many critics remarked upon it as conspicuous and distracting. On the one hand the film subscribes to historical accuracy with meticulous mimesis in costumes, settings and palette; on the other hand casting and language perforate any attempt at verisimilitude. As we shall see in the next chapter, Tarantino adopts the opposite strategy in *Inglourious Basterds* where linguistic competence and incompetence have plot relevance and where characters' nationalities correspond to actors' nationalities.

22. Peter Bradshaw, 'Valkyrie', *Guardian*, 23 January 2009, available at <http://www.guardian.co.uk/film/2009/jan/23/tom-cruise-valkyrie-film-bryan-singer> (last accessed 4 February 2012).
23. The SS Uniform was designed by Prof Dr Karl Diebitsch with the help of graphic designer Walter Heck, both of whom also created many runes, insignia and china. It is harder to trace the design of the Wehrmacht uniform, which is predominantly worn in *Valkyrie*. See Lumsden 2001: 53. The fashion designer Hugo Boss is often erroneously named as the uniform designer. His firm merely manufactured uniforms for the German Wehrmacht, SA and SS; see Timm (n.d.).
24. All statements here are taken from *The Journey to Valkyrie*.
25. Not all directors, of course, want to achieve ironic specularity, and not all topics lend themselves to it. For his representation of a Hitler Youth boarding school in *Der Unhold*, Schlöndorff insisted that to make fascism's seductiveness credible one simply had to seduce the audience with its theatricality. Reproduction was the point.
26. This point is also made in Hava Kohav Beller's documentary *The Restless Conscience*.
27. This account closely follows Peter Hoffmann's (1996: 528–9) but it omits the detail the condemned man cannot know or make sense of.

Chapter 5

'Operation Kino': Quentin Tarantino's *Inglourious Basterds* as Meta-cinematic Farce

Quentin Tarantino's foray into the war film takes its cue from Enzo Castellari's *Inglorious Bastards* (1977) but it is hardly a straightforward remake of 1970s 'macaroni combat'. True to Tarantino's highly allusive style, the film's intertextual archive is much larger and, as the misspellings in his title indicate, much more self-consciously playful. One would not enlist *Basterds* among the earnest hyper-realist war films and TV-series that, beginning with Spielberg's *Saving Private Ryan*, have re-introduced audiences to the heroic protagonist and the good fight. As we have seen in the last chapter, these productions often boast historical consultants and original location shooting to support the conflation of verisimilitude and authenticity. In contrast, Tarantino's costume designer Anna B. Sheppard (whose earlier work included *Schindler's List* and Polanski's *The Pianist*) commented on the 'degree of looseness' in Tarantino's rendition of the period detail. Sheppard altered Nazi uniforms and invented dress jackets, and her lavish chic for the female characters feels more like Hollywood than wartime Europe (Caranicas 2009: 4).

Inglourious Basterds signals from the very beginning a rather complicated relationship between fiction and its historical base: the first chapter title 'Once Upon a Time . . . in Nazi-Occupied France' points at Sergio Leone's Spaghetti Western *Once Upon a Time in the West* (1969), while the first wide-angle shot – an isolated farm on the edge of a forest, with a man chopping wood – reminds us of the beginnings of George Stevens's classic Western *Shane* (1953), John Ford's *The Searchers* (1956) as well as Clint Eastwood's *Unforgiven* (1992). Even before the story is set in motion, the doors of the cinematic archive have been flung wide open. As we see an army car and a motorbike approaching, the soundtrack accompanies the arrival of uniformed strangers with a track from Sergio Sollima's Spaghetti Western *The Big Gundown* (1966), in which Ennio Morricone alternates Beethoven's 'Für Elise' with Spanish guitar solos to illustrate musically a duel between an Austrian arms dealer and a Mexican bandit. So the cues from text, image and audio track shift our frame of reference from the war film to the western, and back and forth between the classics of the genre and their revisions.[1] The oscillating movement between immediate text (the story that unfolds on the screen) and context (cinema history; casting; genre; trope) continues throughout the movie. This persistent intertextuality should alert the spectator to the kinds of foreknowledge and expectations on which genre film depends.[2] Marsha Kinder has argued that Tarantino's earlier films *Pulp Fiction* and *Jackie Brown* are database narratives in which the paradigms of screen violence and the process of their selection are made blatantly obvious (2001: 81–3).[3] The popular canon underpinning *Basterds* could be seen as a cultural database whose myth-making and meaning-making strategies the spectator is asked to examine critically: how does popular cinema shape our cultural narratives of war, fascism and violence? Here the data narrative is taken one step further towards postmodern pastiche, by literally making the cinema central to dealing with the Third Reich. A more appropriate title for *Inglourious Basterds* might be 'Operation Kino' because it is primarily a film about 'fascism' as an aesthetic perpetuated by the cinema rather than a movie about fascism as a historical reality.

Set in occupied France, *Basterds* develops two separate revenge plots which converge in a Parisian cinema where Hitler and the Nazi government are gathered to watch the premiere of a propaganda film and where they are all killed ('Operation Kino'). In the first storyline the Jewish cinema proprietor Shosanna Dreyfus sets her locked auditorium alight with highly flammable nitrate film in retribution for the killing of her family. The second storyline gestures heavily towards Robert Aldrich's *The Dirty Dozen* (1967): US Lieutenant Aldo Raine (Brad Pitt) trains a motley crew of Jewish renegades ('the Basterds') to ambush German soldiers. The sole survivor of each attack has a swastika carved into his forehead and is sent back to his lines, reporting on the killing and scalping of his comrades. The Basterds seize the chance to end the war by interrupting guerrilla warfare and cooperating with an Allied plan to blow up Shosanna's cinema at the premiere. In this alternate history, the plan to blow up the cinema repairs as it were the bungled theatre assassination plot in Lubitsch's *To Be or Not to Be* (1942).

The plot is full of cinephiles: Hitler, the movie fan; Goebbels, the ideological mastermind of UFA under the Nazis; the British agent is a cinema critic and the German double agent, Bridget von Hammersmark, a UFA star; the card game German soldiers play in the tavern La Louisiane depends on film knowledge; Frederick Zoller, the German war hero turned actor in the propaganda film *Nation's Pride* reads his war record as a data narrative ('I'm Germany's *Sergeant York*'). Shosanna's cinema becomes a shelter for the subaltern, the persecuted Jewess and the black projectionist she loves, but cinema is also the death of Nazism. In real life, cinema is the guarantor of the discursive longevity of 'fascism'. Correspondingly in *Basterds*, it is literally the locus for the fulfilment of all sorts of dreams: Nazi victory and Jewish revenge; riotous entertainment and unconscionable scenes; glorious heroism and abject abasement. That these contradictory desires are satisfied simultaneously makes for a laden storyline that has its moments of loquacious *longueur* and needs a perturbing double ending, but this meta-cinematic strategy also points to the incongruity of the spectator's desires and expectations shaped by cinematic consumption. How is the spectator positioned (implicated, interpellated, distanced, insulated) vis-à-vis 'fascism' and the visual archive through which it is refracted by references to *The Dirty Dozen*, *Kelly's Heroes*, *Where Eagles Dare*, *Die weiße Hölle vom Piz Palü*, *Kolberg*, *Die große Liebe*, *The Great Dictator*, *To Be or Not to Be*, *The Producers*, *The Searchers*, *The Wild Bunch*, the 'Dollars' trilogy, *The Damned*, *Salò*, or *Salon Kitty*? This chapter will focus on Tarantino's strategy of highlighting the importance of cinema in shaping notions of history; or rather, in replacing historical knowledge with a composite visual myth. I am particularly interested in the ambivalent juxtaposition of comedic representations with paradigms of violence (what Raine calls 'killin' Nazi business' in the film). The relationship between diegetic (in-film) and cinema audiences in both Tarantino's film and his database will tell us much about the changing face of 'fascism'. Whether such an interrogation of popular culture actually succeeds with younger audiences, habituated to representations of hyperviolence, remains a moot point.[4] Has the cultural wheel, to borrow from Susan Sontag, turned too often? Is Tarantino's film further evidence of the fact that the allure of fascism 'seems impervious to deflation by irony or overfamiliarity' (Sontag [1975] 1996: 101)? Or does *Inglourious Basterds* actually achieve this deflation by irony, hyperbole and incessant quotation precisely because it eschews realism and constantly reminds us of familiar tropes?

Comedic theatricality and celebrity: *The Great Dictator*

Although the Nazis were satirised in Britain and America almost as soon as they came to power, and although comical representations existed throughout the war alongside more alarming propaganda images,[5] retrospective satire is perhaps more problematical given the known scale of their crimes. What most of these comedic representations focus on is the essential grotesqueness of all demonstrative power and the incompatibility of power with humour. Non-democratic regimes are notoriously hostile to satire precisely because it can and does work as a form of political resistance. Comedy, according to Gerald Mast, deflates and destroys (objects, egos, social assumptions) but does not necessarily offer a solution to the issues it raises. In reminding us of the fictions we construct to give our lives meaning, comedy reveals power to be merely one such illusion. It points to the hubris of those in power, but it also humanises them, or at least points to the humanity we share (Mast 1979: 338–40). (The latter, when applied to the Nazis, is perhaps the real representational transgression that is often perceived as inappropriate.) It is the nature of the grotesque to combine incongruous elements in which the lower form perforates and punctures the higher: amateurish bumbling ruins elaborate stage management; aphasia disrupts grandiloquence; buffoonery shows up high-mindedness; gross vulgarity chafes against the consciously artistic; the portentousness of ritual meets with haphazard accident. By the time the Nazis became the subject of satire abroad they had a recognisable identity, one that had initially at least helped to make them not just visible as a political group but given them the aura of well-organised critical mass. It is this performativity of political weight, and the portentous enactment of ideology, that lends itself to ridicule.

Chaplin's Adenoid Hynkel in *The Great Dictator* (1940) remains the comic template for satirical Hitler portrayals. Chaplin's comedic persona and Hitler's performances had little in common other than a trademark toothbrush moustache and plenty of hyperbole but it was hard to take either seriously after the megastar of comedy had taken on political celebrity. The seal-and-ball scene reveals Hynkel's childish delight with the world-as-toy. It exposes his megalomania but it also reduces the great dictator to a little boy. Yet while Chaplin's satire has always delighted audiences, the film had considerable difficulties in the production phase that centred upon the potential reception of the film in Nazi Germany: would its release worsen the situation of the European Jews?[6] Was humour the appropriate response towards a regime that had plunged Europe into war? Indeed, Chaplin himself voiced some doubt in his autobiography over the appropriateness of the film's satire in the light of the unconscionable crimes committed by the Nazis of which he could not have known when he was writing and shooting the film (1966: 148). Ernst Lubitsch's *To Be or Not to Be*, released two years later, had a very different reception although it too sent up Nazi theatricality

(Gemünden 2003: 76). While Chaplin's long film has entered the cultural archive through iconic scenes (chiefly, the stateroom scene and the final speech), Lubitsch's film cannot be excerpted in such a way, nor is its plot easily summarised. Its satire lives off the sparkling wit of Edwin Justus Mayer's script as much as its visual jokes. One of its tenets is that it requires ham-fisted acting to impersonate Nazis, who themselves are all sound and fury despite the very real atrocities the film reports them committing. Twice, before the plot gets underway, Lubitsch tricks the spectator into believing that what they are watching is 'real' rather than an impersonation put on for a diegetic audience. Both times it is the incompetent actor Josef Tura (Jack Benny) who dresses up as a Nazi: first as 'Concentration Camp Ehrhardt' to test whether the citizens of Warsaw are fooled (they are not), and secondly as Hitler in the rehearsal of a play, which we only realise once the camera pans to the right to reveal the stage and the director.

While Lubitsch chose the milieu of the theatre as the most appropriate metaphor to satirise the pompous performativity of Nazism (how the Nazis present themselves), Tarantino is more interested in the manner in which cinema presents the Nazis (what we have made them look like). Both Chaplin and Lubitsch needed diegetic audiences to satirise Nazism and this paradigm becomes the defining feature of the farcical treatment of Hitler from these early satires to contemporary alternate histories such as Daniel Levy's *Mein Führer* (2007) and Tarantino's *Basterds*.

We meet Hitler in chapter two of the film in scenes intercut with the Basterds' story (their recruitment, the back stories of some individuals, and their 'apache' ambushes). The Führer wears dress uniform and white cape for a monumental state portrait which is being painted in the background. The scene contrasts official truth with political reality: the impotent fury of the man receiving yet another despatch about the Basterds belies the composure of the statesman in the portrait; the fabric and colours of his actual attire are significantly different from their artistic rendition, reminiscent of Tamara de Lempicka's large and angular males. Banging on the table in front of him, gesticulating wildly and screaming 'Nein! Nein! Nein!' at two generals seated before a gigantic, swastika-riddled map of Europe, Tarantino's Hitler (Martin Wuttke) is immediately recognisable as the ranting megalomaniac dictator Charlie Chaplin satirised in 1940. A mere former corporal rather than a general; an *Anstreicher* ('house painter'), in Brecht's words, rather than an accomplished artist; a dyspeptic ranter rather than a rhetorician, Hitler is never a threat in any of the scenes in which he appears. Most importantly, perhaps, the size of the room, the painting and the map on the wall characterise the ambitions of the man who is dwarfed by them,

They seem to be able to elude capture
like an apparition.

Figure 5.1   Tarantino's Hitler

even though the low camera-angle emphasises the mechanics of aggrandisement (Fig. 5.1). Instead, these props and techniques underline the manner and effect (on the characters in the story and on the audience) of the careful construction of what we would now call celebrity.

What is being mocked, when we laugh at Nazis on screen, is the seriousness of their habitus, their portentous self-dramatisation. It is easy to dismiss the reliance on pageantry and ritual as so much mumbo jumbo, but such cynicism is ahistorical. Above all, it fails to recognise Nazism's appeal through a manufactured affect. As a mass-experience, Nazism was very carefully stage-managed, within a quasi-religious völkisch-nationalist framework, to enthral. We have seen in the last chapter that any attempt at documentary replication of iconography and habitus merely replicates this enthralment. Even films that offer case studies of the seductions of fascism – Louis Malle's *Lacombe Lucien* or Volker Schlöndorff's adaptation of Michel Tournier's novel *Le roi des aulnes*, *Der Unhold* (*The Ogre*, 1996) – cannot escape this impasse. Filmmakers who have eschewed realist modes of representation have notably fallen prey to Hitler's celebrity status, as if they could not resist the fictitious encounter of a character with the real historical 'monster'. In Spielberg's *Indiana Jones and the Last Crusade* (1989), Harrison Ford is swept along with a group of adoring Nazi youth towards the Führer who obligingly autographs his book for him. Woody Allen's mock documentary *Zelig* (1983) features a human chameleon who manages to be part of a Nazi party rally and meets the Reichchancellor.

The construction of the Führer as celebrity into a Führerkult with the most sophisticated media available, and the exploitation of the celebrity effect as affective bond to a charismatic, messianic leader is one of the hallmarks of Nazism's modernity, and a cornerstone of its propaganda (Kershaw 2001). Its strategists utilised the kind of marketing that creates a 'brand': a swastika is still as globally recognised as the shape of a Coca Cola bottle, and Hitler remains one of the most globally well-known historical persons because he became literally the face of fascism.[7] From the mid-1920s onwards that 'face' was carefully constructed and disseminated through photography, public appearance, radio broadcast and media reportage. Leni Riefenstahl's chief cameraman, Walter Frentz, developed the hand-held vérité style that gave Hitler's speeches such immediacy while Heinrich Hoffmann photographed and marketed Hitler in the same manner one would control the publicity of a major movie star, with orchestrated photo opportunities for national and international magazines, souvenir booklets for events, cigarette cards and other collectors' items. According to Robin Muir, Hoffmann's income from such publications was so stupendous that he was indicted at Nuremberg for profiteering (2005: 61). The mass production and dissemination of Hitler memorabilia and collector's items during Hitler's reign – Hoffmann's profitable business line – guaranteed the postwar availability of such 'relics'. Hitler's celebrity status now ensures his convenient citability: even an audience with virtually no historical knowledge of Nazism or the Second World War can grasp what he 'means'.

In *Basterds*, Hitler is not the only historical character accorded celebrity status. Tarantino plays with the audience's desire to see historical 'stars' in a war film – Goebbels, Göring, even Churchill – in every scene in which they appear. We encounter Churchill very late, in chapter four, where his staff brief the British film critic turned secret agent. Seated in the back of a vast stateroom at a country estate, at a piano, he is easily recognisable through his iconic omnipresent cigar and his lugubrious bulk. Rather tellingly, *his* globe contains a bar.[8] Göring has to wait until chapter five to make an appearance amongst the fascist luminaries in the cinema lobby at the premiere, and even then his white bulk has to be pointed out through a handwritten white arrow marked 'Goering' scribbled, as it were, on the frame, as if the scene were a shot for a celebrity magazine, pointing out a C-lister. This superscription, I would suggest, plays with the notion of 'historical capital'. Churchill is a household name; Hitler is instantly recognisable; Himmler remains the petit bourgeois architect of evil, a schoolmaster in SS uniform; but vulgar Hermann Göring, President of the *Reichstag*, Ministerpresident of Prussia, Reich Minister for both Aviation and Forestry, owner of *Karinhall* and wearer of fanciful costumes, the canny survivor indicted at Nuremberg for war crimes – he does not quite fit the mould of 'fascism' just as he did not quite 'buy' fascism and thus fell out of favour.

Goebbels, on the other hand, the architect of the Nazi propaganda machine and the mastermind of the premiere, has more screen time than the dictator he adores.[9] Goebbels is central to Tarantino's projection of Nazi celebrity because he helps to manufacture it. Yet in the portrayal of Nazi film culture, historical referents and the tropes of 'fascism' collide. The references to mass culture under the Nazi regime are plentiful: there are *Durchhaltelieder* (perseverance songs) from Rolf Hansen's box-office hit *Die Große Liebe* (1942), a Zarah Leander vehicle but also a 'modern war film' according to the minister for propaganda, that shows some of the reality of war while encouraging national unity and sacrifice. There's a well-known song from the musical comedy *Glückskinder* (1936), featuring the popular couple Willy Fritsch and Lilian Harvey. The soldier's card game includes Winnetou, bestselling author Karl May's Native American hero, a staple of boys' literature in Germany (and early postwar cinema) as well as one of Hitler's favourite writers. When Zoller and Shosanna meet for the first time she is fixing the neon display that advertises Pabst's *Die weiße Hölle vom Piz Palü*, a silent mountain film starring Nazi Germany's most influential director, Leni Riefenstahl. Von Hammersmarck, as Tarantino tells us, is meant to be 'the Dietrich that stayed', rather than the ersatz-Garbo Zarah Leander whose contralto so memorably underpinned the exotic melodramas she starred in (in Gilbey 2009). In the screenplay, von Hammersmarck also refers to *Tiefland*, a film Riefenstahl only completed in 1955 and asserted to have been beyond Goebbels's influence. Many of the film's references to fascist mass culture suggest that the Nazi culture industry indeed produced predominantly vacuous, apolitical entertainment. However, as both Georg Seeßlen (1994: 56) and Lutz Koepnick (2002a: 76–8) have argued, such films shrewdly pursued merely different, more subtle strategies in contrast to overt propaganda such as *Hitlerjunge Quex* or the vile *Jew Süß*. These films turned out to be both unpopular and commercially unsuccessful. Mass entertainment interpellated the audience much more easily into a system of social conformity under fascism. Part of Goebbels's *Gleichschaltung*, Nazi film culture standardised desires and emotions but the strategies employed were by no means crude or unambiguous. However, the references to UFA – its stars and its directors – marry the construction of political celebrity with the film star system and underline the interdependence of ideological and cultural personality cult under fascism *and as* 'fascism'. In highlighting a figure like Goebbels, with his power over the iconographic and the cinematic phenomenology of German fascism, Tarantino reminds the audience of the interplay between ideology, historical capital and cinema: what we 'know' about fascism – its self-representation, its cultural production, its documentary evidence and its fictionalisations – may be largely the result of moving pictures. Goebbels, as the Reichsminister for propaganda and people's enlightenment, is the father of 'fascism' and he is an important character in the story because we are made to watch him 'at work', as it were.

There is, however, a remarkable gulf between the shrewdly packaged historical Nazi film culture that is referenced and the propaganda film *Nation's Pride* we see at the premiere and which resembles nothing ever made under Goebbels's firm grip on UFA. As Aaron Barlow has argued, it is much more reminiscent of postwar war films, notably *To Hell and Back* (1955) in which the real-life war hero Audie Murphy plays himself (2010: 149). The decorated soldier as a Hollywood war hero is a unique American creation. In Tarantino's *Inglourious Basterds* the film in the film – *Nation's Pride* – is directed by the actor and director Eli Roth. In the main narrative Roth plays Sgt Donowitz aka 'the Bear Jew'. (In real life he is a director of schlock horror films.) *Nation's Pride* constitutes one of those anachronistic intertextual loops in which fascism is represented through 'fascism', even models of Allied national mythology, while the more accurate references to Nazism's cultural landscape are reduced to in-jokes, movie posters, snippets of audio track, or card games. The spectator certainly has to have considerable knowledge and linguistic skills to distinguish clearly between those different versions of 'fascism', and herein lies a problem with Tarantino's loose understanding of history and the precision with which some of the German and French intertexts are deployed: the effort to demonstrate the linguistic challenges of the European theatre of war certainly produces a level of authenticity that is a corrective to the bungled accents in Castellari's *Inglorious Bastards*, and it avoids the suspension of disbelief required in the Bavarian tavern scene in *Where Eagles Dare*, the model for La Louisiane in chapter four. But this effort is fundamentally at odds with the tropes of 'fascism', however ambiguously used or ironised. Before we examine the way in which *Nation's Pride* functions in the film's engagement with 'fascism', it is helpful to have a closer look at two precursors of such self-reflexive strategies, Mel Brooks's *The Producers* (1968) and Helmut Dietl's *Schtonk!* (1992), two comedies that foreground the audiences of 'fascism' in very different ways.

'Fascism' and its diegetic audiences: *Schtonk!* and *The Producers*

Helmut Dietl's satire *Schtonk!*, whose non-sensical title references Adenoid Hynkel's Germanic sounding rants in *The Great Dictator*, fictionalises the scandal of the fraudulent Hitler diaries, excerpted in

1983 by *Stern* magazine after experts such as the historian Hugh Trevor-Roper confirmed their authenticity (Harris [1986] 1991). The publishing industry strongly suspected a fraud, but reckoned that the enormous profits from selling copy outweighed any scruples. What Dietl's Oscar-nominated film teases out with masterful malice is the powerful fascination Hitler continues to exert over the public imagination; how thin the veneer of liberal democracy was whenever the old fascism promised lucrative income; and how antiquarian interest in Nazi memorabilia often merely cloaks old-boy fascist loyalty. More importantly, *Schtonk!* suggested that the aura of the Third Reich was so powerful that *any* artefact ostensibly connected with Nazism became a sublime relic. To own such an object, however trivial, or to establish a connection with it, however tenuous, meant to participate in this aura, to bathe in a hallowed reflection: somehow, you too were 'there'. Dietl's comedy is not at all about fascism, but, like Brooks's *The Producers*, about 'fascism' as an ersatz sublime: consumable history, entertainment and lucrative business venture.

We recall the full-sized Hitler portrait from chapter two in *Basterds*. *Schtonk!* too makes use of a painting to expose the desire for ersatz Nazism through historical relics. The bogus art expert 'Prof. Dr.' Knobel makes a living from forging and manufacturing Nazi memorabilia. When he tries to sell an 'unknown' painting by Hitler of Eva Braun *in statu nascendi* in front of the Watzman mountain to the wealthy Swabian industrialist Lenz, his customer calls on a second expert to authenticate the painting, distinguished Professor Strasser.

Strasser's paradoxical mode of verification is not a scientific or technical analysis but to provide a detailed narrative of production that

Figure 5.2   A 'genuine' Hitler! Dietl's *Schtonk!*

includes him as a witness. The narrative vouchsafes for the authenticity of the artefact since it turns him into a secret audience to Hitler's opaque love life and unknown artistic endeavour, and because of this proximity to Hitler, the painting gains a paratext that also augments the expertise of the expert. The market thus creates its 'experts', and the experts narrativise its objects.

> Strasser: Ich war nämlich dabei als er's gemalt hat.
> Knobel: Da war'n Sie. . . dabei?
> Strasser: Ja! Ich war Sommergast auf dem Berghof. Es war ein wunderschöner Sommertag: der 7. Juli 1939, gegen Nachmittag. Es muß so um fünf Uhr gewesen sein. Ich gehe durch die weite Wiese, durch die Kornblumen, hinterm Berghof, da – plötzlich – steht Er. Und malt *sie*, wie Gott sie schuf. Es war genau vor diesem Bergpanorama.
> Frau Lenz: Wasch wolle sie jetz damit sage, Herr Professor? Isch des jetz oi Hitler oder is des koi Hitler?
> Strasser: Gnädige Frau, eines kann ich Ihnen zweifelsfrei und verbindlich sagen: das ist aller, aller, allerechtester Hitler!

> [Strasser: I was actually there when he painted it.
> Knobel: You were . . . there?
> Strasser: Indeed! I was a guest at the Berghof that summer. It was a beautiful summer's day, the 7th July 1939, in the afternoon. It must have been around five o'clock. I am walking through the open fields, through the cornflowers, behind the Berghof. There – all of a sudden – is HE, painting HER, as God created her. It was exactly in front of this mountain view.
> Frau Lenz: What'ya trying to say here, Professor Strasser? Is this a genuine Hitler or ain't it?
> Strasser: Ma'am, if I can guarantee you one thing without any doubt: this is an utterly and totally genuine Hitler!] [my translation]

Earlier the audience saw Knobel working on the painting from old magazine clippings of Braun's face while a young agricultural labourer was posing for the body, so Strasser is immediately exposed as just as much of a fake as the 'genuine Hitler'. What makes such fraud possible and lucrative – and this is a theme that runs throughout the film – is the desire that creates the narrative, the artefact *and* the market: the longing for a transcendent experience by proxy, brought about by the totemic artefact. Like Tarantino, Dietl makes a point here about the continuity between the celebrity cult *under* the Nazis and celebrity cult *about* the Nazis that echoes Saul Friedländer's argument in *Reflections of Nazism*, Alvin Rosenfeld's in *Imagining Hitler*, and Art Spiegelman's in *Metamaus*. For them, 'Nazism' is consumable history, even 'Holokitsch', prolonged endlessly because it is lucrative: it sells fakes, it sells magazines, it sells films and books.

We may want to ask whether Dietl's audience is encouraged to make connections between the vulgar story on the screen and the perhaps equally risible act of consuming the film, or whether the comedy distances us from those bathing in the glow of a 'genuine Hitler'. This is a crucial question for Tarantino's film as well, and perhaps for all films dealing with 'fascism', comedic or not. *Schtonk!* like *The Producers* makes us gasp at 'fascism' before we are allowed to laugh at it. Having insinuated himself into the circles of Old Nazis that are his most profitable market Knobel is invited to a nocturnal celebration of Hitler's birthday. Through a long, low-angle shot panning upwards the camera reveals row upon row of umbrella'd guests in tuxedos and evening dress moving along a torch-lit serpentine path up to a gothic castle (and the gothic is of course merely of the 'mock' variety: Schloss Drachenburg in Königswinter, a late nineteenth-century neo-gothic folly of a banker's dream). The audience, however, is momentarily taken aback by this spectacle (Fig. 5.3). We have grasped that the lucrative venture of Hitler forgeries must certainly depend on a sizable market, and by now we have seen some of the gullible fools who buy such kitsch, but that there are so many old (and new) Nazis who crawl out of the woodwork with pageantry and occult rituals comes as a shock. Nocturnal pageantry was part of fascist ritual, from the torch-lit march of hundreds of thousands of SA troops through the Brandenburg Gate on the night of Hitler's seizure of power in January 1933, to Christian Weber's Night of the Amazons (Munich 1936–9) – kinky evening entertainment for the Munich derby – to the nocturnal marches of the Hitler Youth at their camps and fortresses. Dietl's scene plays out to a well-known

Figure 5.3   Fake diaries, bogus experts, mock castles, ersatz stars. Dietl's *Schtonk!*

song by Zarah Leander (Goebbels's ersatz-Garbo): 'Ich weiß, es wird einmal ein Wunder gescheh'n' from *Die große Liebe* (*The Love of My Life*, 1942):[10] 'I know eventually there'll be a miracle' – presumably the miracle of Hitler's diaries, but given the choreography of this scene one might as well anticipate the miracle of Hitler's survival (another staple of 'fascism' the film alludes to at the end).

Volker Schlöndorff makes much of romantic castles and pageants in *The Ogre*, and while he deliberately encourages the audience's enthrallment with such *mises-en-scène*, Dietl's use of it seems at odds with the comedic tone of the film and the contemporary setting: the gothic pageant and the nocturnal gathering are literally out of place and out of time, and so are the people participating in it. Thirty minutes into the film Dietl reminds us what we are also dealing with in the remnants of Nazism in the 1980s, not just fascist objects (fake or otherwise) but unapologetic fascist subjects and their desire for transcendence. In its probing of the hypocrisies and capitalist interests of the publishing industry (part of the engine of 'fascism'), the film also reveals how historical inquiry (and its fetishistic version of antiquarian collecting) can also be a convenient pretext for engaging 'fascism'. While the audience certainly enjoys a funny film about two fraudsters who are presented as likable wheeler-dealers, we cannot help siding with them because the people they take for a ride are vile, opportunistic and greedy. When *Stern* first published extracts from the forged diaries, its sales figures soared sky-high, with million-dollar foreign deals beckoning, so the historical background of the film suggests that its audience might just as well consider itself part of the gullible world that deserves to be fooled: we would have bought the magazine and read the diaries just as we now watch the film, believing ourselves safely distanced through the device of satire.

Brooks's *The Producers* is a more aggressive assault on audience taste. The plot features two Jewish crooks – an overselling musical producer (Zero Mostel) who wheedles 'checkies' out of old ladies in exchange for fulfilling their sexual fantasies, and a highly neurotic 'creative' accountant (Gene Wilder). Together they put on stage *Springtime for Hitler: A Gay Romp with Adolf and Eva in Berchtesgarden*, counting on a sure-fire flop that will have made them a fortune in checkies. Contrary to their expectations that a pro-Nazi script, a horrific cast and a camp version of Nazism will cause uproar, bad taste is a roaring success, and because they cannot pay out dividends to their investors they land in prison. The Busby Berkeley dance number 'Springtime for Hitler' with its goose-stepping Aryans in patent-leather miniskirts is the Brechtian play-in-the-play, and caused considerable offence on the film's first

Figure 5.4   The human swastika in Brooks's *The Producers*

release. It was only due to Peter Sellers's public endorsement of Brooks's comedy in *Variety* that the film gradually built up a cult audience (Symonds 2006: 25–32). Undoubtedly the number is excessive, vulgar and 'in bad taste' but so is everything else in the film: the stereotyping of the two main characters as Jewish crooks; the director de Bris and his assistant as camp queens; the Swedish dumb blonde Ulla as a gyrating sex object; the Yankee Doodle Nazi as the fascist in hiding; the representation of old people's sexuality as inappropriate and revolting. The list could be continued with the bourgeois audience who rescue the play from commercial failure because they re-interpret trash as 'funny' and 'ironic'. Brooks comments on the cultural wheel that makes 'fascism' funky before Susan Sontag raises her modernist eyebrows on mass culture.

The opening dance number of *Springtime* is intercut with reverse shots that show the theatre audience's changing reaction from bewilderment to open-mouthed consternation to outrage. The diegetic theatre audience cannot see some effects of the choreography because they are produced via an aerial down-shot for the film audience, particularly the swastika formation (Fig. 5.4). Susan Gubar rightly points out that this frame replicates some of the techniques that were used in the party rallies and Riefenstahl's cinematic renditions of mass events. The embodiment of ideological semiotics through humans in mass formations of course depends on this technique (Fig. 5.5 shows a swastika formation at such a mass event). For Gubar, however, Brooks's editing amounts to 'racial camp mock[ing] the shoddy theatricality of fascism' (2006: 30). Neither

Figure 5.5   Rotating ideology: German youth forming a swastika in honour of an unknown soldier (The Associated Press)

the theatricality nor the camera work is shoddy, I would argue. Both were highly effective propaganda tools and Riefenstahl's perspectives on mass events and the human body are recognisably influential on modern sports reportage, whether we like to credit her with this or not. The human swastika shot makes us aware of another audience than the diegetic one – ourselves – and draws attention to the *mise-en-abîme* of watching the watchers. If we haven't grasped it already, here we are certainly as implicated in the 'bad taste' of this performance, and of the entire film's spectacle, as the audience in the theatre, whose response is more than questionable. That the theatre audience is 'aghast at the bad taste of German propaganda', as Gubar claims, is another misreading of the scene: they are aghast at what passes for acceptable entertainment on stage. We may believe that the audience's initial responses are appropriate (consternation, outrage, leaving the theatre in protest of 'bad taste'). We may equally ask what an audience expects who attends a play entitled *Springtime for Hitler: A Gay Romp with Adolf and Eva in Berchtesgarden*? A gay romp it is, so why be surprised, let alone scandalised? The one audience member who enthusiastically applauds the opening number is immediately censored by those sitting next to him. When the audience make for the doors while the play continues they are stopped in their tracks by L.S.D.'s (Dick Shawn) languid rendition of Adolf's placatory serenading of a querulant Eva: 'I lieb ya, baby. Now lieb me alone.' Again the stage play is intercut

Figure 5.6 'Harry, he's funny!' Spectacular mirth in Mel Brooks's
The Producers

with shots of a revised audience reaction: people returning to their
seats; a woman near the door exclaiming to her husband, 'Harry, he's
funny!'; another shouting into the corridor for her companions to come
back. When we next get a full-frontal shot of the audience, the mood
has turned to ribald amusement, thanks to a hippie Hitler (Fig. 5.6).
There is something very peculiar about this reaction, because what we
have seen on stage is in a different register from the outrageous opening
number. L.S.D.'s Hitler (recognisable again by the toothbrush moustache and the 1960s version of a side-parting) is merely silly but not
really funny. Why should this performance change the audience's mind;
why might this psychedelic Adolf enable an interpretation of *Springtime*
as 'ironic'? Who is 'he' in 'Harry, he's funny!'? Is it L.S.D. or is it
Hitler?

    If the diegetic audience is not susceptible to a camped-up version of
Nazism, they certainly respond to a rendition of Hitler precisely because
this updates Chaplin's efforts in exactly the way in which period drama
produces contemporaneous versions of the past. L.S.D.'s Adolf can rely
on Hitler's status as a historical celebrity, who gets the star billing of
the show. But note the intimate first-name footing on which the audience is placed through the play's subtitle. In the first dialogue scene we
see 'Adolf' and 'Eva' as private individuals, a romantic couple in their
domestic environment. They are treated in precisely the same manner
as Hollywood stars in gossip columns – public figures of whose private
lives the audience catches a privileged glimpse. The tremendous interest
in Hitler the private man stands perhaps in stark contrast to his wilful

vanishing act through suicide and incineration, as if the most trivial of details could uncannily return the materiality of his person: his vegetarianism, his love of 'Blondie' the Alsatian, the interior furnishings of the Berghof, his relationship to Eva Braun, the stories of his valet, the contents of his library, his table talk, his favourite films, speculation about the brutality of his upbringing, his niece Geli or his sexual identity – none of this fug of detail could possibly help to 'explain' Nazism or indeed the man who embodied it. It satisfies salacious curiosity and a prurient imagination, but it also testifies to a desire to domesticate the dictator, to diminish him to the merely monstrously human. As we have seen in Chapter 4 when discussing the criminal celebrity, it is one of the paradoxes of modern celebrity culture that it both elevates individuals in the public sphere (so that we can vicariously participate in their aura) and courts their deflation. The transvestite director Roger de Bris's queer (mis)interpretation of the fascist Franz Liebkind's play manages to deliver just such domestication: it turns Hitler into Adolf, a bathetically silly, hen-pecked Romeo. One couldn't possibly find genocide funny, but one can laugh at common and recognisable domestic bickering.

The premise of *The Producers* (and *Springtime*) is that the Shoah is unmentioned and unmentionable. Bad taste consists in a cultural process of disavowing historical knowledge. In that sense, *The Producers* is also a film about the complicity of the entertainment industry in all manner of lucrative vulgarity. While the editing exposes the poor taste and moral uncertainty, not to say fickleness, of the theatre audience, the film's spectators are by no means excluded from critique. It is no coincidence that the film's history – from flop to rotten-tomato cult status to its entirely uncontroversial success as a Broadway production and re-make in 2001 – mirrors the reception of *Springtime* in the theatre, to the point where it takes the public endorsement of a single individual (Harry's wife; the comedian Peter Sellers) to turn bad taste into dollars and comedy history. What happens before the curtain rises to the now iconic Busby Berkeley dance number – a very long hour into the film – is a long-winded emptying of fascism of its lethal historical referent via an accumulation of other vulgarities, and by that point *Springtime* is hilarious. *The Producers* and *Schtonk!*, then, really are about the lucrative transition of fascism to 'fascism', from its roots as Nazi aesthetic to its permutations in camp, fetish gear, memorabilia, celebrity culture and period drama.

'The killin' Nazis business': 'fascism' and violent cinema

This brings us back to Tarantino's *Inglourious Basterds*. What does an audience expect that goes to see a film that carries the misspelled title of a minor 1970s 'dirty war' movie, by a director notorious for his allusive postmodern style and his use of violence on screen? Clearly they would be entitled to an army of screen Nazis who would, in the course of a story syncopated with special effects and spectacular violence, be thoroughly defeated, killed by the dozen through both ballistic and ingenious means and possibly by adversaries who are little better in moral stature than the fascists they often impersonate and reduce to blood-soaked corpses. Such is the plot of Mark Robson's *Von Ryan's Express* (1965), Aldrich's *The Dirty Dozen*, Hutton's *Where Eagles Dare* (1968), and Castellari's *Inglorious Bastards*. One must also add Sam Peckinpah's *The Wild Bunch* (1969), which features the same structure in a historic Anglo-Mexican setting and, together with *Cross of Iron* (1977), was highly influential in its representation of aestheticised slow-motion violence on Tarantino and other filmmakers. Many of these productions in the late 1960s and 1970s were ostensibly not about the historical conflicts they depict but indirect comments on the Vietnam War and the political violence in American public life and culture: the assassinations of Martin Luther King and John F. Kennedy; the violent responses to the anti-war protests; and the crisis of confidence in American exceptionalism (Landy 1996). Like the Spaghetti Westerns that appeared around the same time (Frayling 2006: 121–37), they were often panned by reviewers because of their moral ambivalence and their unapologetic foregrounding of violence. Aldrich's combat film finishes with an apocalyptic scene in which a group of disposable and steadily decimated criminal US soldiers conclude a mission to eliminate the German High Command gathered at a French Chateau by locking them into the cellar below and incinerating them and their wives with explosives thrown into air vents. This fictitious assassination, alongside Lubitsch's bungled bomb plot in *To Be or Not to Be*, is Tarantino's obvious inspiration for 'Operation Kino' in *Basterds*. Aldrich claimed that his use of violence was not gratuitous but deliberately critical of US military strategy:

> The whole nature of war is dehumanizing. There's no such thing as a nice war. Now American critics completely missed that, so they attacked the picture because of this violence, and for indulgence in violent heroics. Now fascinatingly, European critics all picked up on the parallel between burning people alive and the use of napalm, whether they liked the picture or not. (Cited in Sauvage 1976/7: 59)

Indeed Tony Williams in his persuasive reading of Aldrich's film goes further in suggesting that the incendiary apocalypse forges connections between the use of such weapons in the Second World War, Korea and Vietnam, indicting the US military and political establishment for a continuity of ruthless and disproportionate destruction (2004: 352). As Aldrich emphasises here, the 'dirty war' movie is not necessarily an anti-war genre; it can't be, nor can it dispense with violence. Rather, it challenges any simplistic notion of heroism or the myth of 'the good war' propagated by the classic Second World War combat film.

This is not to say, however, that the audience who made *The Dirty Dozen* the run-away box-office hit of 1967 could not have read it as a critique of US foreign policy *and* a highly entertaining action and adventure film in which the spectator can unashamedly indulge in combustible anti-fascist violence precisely because the double-standard pertaining to that violence (*any* violence against fascism is justified) is so ingrained that it supersedes moral ambivalences or representational ambiguities. (The dropping of incendiaries and hand grenades through air vents in *The Dirty Dozen* had led some critics to draw parallels between Germans in cellars and Jews in gas chambers; Williams 2004: 352.) In contrast, there is no room for such interpretive looseness in the Manichean universe we see in fantasy films that reference fascism such as Spielberg's *Indiana Jones* series and George Lucas's *Star Wars*. But the boundaries between the methods of friends and foes are habitually blurred even in 'classic' war films. While many war films including *Basterds* make distinctions between ordinary German soldiers (conscripts and professionals) on the one hand, and ideological Nazis on the other, preferably black-uniformed SS troops and officers, this often makes little difference when it comes to the body count. The fact that many storylines include sabotage plots in which Allied soldiers have to impersonate Germans makes for further ambiguity: the German uniform seems to mobilise hitherto unknown resources of ingenious brutality in the wearer. Castellari's bastards spend most of the film in German uniforms killing Germans; they even manage to massacre a genuine Allied intelligence unit wearing German uniforms. In many scenes of carnage, then, it is rather hard to distinguish between the warring sides: it just looks like Germans killing one another – perhaps the underlying prime fantasy. Given Castellari's strategic use of slo-mo sequences when the German lines come under attack, a casual viewer might be forgiven for confusing *Bastards* with Peckinpah's *Cross of Iron*, a film about German troops on the Eastern Front.[11]

From these genres Tarantino's film retains a morally dubious group of Jewish avengers whose preferred mode of killing Nazis – scalping and baseball-bashing – is thoroughly Americanised.[12] This guerrilla M.O. combines in one fell swoop sports movie, gangster film, combat film and Western. Slasher and horror films are rather fond of such mutilations, for instance in *Maniac* (1980) and *Deathwatch* (2002),[13] and the casting offers a particular in-joke with 'Bear Jew' Donowitz played by Eli Roth, director of *Hostel* (2005), a film that epitomises the so-called 'torture porn' genre. For Aaron Barlow, Aldo and his Apaches are not merely a fantastical version of muscular Jewish vengeance in the manner of *Defiance* (2008), or Spielberg's *Munich* (2005), but a particular twist of early American myth: the Apaches behave with a savagery convention-ally associated with the historical 'losers', Native Americans, against white settlers whose exterminationist imperialist practices acquire fascist connotations (Barlow 2010: 147).[14] Alvin Rosenfeld identified the trope of the obsessive, knife-wielding avenging Jew as a byproduct in popular Hitler fiction that drew extensively on fascist symbolism. For Rosenfeld, this mass-market Jewish avenger, driven by a furious 'Holocaust mental-ity', is not so much a revaluation of racist stereotypes from *Der Stürmer* but merely their continuation: the Jew thrives on violence as much as the fascist perpetrator (1985: 48–9; 51). The pernicious logic of fascistoid anti-fascist violence is dismissed by Eli Roth, who called the scenes of slaughter in *Basterds* 'kosher porn: it was an orgasmic feeling to swing that bat': 'when we filmed the scenes where I killed Nazis, the German cast and crew were as excited about it as the Jews were – it was like we were killing them together . . . They were so happy. And they wanted the deaths to be as violent as possible, because they're tortured by the Holocaust as much as we are.'[15] Tarantino's 'killin' Nazis business' sup-posedly operates as a release mechanism of historic guilt and relief from transgenerational trauma. Roth's father, visiting the set in Berlin and commenting on the scene, maintained that Tarantino's film represented 'a psychological reality', namely the individual and collective fantasy of Jewish revenge, of killing Hitler.[16] This logic makes a clear distinction between historical reality and psychological reality, between history and fantasy, fact and film, but the relationship between reality and cinema in *Basterds*, I would argue, is not quite so clear-cut.

'Operation Kino': watching fantasy

It is notable that almost every scene of violence in this film is performed in front of an in-film audience, and, as in *The Producers*, these spectato-rial orchestrations highlight the medium's (and cinema history's) politics of representing 'Nazism'. The first chapter reminds the audience of familiar historical knowledge – that officious SS officers were employed in rounding up and executing Jews; that the French were coerced into collaboration. Its *mise-en-scène* and audio track, however, is that of the Western. This hybridisation draws our attention to the way in which different genres narrativise (justify, choreograph, dramatise) violence. The different chapters offer different paradigmatic choices even if this makes for a rather episodic (or as Tarantino puts it, 'novelistic') structure overall: Western (classic and Spaghetti); comedy; combat film (classic, 'dirty', macaroni style, adventure), until the last chapter offers the usual explosive culmination in a spectacular overkill. Each chapter ends with a different orchestration of violence. At the end of the first chapter a Jewish family hiding under the floorboards of a farmhouse are machine-gunned. The camera pan-down that had earlier revealed their refuge does not follow the same route when they are killed but stops above ground substituting sawdust and wood for flesh and blood. There are taboos, it seems, that even a staunch advocate of graphic screen violence does not easily break.[17] This visual displacement of death onto blasting wooden planks is similar to the aural displacement of violence in the ear-cutting scene in *Reservoir Dogs* and the sounds of whipping behind a long shot on a firmly closed door in the torture scene in *13, Rue Madeleine* (1947). They serve primarily to characterise the perpetrator as brutal and sadistic; for this purpose it is simply not necessary to see the victim suffering. (This narrative economy defines voyeurism as watching pain rather than watching the infliction of pain.)

However, by the same token scenes of perpetration often act as justifications for retributive violence (even though the Hays code that applied to classic war films prohibited revenge as a motivation). In *13, Rue Madeleine*, torture contributes to justifying the concluding act of violence in the film, an air raid on the Gestapo Headquarters. The fascist violence in the first chapter of *Basterds* dramatises 'evil' in this conventional sense, and conforms to the narrative dynamics we see in Spaghetti Westerns like *A Fistful of Dollars* or *Once Upon a Time in the West* that open with the destruction of families.

Chapter two introduces the Basterds, demonstrates their methods and intercuts anti-fascist terror with the scenes from Hitler's stateroom so that we can learn of the physical and psychological impact of the Basterds' actions by juxtaposing visual and verbal representations of violence. German troops are ambushed and their corpses desecrated and robbed (with a nod to the venality of the bounty hunters in *The Wild Bunch*). Three survivors are made to observe the graphic scalping (in close-up) of their comrades: 'We in the killin' Nazi business', explains Lt Raine and the following scenes provide graphic illustration of what this means. In flashback we learn of the amateur-turned-professional Nazi assassin Hugo Stiglitz who has attracted the Basterds' attention by murdering Gestapo officers by garrotting them, stabbing them, smothering them with pillows or with his fist. For his valiant efforts he is rescued from prison by the Basterds who machine-gun his guards. This montage of Nazi killing is presented as if reported through sensational journalism – Stiglitz the rising sports star who is 'discovered' by Aldo's talent spotting: 'you wanna go pro?' Even before the Basterds go to work with their top performer, the renowned 'Bear Jew', the pervasive references to notoriety, celebrity and stardom (historical, criminal, sporting, cinema) highlight to what extent both cinematic and historical violence depend on media culture; violence is never contained in the act but seeps into and continues through representation.[18] Popular culture has been in the lucrative and emotionally satisfying 'killin' Nazi business' for a long time and has turned it into a spectator sport that, for the most part, escapes the moral censure that polices the representation of the Holocaust. Killing Nazis, chapter two tells us, is part of the American entertainment industry: 'Frankly, watchin' Donny beat Nazis to death is the closest we ever get to goin' to the movies', enthuses Raine (anachronistically but meta-cinematically) before he calls upon his star performer, Donny Donowitz. The scene that follows literalises 'killin' Nazis' as a spectatorial delight and links it to a quintessential American sport, baseball.

Sgt Rachtman, who refuses to divulge information about German placements, will be battered to death by the 'Bear Jew'. The tension builds up as we hear the sound of the baseball bat against rock over a long shot into the complete darkness of a cavernous space. The editing cuts between close ups of Rachtman's tense face, his point of view in tantalisingly long shots of the dark cave, and coach Aldo's dispassionate position on the sidelines of the 'action'. These cuts offer us three different emotional possibilities (amusement, imminent fury, terror). When Donowitz saunters out, to a Spaghetti Western audio track – his shape aggrandised by the camera's low-angle position, as if emerging from a stadium's changing rooms to the cheers of an adoring crowd, an amalgam of working-class hero and primitive masculinity – the effect of this hysterical over-dramatisation is comic relief. Shortly afterwards Rachtman is pummelled to death; the first two blows in over-the shoulder perspective give way to a steady crane pull-back to distance the spectators from the bloody pulp on the ground. Simultaneously this perspective positions us on the same level as the Basterds in the surrounding 'stadium' who are cheering another home run (Fig. 5.7).

The violence inflicted on the remaining German soldier, Private Butz, follows an identical pattern of merging humour with revulsion.

Figure 5.7   Home run! The 'Bear Jew' in the arena (*Inglourious Basterds*)

Tarantino cuts between the forest clearing and the stateroom scene where we see the Private removing his cap before Hitler to reveal a swastika carved into his forehead. The jump cut that returns us to the forest displaces the violence as the camera's low angle assumes Butz's point of view after Aldo the Apache inspects his handiwork. The contrast between the displacement of anti-Semitic violence in chapter one and the violent anti-fascist sport in chapter two could not be more blatant. Emotionally we are more affected by what we don't see but have to visualise ourselves. One may blame the Hays Code for the off-screen slaughter that ostensibly motivates the quest in John Ford's *The Searchers*; but what Ford's ellipses underline is precisely *the effect* of looking upon raped, scalped and mutilated female bodies. This gaze does more lasting damage to John Wayne's character than the civil war he has just returned from, triggering an obsessive racist search that perpetuates violence. The violent sport we watch in *Basterds* is explicitly framed as an entertaining spectacle for consumption and exhilaration. These scenes are very different from say, the end of Pasolini's *Salò*, where the *mise-en-scène* is ostensibly quite similar: those with absolute power watch from an elevated position, through binoculars, how their flunkies torture and kill a group of naked youths in the courtyard below. The gouging out of eyes, the cutting of a tongue, genital mutilation, scalping, rape and hanging – all this medieval horror is staged from the point of view of the fascist spectator, and because we too visually consume this suffering, our act of voyeurism implicates us. Tarantino's referencing of the violence of spectating does not have Pasolini's earnestness, nor could one even call it a critique (in the manner of, say, Oliver Stone's *Natural Born Killers*), given his frequently declared view of not taking violence very seriously. Yet he stages violence as a dubious pleasure (rather than kosher porn) to make us aware of its absurdity – or rather, our absurd reaction to it, which has been naturalised, since the 1980s, through the habitual exposure to casual carnage on TV and cinema screens. As he commented, 'You can enjoy what the Basterds are doing, and I set it up for you to enjoy it. But I don't make it that easy' (in Gilbey 2009). The Basterds' thuggish delight in mayhem and terror contrasts sharply with the old-fashioned bravery of Sgt Rachtman and the sniper-turned-actor Frederick Zoller, and this underlines the cultural double standards that underpin 'killin' Nazi business'. The war-and-adventure films of the 1960s and '70s (and even Holocaust narratives like Spielberg's *Schindler's List*) usually reserve cruelty and sadism for the men in black SS uniforms so that when they are finally disposed of, they present the opportunity of a satisfying and spectacularly gruesome exit: Gregory Peck's Mengele killed by his creepy creation in *The Boys from Brazil*; Derren Nesbitt's grotesquely Aryan SS officer in *Where Eagles Dare*; the psychopathic lunacy of Klaus Kinski's SS Colonel Hans Mueller in *5 per l'inferno*; Laurence Olivier's Christian Szell gobbling diamonds in *Marathon Man*; Malcolm MacDowell's Cpt. von Berkow in *The Passage*; the medieval slaughter of the SS officers in the castle in *Inglorious Bastards*; Ronald Lacey's divinely occasioned melt-down in *Raiders of the Lost Ark*. In the cinema, evil cannot be 'banal'. The audience's satisfaction is twofold: our revulsion at Nazi violence is morally elevating (and cloaks our voyeurism as an act of witnessing), and our exhilaration at their demise is passed off as just punishment.

These screen Nazis, as Uklański's frieze demonstrated, are now so paradigmatic in their impersonation of 'evil' that they have become part of our cultural inventory. Christoph Waltz, as SS Colonel Hans Landa, aka 'The Jewhunter', is a further entry in the catalogue, but also a commentary on it. It is notable how many critics were surprised that he (or his character?) stole the show from the film's most well-known box-office star, Brad Pitt. The unknown Waltz mesmerised audiences and critics with a screen presence that combined polyglot panache with cunning menace, grotesque vulgarity with unpredictable violence. Landa (like Littell's literary equivalent Maximilien Aue) is a composite character, made up from templates of screen Nazis. He is both Lubitsch's 'Concentration Camp Ehrhardt', infantile in his humour and ludicrous in his penchant for dairy products and enormous calabash pipes, and in his one unidiomatic linguistic blunder ('It's a bingo!'). And he is Lubitsch's extremely dangerous agent Savitzky, in his dispassionate blackmail of farmer LaPadite as he outlines his pragmatic, culturally ingrained anti-Semitism with the officiousness of an Adolf Eichmann; menacing in his appreciation of beautiful young women, as he holds their hand or their gaze for a fraction too long; psychopathic like Litvak's General Tanz in his explosion of rage as he strangles von Hammersmark; oozing Old World sophistication in his command of European languages; and highly intelligent in the engineering of his survival. Whenever Landa enters a frame he commands the scene, and our attention. Like the 'final girl' in the slasher film, he is the only character who has been given a complex psychology; the rest of the cast are plot functions or truncated citations. And like the 'final girl', he survives, scarred by the past.

According to convention, the massacre in chapter five that rids the world of the Nazi High Command and ends the war a year early should be most satisfying. Again, Tarantino 'doesn't make it easy'. The over-kill (bombing, burning, machine-gunning) reads like a culmination of postwar anti-fascist screen violence and, ironically, it is the cinema that both kills the Nazis and periodically resurrects them to kill them all over again, as the perennially undead of the historical genre. The premiere of the propaganda film *Nation's Pride* before an audience of Nazi bigwigs in Shosanna's cinema features Zoller's three-day defence of a tower against Allied attack, during which the sniper kills over 300 enemy soldiers. *Nation's Pride* consists entirely of a montage of serial carnage which is frequently intercut with shots of ribald cheering from the diegetic fascist audience (Figs 5.8 and 5.9). That this scene is an uncom-fortable parallel to chapter two, in which mayhem was also treated as a sporting event applauded by an on-screen audience, may make us feel uneasy enough. In the following massacre of the cinema audience any simplistic enjoyment of anti-fascist violence is surely tempered by the way in which Tarantino holds the mirror up to the audience: now the spectator's exhilaration at 'killin' Nazis' directly duplicates the fascists' earlier delight at screen violence. As Shosanna's face appears on the screen proclaiming boldly: 'I have a message for Germany: you are all

Figure 5.8   Zoller, the heroic fascist (*Inglourious Basterds*)

Figure 5.9   Hitler, the amused fascist (*Inglourious Basterds*)

Figure 5.10   Kosher porn: Donowitz, the fantasy assassin
(*Inglourious Basterds*)

going to die!', her projectionist lights the cans of nitrate film behind the screen, and the ensuing destruction is accompanied by the projected sound of her laughter which even overlays the diegetic sound of flames, machine-gun fire and explosions. It evokes the canned laughter so ironically deployed for screen violence in *Natural Born Killers*. The violence we are invited to enjoy is not couched in the sporting terms of marksmanship or the rhetoric of patriotism; it is unashamedly vindictive and excessive with a now classic use of slow-motion machine gunning and explosion.

As Matthew Boswell points out, Tarantino's film asks important questions about the kind of pleasure we derive from cinematic violence, including the gratuitous violence he offers us in his own productions (Boswell 2011: 181). If we cheer loudly at seeing Hitler's body riddled with machine gun bullets, what distinguishes 'our pleasure' from that of 'cheering Nazis'? What makes the consumption of *Nation's Pride* more (or less) offensive than the mayhem we eagerly await? How does the uncontrollable hatred that distorts Landa's face as he strangles the UFA star sit alongside Donowitz's crazed determination as he massacres the audience below him (Fig. 5.10)? As Frederick Zoller carves a swastika in the floorboards of his tower refuge (to the applause of the fascist audience) we also find it hilarious that Nazi soldiers should be marked by their ideological affiliation. Whether or not such parallels are in 'bad taste' is a moot point given the politics of 'dirty war' movies. Whether the film's audience has the historical capital and the cinephile register to recognise Tarantino's technique is the more important matter, as is the question of whether this technique can escape the problem of having to show violence in order to make us aware of our now pervasive spectatorial responses with incongruous feelings of exhilaration *and* revulsion, laughter *and* terror.

Those directors most criticised for their use of violence regularly defend themselves by stating that their stylisation is not an aestheticisation but rather a means to break spectatorial habituation to violence. Peckinpah was deeply disturbed by the exhilarated reception of the Agua Verde massacre in *The Wild Bunch* by Nigerian soldiers who left the cinema wanting to go die in a hailstorm of bullets (Prince 1998: 98–9). The controversies surrounding the concluding killing spree in *Taxi Driver* or the rape scenes in *A Clockwork Orange* are well known. What kinds of associations intertextuality triggers cannot always be tightly controlled either. For Tarantino, the Sherlock Holmes calabash pipe Landa pulls out of his pocket in chapter one underlines his ability as a detective; almost all reviewers (and all audiences I observed) were amused by its size as an ironic comment on Landa's masculinity. In the screenplay, Shosanna's giant face projected onto the screen and the billowing smoke in the final massacre 'brings to mind Orwells [sic] "1984" Big Brother' (Tarantino 2009: 159). Critics, however, pulled different indices of cinematic references, from the close-up on the robot Eva's metal face in Lang's *Metropolis* to the projection room in *The Wizard of Oz* (for instance, Barlow 2010: 142). Some reviewers were reminded of the burning of Jewish bodies during the Holocaust – a reference they found offensive and tasteless. The problem with 'database narratives', to use Marsha Kinder's term again, is that the furious frequency of allusion encourages a reading strategy that directs attention away from the story and focuses on intertext 'recognition'. The boundary between connotation verified by narrative context and free association is increasingly hard to police, not least because Tarantino's own data use in *Basterds* can be quite loose.[19] What his hybrid narratives highlight, however, is how cluttered our popular archives of 'violence' and 'fascism' are; how little we can make sense of history without projecting onto it the 'drama' and 'spectacle' of our fantasies or the 'already seen'.

Irony, virtuosity and excess are no longer effective ways of questioning the spectator's enjoyment of screen violence (if they ever were in the first place) because the predominantly young audience that is attracted to such spectacles manages to either miss the irony or accepts it as a now customary mode of representation that accounts for much of the pleasure. As Vivian Sobchack astutely comments, watching an ultraviolent film like *Pulp Fiction* is a very different experience from attempting to endure the eyeball slicing in Bunuel's *Un chien Andalou* or the historic suffering in *Beloved* (2000: 124). Much of the pleasure of casual carnage (and 'fascism') hinges on watching perpetration rather than pain: this puts paid to Landsberg's notion of prosthetic memory as a route to empathetic history. Even the scalped soldiers in chapter two are already dead. Their bodies' desecration is 'gross' but we are not subjected to Pasolini's torture scenes. When we see Landa's forehead being carved with a swastika, he has conventionally 'earned' his pain and we certainly do not in any sense 'feel' his physical suffering, let alone empathise. In fact, Tarantino offers a semiotic joke in which Nazism is written on the fascist body. This is Raine's objection to the postwar vanishing act of Nazis escaping punishment and forms part of the fantasy structure of the film (e.g., to be able to pay back Nazis, end the war early, mark them with their historical responsibility). But it is also (once again) a play on our insistent evocation of 'Nazism', on handsome SS uniforms, gigantic swastikas and toothbrush moustaches. Like Aldo, we don't seem to be able to 'abide' the passing of Nazism into the history books. Like the final girl, Landa will live, marked by and as monstrosity, but only as 'our Nazi'. The joke is on him and on us: the final frame, shot from Landa's point of view looking up at Utivich and Raine, puts us in his position. We too have been marked as a 'masterpiece' of 'fascism'; by participating in the pleasure of its evocation we continue its cultural posthumous existence (Fig. 5.11).

Tarantino's 'nutbrain fable' of a historical fantasy, I would argue, does a very good self-reflexive job of foregrounding our own nutbrain fantasies vis-à-vis traumatic history. Largely generated by the screen they are situated somewhere between glamorised fascism and glamorised resistance. These are mutually contradictory fantasies about agency: permissible dreams of heroism and inadmissible scenarios of omnipotence; scenarios of moral righteousness and exculpating admissions of history as *force majeur*. Perhaps this also demonstrates Tarantino's own ambivalence towards cinema history and history-as-cinema:

Figure 5.11   The 'masterpiece': our Nazi (*Inglourious Basterds*)

> On the one hand, it's a really juicy metaphor, the idea of cinema bringing
> down the Third Reich. On the other hand, it's not a metaphor at all, it is
> actually what's happening: 35mm film is bringing down the Third Reich!
> . . . so there's that, but there's also more in that ending. Let's contemplate:
> that pile of film stock for a second now. What if that pile of film . . . what if
> it is Shosanna's collection of 35mm films that've been banned by the Nazis?
> Let's say that's *Grand Illusion*. Let's say that's *Mayerling. Duck Soup. The
> Kid*. Let's say it's all those. If that's the case then it's almost as if Papa Renoir
> himself is helping to bring down the Nazis! Ok. But now, let's look at the
> other possibility. Let's say those are all Goebbels' films. You're looking at
> 300 prints of Nazi propaganda, so now it's Goebbels' own creations that are
> bringing down the Third Reich. (Quoted in Gilbey 2009)

The looseness of the cinematic metaphor, its literalisation (Hitler dies in a
cinema) alongside Tarantino's concrete examples of what kind of cinema
might set alight Hitler (never specified in the film's final version), chafes
against the encyclopaedic 'fascism' that furnishes *Inglourious Basterds*.
How can the cinema bring down the Third Reich, when it perennially
reconstructs it in a *mise-en-abîme* of intertextuality, precisely by drawing
on earlier cinematic constructions of fascism (just as the apocalyptic
Spaghetti Western cannot help but reference its classic predecessor). Note
Tarantino's reliance on such a canon of 'fascism' in the script: 'the lobby
of Shosanna's cinema, pimped out in Nazi iconography . . . which now
resembles something out of one of Tinto Brass's Italian B-movie ripoffs
of Visconti's *The Damned*' (2009: 72). And, of course, the pre-massacre
gathering in the chateau in *The Dirty Dozen*, just as the set piece of impersonating Nazi soldiers in the tavern La Louisiane recalls the inn scene in
Where Eagles Dare. The 'pimping out' applies to décor, to history and to
the cinematic archive. Cinema, as I hope to have demonstrated, does the
exact opposite of bringing down the Third Reich; it continually resurrects

it with one war film after another, with Holocaust movies, docudrama and historical documentary. Tarantino's film reminds us (having paid for our ticket at the box office) why the 'killin' Nazi business' continues to be 'boomin': it is 'dramatic' history; it lends itself to the ideological sentimentality of *Saving Private Ryan* as much as to nutbrained fantasy or – most recently – vampire slasher film (for those amongst the numb and dumb who like their fascists literally ghoulish and undead, there's always *Zombie Lake* or *Bloodrayne: The Third Reich*). Ultimately, 'killin' Nazis' offers even those with the scantiest historical capital merely reel changes: a familiar history made safe as cinematic déjà vu.

Notes

1. Tarantino's hybridisation of war film and Western is entirely apt but not new: *Kelly's Heroes* (1970), for instance, has a notable scene before the robbery of Nazi bullion in Clermont-Ferrant when Donald Sutherland, Clint Eastwood and Telly Savalas step out into the street with hip holster and pistol to a Spaghetti Western audio track. The casting of so much recognisable Hollywood testosterone (Lee Marvin, Yul Brynner, Ernest Borgnine, William Holden, Charles Bronson, Clint Eastwood, Gregory Peck) in several war films and Westerns further contributes to creating a generic phenomenology of masculine violence. As Robert Warshow pointed out in his classic early essay 'The Westerner', both the war film and the Western are genres that (in their classic period) negotiate civilisation's refusal to acknowledge the value of violence. Yet while the war film may be marred by 'ideological sentimentality', the Western constructs an image of self-controlled masculinity through purposeful and restrained violence. Warshow [1954] 2004: 715–16.
2. For an impressive and helpful but by no means exhausting listing and contextualisation of the popular canon informing *Inglourious Basterds* see Seeßlen 2009.
3. The critical cliché that Tarantino makes films about films also accounts for the peculiar competitiveness with which middle-aged cinephiles discuss his work, rattling off long lists of references they insist on recognising while a younger audience in their teens and twenties appear to simply enjoy the story through its comical, hyperviolent aesthetics.
4. The assumption that violent films, toys or computer games appeal predominantly to an adolescent male audience has been questioned by a variety of studies from different disciplines. See Goldstein 1998. There seems little doubt about the social function of such entertainment: it is predominantly a group activity and it seems to serve purposes of shoring up gender expectations, but this in itself has not been deemed sufficient by researchers to propose any theory about the nature of the appeal of violent representations – we watch representations of violence with a range of responses, but we do not know why we watch and how our responses relate to our cultural identity and to the nature of what we see.

5. See for instance Jules White's *You Nazty Spy!* (1940) and *I'll Never Heil Again* (1941), and Walt Disney's *Der Fuehrer's Face* (1942). Propaganda film such as Litvak's *Confessions of a Nazi Spy* (1939) in contrast, highlighted the international reach of Nazism through espionage, local fascist organisations such as the American *Bund* and Gestapo surveillance. For an overview of comical representations of cinematic Nazis see also Reiner 2009.

6. For the problematics of production and reception see the documentary *The Tramp and the Dictator* (2002).

7. Reduction to these features lent itself to satire and even to use on propaganda posters (such as Fougasse's *Careless Talk* series in which Hitler's face became a synecdoche for Nazism).

8. We are reminded here, of course, of the globe in Adenoid Hynkel's stateroom and the megalomania that its balletic use suggests. Dani Levy's satire *Mein Führer: Die wirklich wahrste Wahrheit über Adolf Hitler* (The Truest Truth About Adolf Hitler) (2007) also uses the stateroom globe, this time to hide an ample medicine cabinet for the teetotal, hypochondriac and tongue-tied Hitler.

9. Grothe already had that part in *Mein Führer*, which may have influenced Tarantino's casting. Levy presents a weak and moody Hitler built up into a national messiah by Goebbels's relentless grip on, and grasp of, media manipulation.

10. The song is proverbial in Germany and was revived by Nina Hagen's punk version in the 1980s. *Die große Liebe* also features another big hit of Leander's musical career, 'Davon geht die Welt nicht unter' (it's not so bad, literally: the world won't fall apart), used for the bombing scenes in Florian Henckel von Donnersmarck's *Der Untergang* (2004).

11. In an interview with Enzo Castellari that is part of the recent reissue of *Inglorious Bastards* on DVD, Tarantino asked the Italian director about Peckinpah's influence on the representation of violence in his film, but the Italian pointedly denied it. Castellari and Tarantino 2009. Kurosawa's work might be another likely source for these balletic scenes given his importance for both Sergio Leone's Spaghetti Westerns and Peckinpah's work. See Prince 2004: 331–45.

12. Scalping, although popularly associated with Native American combat, was not a universally practised ritual. Nor was it specific to Native Americans. Herodotus reports of scalping in his Histories; Central European tribes like the Visigoths used it, and European settlers, in various campaigns against Native Indian warriors and civilians used it as a tab of the body count.

13. Brad Pitt, who plays Lt. Aldo Rain aka 'Aldo the Apache' in *Basterds*, brought 'his' expertise in scalping German soldiers from the earlier *Legends of the Fall* (1994).

14. Joseph Natioli (2009) saw the Jewish avengers as 'Barbarians of the Good', for whom the conviction of moral righteousness sanctions the most gruesome means. He explicitly linked their dubious rationale to the advocacy, within the Bush administration, of torture at Guantanamo, thus erasing in both the film and its contemporary real-life political context the difference between fascist and anti-fascist violence.

15. Naomi Pfefferman, 'Eli Roth fuels Basterds' role with Holocaust fury',

JewishJournal.com, 18 August 2009, available at <http://www.jewishjo urnal.com/cover_story/aricle/eli_roth_fuels_besterds_role_with_holocaust_ fury_20090818/> (last accessed 2 August 2011).

16. Sheldon Roth, 'My son killed Adolf Hitler', *JewishJournal.com*, 9 December 2009, available at <http://www.jewishjournal.com/opinion/article/my_ son_killed_adolf_hitler_20091208/> (last accessed 4 August 2011).

17. See Gilbey 2009. Interestingly, the script offers more scenes of violence that didn't make the final cut, specifically scenes that underline the willingness of Jews to commit vengeance, as in Donowitz's back story in which he buys and tests the baseball bat in Boston and visits his Jewish community to collect the names of missing European Jews to write on his bat. Some of this violence is uncomfortably reminiscent of the Holocaust, for instance the prizing of gold teeth out of German soldiers' mouths. Tarantino 2009: 23.

18. One might recall here the endless slow-motion replays of such ground- breaking footage as the Zapruder tape of the Kennedy assassination or, more recently, the attack on the Twin Towers on 9/11.

19. For instance, the script offers a much longer version of Shoshanna's death in the projectionist's room, a prolonged intertextual 'DYING' complete with Peckinpah-esque slow-motion falling, Sergio Leone close ups that extend time, her body riddled with bullets, concentrating the carnage in *Nation's Pride* on one body, but making a superhuman effort to manage the reel change that will instruct her lover to set fire to the nitrate film: 'Like the German heroine in one of Riefenstahl's mountain films, Shosanna CLIMBS UP the 35mm film projector, like it was Pitz Palu' (Tarantino 2009: 156–8). The script highlights the process of Tarantino's postmodern bricolage – the privileging of style over content, archive over story. That this sort of data narrative does not always make for coherent storytelling is perhaps endorsed by the fact that in the final film version, the scene is mercifully simple: no DYING, no close ups, no slow motion, no Pitz Palü.

Coda

In the summer of 2011, the Chapman Brothers mounted a widely reviewed installation entitled *Jake or Dinos Chapman* at the White Cube in London, one part in Hoxton, one part in the Mason's Yard gallery off The Strand. As I descended the stairs to the basement gallery of the central London venue, I caught a glimpse of the main exhibit before I fully entered the room. I remember that I froze on the steps although it is not clear to me precisely what I felt – shock, horror, fear, or a mixture of all three. I had seen the reviews, most of which came with photographs of the most controversial exhibit, but they had evidently not prepared me for how I would affectively respond to what I saw, or thought I saw. The large white room was filled with over a dozen tall black-fleshed mannequins in black uniforms which looked like SS uniforms, complete with swastika armbands, insignia, boots and helmets. They stood in groups contemplating drawings on the wall or abstract art exhibits (cardboard models, deformed mutant child mannequins, stuffed ravens on steel frames), some of them visibly amused and joking, others ostensibly so bored they started sodomising one another. On closer inspection, the identical black mannequins, all with the same bared white teeth and popping eyeballs, did not wear swastika armbands above their Sütterlin cuff bands but smiley faces. The more one looked and wandered around this exhibition, the more one's responses began to resemble those of the figures: slightly perplexed, amused, bored after a while, one could approach them and have a really good close look at these phoney Stormtroopers. Visitors chuckled over the one which had been shat on by a stuffed raven ascending in flight. Young men in particular found themselves drawn to the copulating pair, and had one been permitted to touch the exhibits, the jacket of the officer happily sodomising his bent-over colleague might have been lifted for better scrutiny of detail. Had the Chapmans been realistic here or merely teased the audience with a promise?

I spent an hour in the gallery, increasingly more interested in the visitors' responses than in what most critics had dismissed as a repetitive trope, tired provocation or 'the worst possible taste'.[1] The audience on this Friday afternoon included young couples, small bunches of teenagers, tourists who had wandered in by chance to avoid the rain, senior citizens, or the odd corduroy-clad middle-aged man, clutching an art book. Amongst this diverse bunch of people, the reactions were near identical. Initial aghast expressions relaxed into relieved faces that might further morph into bewilderment or mirth: thank god, this is merely a joke. Thank god, this is merely bad taste. If this is contemporary art, perhaps we'd better schlepp back to the National Gallery at Trafalgar Square. We experienced a collective relief that we would be spared a painful or frightening encounter with fascism, or the kind of *Betroffenheit* Adorno had associated with radical art (a tremor in our emotional landscape, a shift in our perceptive register). Perhaps we all too gladly ignored any potential for self-reflection, shrugging at this exhibition the way these mannequins laughed at rubbishy cardboard models. We walked up to them the same way they hovered over installations; we peered at their uniforms in the way they scrutinised details of paintings. Had I been allowed to use a camera, I would have been able to snap countless members of the audience duplicating the mannequins' poses.

Nazism has of course featured before in Jake and Dinos' Chapman's installations, notably in *Hell* (1999–2000; destroyed 2004). *Fucking Hell* (2008) consisted of nine glass cases with thousands of miniature plastic figurines, painstakingly painted, in scenes of carnage and mass murder that looked like a better effort at realism than the scale-model of the gassing process in the Museum at Auschwitz. The excess of this miniaturised mass display is immediately obvious: no visitor could possibly take in so much detail. And yet the form of this display is still deeply familiar. Throughout the twentieth century, toy manufacturers sold millions of replica miniaturised soldiers that engaged millions of boys (and men) in playing war. Every model shop on every high street still sells this merchandise, with editions of replica soldiers going back to the Napoleonic wars. The Chapman Brothers in fact used mass-produced figurines sold in kits and recast them, pointing to the pre-existence of such material as a commentary on the cultural presence of ludic belligerence (Harris 2010: 174). Miniaturising battle was once part of every healthy boy's childhood. Today such desires are upgraded (and deferred) to online sessions of *Call of Duty 2* for adolescents and adults, to 're-enactment societies' whose middle-aged members claim to have historical interest at heart when they don Wehrmacht uniforms, and to the attic rooms of pensioners who lovingly restage their dad's invasion of Normandy or Uncle Doug's part in the siege of Tobruk. 'Normal' war, no matter how atrocious, is still an object of ludic interaction since its lethal or traumatic violence is never replicated as long as you press QUICKSAVE in time and restart the mission before you tread on a mine. Yet 'normal' war features consistently in the Chapman Brothers' installations, notably through overt references to Goya's series of etchings *The Disasters of War*, about the brutal Franco-Spanish war in the early nineteenth century. It is a constant reminder that art is justified in shocking us and that there is no such thing as 'conventional' war. Such parlance is the invention of politicians or armaments manufacturers to cloak the reality of what war does to the human body. Goya's deliberate and shocking display of atrocity – raped, tortured and mutilated bodies, hung from trees or abandoned in the dirt – merely mirrored the way in which violence had become a spectacle for the combatants, an advertisement of what might befall the enemy. But how do we perceive such art, and can we bear to look at the horrors it shows us?

For the Chapmans, perspective and distance, too, played a role in *Fucking Hell*. At close range the figurines in the display cases were not Nazis engaged in the slaughter of Jews but Nazis killing other Nazis (that is, themselves) in an endlessly played-out scenario of death drive and abjection. Seen from above, *Fucking Hell*'s display cases were positioned in the shape of a swastika, but the visitor on the ground would not perceive that in scrutinising the models from all sides they were 'skirting around' a specific take on 'fascism'. *Fucking Hell* is what is occluded in 'ordinary' ludic belligerence but is nonetheless a fundamental part of it, its ideological underbelly, its lazy assumptions and its falsifying prettification of combat (note the ubiquitous juxtaposition of pastoral scenes with wastelands in models). The audience, then, is always too close and at insufficient (critical) distance to see all of the installation. With our noses pressed against a replica atrocity that turns out to be both more and less of what we bargained for, we still fail to recognise that what we have come to want is what Gillian Rose called the fascism of representation, that is, precisely and predictably what we want fascism to be rather than what historical fascism was. Jake or Dinos Chapman did not present us with Nazism either, but with a version of it we could walk up to and look at, plastified images from our dreams or our cultural inventory of films. These truly were 'our Nazis'.

Rather than dismiss the Chapmans' installations as tasteless jokes about the degenerate state of the art scene (or the nature of taste), I would like to return to the noticeable shift in affective response from shock to relief to disengagement that their art engenders, which is not dissimilar to what one might experience in a horror film when the audience exits the cinema laughing at the absurd hyperbole of outlandish violence. We slide from possibly apprehending fascism to being briefly entertained by 'fascism'. The defamiliarising aspects of the mannequins (the unrealistic blackness of the flesh, the smiley faces, the boots they don't quite fill) coax us into a false proximity to them, as if we approached a deadly snake from which we are protected through a pane of safety glass. 'Fascism' is our Perspex. It protects us from apprehending the reality of totalitarianism so much that we can project our worst fears and inadmissible desires into this ideological space until we can fool ourselves into believing that it really is utterly foreign and other, rather than an abjected version of what we are capable of. The cultural function of representations of fascism is not to inform us about historical fascism or to keep the memory of this period alive out of respect for the victims. 'Fascism' is neither educative nor commemorative. It is talismanic. In times when we become a little careless about the civil liberties of those we purport to protect through military intervention or when we feel concerned about our status in the Western world as a liberating force scattering democracy like the seeds from Ceres' cornucopia, we might want to reassure ourselves that it can never get as bad as *this* because we can never be as bad as *they* were. Consequently we dismiss as irrelevant or controversial artworks, films and novels that point to the complacency of such implausible albeit hegemonic constructs of absolute alterity.

What I want to remember about the Chapman Brothers' exhibit is that initial moment of terror before I could begin to rationalise what I had barely apprehended. There, in that moment of fear, lies the true meaning of fascism for me: a sense of what it might do to me, what it might make me do, what I am capable of. 'Fascism' too often neutralises this moment of self-recognition and converts it into someone else's disaster or someone else's crime or retrospectively dismissed risible aesthetics, watched from a safe distance. As historical fascism slides out of living memory and turns into museum display and textbook history, we need to become more inventive about how we remain alert to our fascist potential. The lucrative ongoing existence of 'fascism' in film, literature and gaming culture is in itself a testimony to our desire to inhabit a fiction in which we can play out this potential. That such play might normalise our desires, rather than merely trivialise history, is perhaps already an important contributing factor to what Roger Stahl has called 'militainment'. The recurrence of war and genocide in the twentieth century has done little to displace fascism from its pole position of alterity, and the institutionalisation of Holocaust commemoration as a unique genocide curbs attempts at reading these phenomena

comparatively or paradigmatically. In fact the twentieth-century genocides in Africa and Asia are often seen as different (that is, expressions
of 'savagery') whereas both 'ethnic cleansing' in former Yugoslavia
and the systematic starvation of the kulaks in the Soviet Union were
balkanised and slavicised to the point where they were virtually pushed
to the margins of Europe. Yet the very feature that makes fascism and
the Holocaust so frightening – their location in the centre of modern
European, Western culture – also occasions the hegemonic othering and
disavowal that is integral to 'fascism'. Unless 'our Nazis' truly become
a collective responsibility in the contemporary assessment of the West's
potential for fascism, the relevance of 'fascism' will dwindle to the
mockery of a game of 'Cowboys and Indians'.

Note

1. See for instance, Adrian Searle, 'Jake or Dinos Chapman – review', *Guardian*,
   14 July 2011, available at <http:www.guardian.co.uk/artdesign/2011/
   jul/14/jake-or-dinos-chapman-review> (last accessed 15 July 2011); Richard
   Dormant, 'The Chapman Brothers: Jake or Dinos Chapman at the White
   Cube, review', *Telegraph*, 18 July 2011, available at <http://www.tel-
   egraph.co.uk/culture/art/art-reviews/8646040/The-Chapman-Brothers-Jake-
   or-Dinos-Chapman-at-the-White-Cube-review.html> (last accessed 20 July
   2011); and a more appreciative review by Mark Lawson and Matthew
   Collins on *Front Row*, BBC Radio 4, broadcast 14 July 2011.

Bibliography

08/15 (1954–5), dir. Paul May, West Germany: Divina.

13, Rue Madeleine (1947), dir. Henry Hathaway, USA: Twentieth Century Fox.

A Fistful of Dollars (1964), dir. Sergio Leone, Italy/Spain/West Germany: Constantin Film, Jolly Film, Ocean Film.

A Foreign Affair (1948), dir. Billy Wilder, USA: Paramount.

Above Us the Waves (1955), dir. Ralph Thomas, UK: London Independent Prod.

Albahari, David (2004), *Götz and Meyer*, trans. Ellen Elias-Bursać, London: Vintage.

Ambler, Eric ([1937] 1960), *Uncommon Danger*, Harmondsworth: Penguin.

—([1938] 2009), *Epitaph for a Spy*, London: Penguin.

—([1940] 2009), *Journey Into Fear*, London: Penguin.

Amis, Martin (1991), *Time's Arrow*, London: Penguin.

Anderson, Clive (2011), radio broadcast, *Nazi Gold: Publishing the Third Reich*, BBC Radio 4, 17 March, <http://www.bbc.co.uk/programmes/b00zf4hz> (last accessed 20 March 2011).

Anonymous (1990), 'What the PM learnt about the Germans', *Independent on Sunday*, 15 July, p. 19.

Apt Pupil (1998), dir. Bryan Singer, USA/France: Phoenix Pic., Bad Hat Harry Productions, Canal+ Audiovisuels.

Arendt, Hannah ([1955] 2005), *Elemente und Ursprünge totaler Herrschaft*, Munich: Piper.

Astor, David (1969), 'Why the Revolt Against Hitler Was Ignored: On the British Reluctance to Deal with Anti-Nazis', *Encounter* 32/6: 3–13.

Auden, W.H. ([1934] 1977), 'The Liberal Fascist', in Edward Mendelsohn (ed.), *The English Auden: Poems, Essays and Dramatic Writings, 1927–1939*, London: Faber & Faber, pp. 321–5.

Augstein, Rudolf (ed.) (1987), *Historikerstreit: Die Dokumentation der Kontroverse um die Einzigartigkeit der nationalsozialistischen Judenvernichtung*, Munich: Piper.

Barlow, Aaron (2010), *Quentin Tarantino: Life at the Extremes*, Santa Barbara, CA: Praeger.

Barnett, Erin and Philomena Mariani (eds) (2011), *Hiroshima: Ground Zero 1945*, exhibition catalogue, New York: International Center of Photography/ Steidl.

Barta, Tony (1998), 'Film Nazis: the Great Escape', in Tony Barta (ed.), *Screening the Past: Film and the Representation of History*, Westport: Praeger, pp. 127–49.

Bartov, Omer (1996), *Murder in Our Midst: The Holocaust, Industrial Killing, and Representation*, New York: Oxford University Press.

— (2000), 'Reception and Perception: Goldhagen's Holocaust and the World', in Geoff Eley (ed.), *The 'Goldhagen Effect': History, Memory, Nazism – Facing the German Past*, Ann Arbor: University of Michigan Press, pp. 33–89.

Baum, Rachel N. (1996), 'What I Have Learnt to Feel: The Pedagogical Emotions of Holocaust Education', *College Literature* 23: 44–57.

Bauman, Zygmunt (1991), *Modernity and the Holocaust*, Cambridge: Polity Press.

Beevor, Antony (2011), 'The appeal of faction to writers and readers has recently increased in a dramatic way', series 'Author, author', *Guardian*, 19 February, <http://www.guardian.co.uk/books/2011/feb/19/author-author-antony-beevor> (last accessed 13 October 2012).

Beier, Lars-Olav et al. (2008), 'Helden vor Hakenkreuzen', *Der Spiegel* 52, 20.12.2008, p. 128–31.

Bernhard, Thomas ([1979] 1988), *Vor dem Ruhestand*, in Thomas Bernhard, *Stücke 3*, Frankfurt am Main: Suhrkamp, pp. 7–115.

Bielenberg, Christabel (1988), *The Past is Myself*, London: Corgi.

Binet, Laurent ([2009] 2012), *HHhH*, trans. Sam Taylor, London: Harvill Secker.

Bird, Kai and Lawrence Lifschultz (eds) (1998), *Hiroshima's Shadow*, Stony Creek, CT: Pamphleteer's Press.

Blanchot, Maurice ([1948] 1996), *The Most High*, trans. Allan Stoekl, Lincoln and London: University of Nebraska Press.

Blum, John M. (1976), *V Was For Victory: Politics and American Culture During WWII*, New York: Harcourt Brace Jovanovich.

Blumenfeld, Samuel (2006), Interview with Jonathan Littell, *Le Monde*, 17 November, <http://thekindlyones.wordpress.com/littell-interview-with-samuel-blumenfeld> (last accessed 24 May 2012).

Boggs, Carl and Tom Pollard (2007), *The Hollywood War Machine: U.S. Militarism and Popular Culture*, Boulder: Paradigm.

Bohrer, Karl Heinz (2011), 'Der Skandal einer Imagination des Bösen. Im Rückblick auf *Die Wohlgesinnten* von Jonathan Littell', *Merkur* 741: 129–49.

Boltanski, Luc (1999), *Distant Suffering: Morality, Media and Politics*, trans. Graham Burchell, Cambridge: Cambridge University Press.

Borges, Jorge Luis ([1958] 1972), 'Deutsches Requiem', trans. Julian Palley, in *Labyrinths: Selected Stories and Other Writings*, ed. Donald A. Yates and James Irby, Harmondsworth: Penguin, pp. 173–80.

Boswell, Matthew (2011), *Holocaust Impiety in Literature, Popular Music and Film*, Basingstoke: Palgrave Macmillan.

Brecht, Bertolt (1973), *Der aufhaltsame Aufstieg des Arturo Ui*, Frankfurt am Main: Suhrkamp.

Brockhaus, Gudrun (2012), 'The Emotional Legacy of the National Socialist Past in Post-War Germany', in Alida Assmann and Linda Shortt (eds), *Memory and Political Change*, Basingstoke: Palgrave, pp. 34–53.

Broszat, Martin (1964), 'Einleitung', in Rudolf Höß, *Kommandant in Auschwitz: Autobiographische Aufzeichnungen des Rudolf Höß*, ed. Martin Broszat, Munich: dtv.

Browning, Christopher (2001), *Ordinary Men: Reserve Police Battalion 101 and the 'Final Solution' in Poland*, new edn, London: Penguin.

Buruma, Ian (1990), 'There's No Place Like Heimat', *New York Review of Books*, 20 December, pp. 34–44.

Butter, Michael (2009), *The Epitome of Evil: Hitler in American Fiction, 1939–2002*, Basingstoke: Palgrave.

Byg, Barton (1997), 'Nazism as *Femme Fatale*: Recuperations of Cinematic Masculinity in Postwar Berlin', in Patricia Herminghouse and Magda Mueller (eds), *Gender and Germanness: Cultural Productions of Nation*, Providence: Berghahn, pp. 176–89.

Calder, Angus ([1969] 2001), *The People's War*, London: Pimlico.

— (1992), *The Myth of the Blitz*, London: Pimlico.

Camus, Albert ([1951] 2006), *The Rebel*, ed. Anthony Bower, trans. Olivier Todd, London: Penguin.

Canaris (1954), dir. Alfred Weidenmann, West Germany: Fama-Film.

Caranicas, Peter (2009), '*Basterds* rethinks '40s-era styles', *Daily Variety*, 26 August, p. 4.

Carter, Erica (2007), 'Men in Cardigans: *Canaris* and the 1950s German Good Soldier', in Danielle Hipkins and Gill Plain (eds), *War-torn Tales: Literature, Film and Gender in the Aftermath of World War II*, Oxford: Peter Lang, pp. 195–223.

Cartwright, Justin (2007), *The Song Before It Is Sung*, London: Bloomsbury.

Castellari, Enzo G. and Quentin Tarantino (2009), 'A Conversation with Quentin Tarantino and Enzo. G. Castellari', in *Inglorious Bastards*, dir. Enzo Castellari (DVD: Optimum).

Céline, Louis-Ferdinand ([1957] 1969), *Castle to Castle*, trans. Ralph Manheim, London: Anthony Blond.

— ([1960] 2006), *North*, trans. Ralph Manheim, Rochester: Dalkey Archive.

Chandler, Raymond ([1950] 1988), 'The Simple Art of Murder: An Essay', in *The Simple Art of Murder*, New York: Vintage, pp. 1–19.

Chaplin, Charlie (1966), *My Autobiography*, London: Bodley Head.

Chapman, James (1998), 'Our Finest Hour Revisited: The Second World War in British Feature Films since 1945', *Journal of Popular British Cinema* 1: 63–75.

Christianson, Scott R. (1989), 'Tough Talk and Wisecracks: Language as Power in American Detective Fiction', *Journal of Popular Culture* 23/2: 151–62.

Churchill, Sir Winston (1941), *Into Battle: Speeches*, ed. Randolph Churchill, London: Cassell.

— (1974), 'The War Situation: August 2, 1944' (House of Commons), in *Winston S. Churchill: His Complete Speeches, 1897–1963*, ed. Robert Rhodes James, vol. 7: 1943–1947, New York, Chelsea House, pp. 6968–85.

Cole, Tim (1999), *Selling the Holocaust*, New York: Routledge.

Come and See (1985), dir. Elem Klimov, Soviet Union: Mosfilm, Belarusfilm.

Confino, Alon (2009), 'Narrative Form and Historical Sensation: On Saul Friedländer's *The Years of Extermination*', *History and Theory* 48/3: 199–219.

Cross of Iron (1977), dir. Sam Peckinpah, UK/West Germany: EMI films, Rapid Film, Terra-Filmkunst.

Crossman, Richard (1950), 'Opinions of Rommel', *Picture Post*, 1 April, p. 41.

Dargis, Manohla (2008a), 'Innocence is lost in postwar Germany', review of *The Reader*, *Washington Post*, 10 December, <http://movies.nytimes.com/2008/12/10/movies/10read.html> (last accessed 20 March 2011).

—(2008b), 'Mission Imperative: Assassinate the Fuhrer', *New York Times*, movie review, 24 December, <http://www.movies.nytimes.com/2008/12/25/movies/25valk.html> (last accessed 5 February 2012).

Decision Before Dawn (1951), dir. Anatole Litvak, USA: Twentieth Century Fox, Bavaria.

Deer, Patrick (2009), *Culture in Camouflage*, Oxford: Oxford University Press.

Der 20. Juli: Das Attentat auf Hitler (1955), dir. Falk Harnack, West Germany: CCC.

Der Unhold (1996), dir. Volker Schlöndorff, France/Germany/UK: Canal+, France 2 Cinéma, Héritage Films.

Der Untergang (2004), dir. Oliver Hirschbiegel, Germany/Austria/Italy: Constantin Film, NDR, WDR.

Die große Liebe (1942), dir. Rolf Hansen, Germany: UFA.

Die weiße Hölle vom Piz Palü (1929), dir. Arnold Fanck/G.W. Pabst, Germany: Sokal-Film, H.-T.-Film.

Diemert, Brian (1996), *Graham Greene's Thrillers and the 1930s*, Montreal: McGill-Queen's University Press.

—(2002), '"How do you describe the Indescribable?" Representing History in Detective Fiction: The Case of Philip Kerr's *Berlin Noir* Trilogy', *Genre* 35/2: 331–54.

Dithfurth, Christian von (2003), *Der 21. Juli*, Munich: Knaur.

Döblin, Alfred ([1932] 1961), *Berlin Alexanderplatz*, Frankfurt am Main: Deutscher Bücherbund.

Donnelly, Mary Beth (2006), 'Educating Students About the Holocaust: A Survey of Teaching Practices', *Social Education* 70/1: 51–4.

Dostoyevsky, Fyodor (1972), *Notes From Underground/The Double*, trans. Jessie Coulson, Harmondsworth: Penguin.

Dower, John (1986), *War Without Mercy: Race and Power in the Pacific War*, London: Faber & Faber.

Downing, David (2007), *Zoo Station*, Brecon: Old Street.

—(2008), *Silesian Station*, Brecon: Old Street.

—(2009), *Stettin Station*, Brecon: Old Street.

Eco, Umberto (1994), *Six Walks in the Fictional Woods*, Cambridge, MA: Harvard University Press.

Eley, Geoff (ed.) (2000), *The 'Goldhagen Effect': History, Memory, Nazism – Facing the German Past*, Ann Arbor: University of Michigan Press.

Elsaesser, Thomas (1981/2), 'Myth as the Phantasmagoria of History: H.J. Syberberg, Cinema and Representation', *New German Critique* 24/25: 108–54.

Erickson, Steve (1989), *Tours of the Black Clock*, London: Futura.

Es geschah am 20. Juli: Aufstand gegen Hitler (1955), dir. G.W. Pabst, West Germany: Arca, Ariston.

Evans, Peter William (2001), 'James Mason: The Man Between', in Bruce Babington (ed.), *British Stars and Stardom: From Alma Taylor to Sean Connery*, Manchester: Manchester University Press, pp. 108–19.

Evans, Richard J. (1989), *In Hitler's Shadow: West German Historians and the Attempt to Escape from the Nazi Past*, London: Pantheon.

—(2009), *Cosmopolitan Islanders: British Historians and the European Continent*, Cambridge: Cambridge University Press.

—(2011), 'The Wonderfulness of Us', *London Review of Books*, 33/6 (17 March): 9–12, <http://www.lrb.co.uk/v33/n06/richard-j-evans/the-wonderfulness-of-us?utm_source=newsletter&utm_medium=email&utm_campaign=3306> (last accessed 17 March 2011).

Fassbender, Bardo (1994), 'A Novel, Germany's Past, and the Dilemmas of Civilised Germans', *Contemporary Review* 265: 236–46.

Fay, Jennifer (2006), 'Germany is a Boy in Trouble', *Cultural Critique* 64: 196–235.

Five Graves to Cairo (1943), dir. Billy Wilder, USA: Paramount.

Fluet, Lisa (2006), 'Hit-Man Modernism', in Douglas Moa and Rebecca L. Walkowitz (eds), *Bad Modernisms*, Durham, NC: Duke University Press, pp. 269–98.

Forsyth, Frederick ([1972] 2003), *The Odessa File*, London: Arrow.

Foucault, Michel (1980), 'Power and Strategies', in Michel Foucault, *Power/Knowledge: Selected Interviews and Other Writings, 1972–1977*, ed. Colin Gordon, Brighton: Harvester.

Fox, Stephen (1990), *The Unknown Internment: An Oral History of the Relocation of Italian-Americans During World War II*, Boston: Twayne.

Frayling, Christopher (2006), *Spaghetti Westerns: Cowboys and Europeans From Karl May to Sergio Leone*, London: I.B. Tauris.

Fried, Kerry (1993), 'Criminal Elements', review of Ian McEwan's *Black Dogs*, *New York Review of Books* 40/1–2: 36–7.

Friedländer, Saul (1993a), *Reflections of Nazism: An Essay on Kitsch and Death*, trans. Thomas Weyr, Bloomington: Indiana University Press.

—(1993b), 'The "Final Solution": On the Unease of Historical Interpretation', in Saul Friedländer, *Memory, History and the Extermination of the Jews of Europe*, Bloomington: Indiana University Press.

—(1995), 'Trauma, Memory, and Transference', in Geoffrey Hartmann (ed.), *Holocaust Remembrance*, Cambridge, MA: Blackwell.

—(2007), *The Years of Extermination: Nazi Germany and the Jews, 1939–1945*, London: Weidenfeld & Nicholson.

Frölich, Margit, Christian Schneider, Karsten Visarius (eds) (2007), *Das Böse im Blick: Die Gegenwart des Nationalsozialismus im Film*, Munich: edition text + kritik.

Frost, Laura (2002), *Sex Drives: Fantasies of Fascism in Literary Modernism*, Ithaca: Cornell University Press, 2002.

Frostrup, Mariella (2010), *Open Book*, BBC Radio 4, 29 November.

Fuchs, Anne (1999), *A Space of Anxiety: Dislocation and Abjection in Modern German-Jewish Literature*, Amsterdam: Rodopi.

—(2008), *Phantoms of War in Contemporary German Literature, Films and Discourse: The Politics of Memory*, Basingstoke: Palgrave.

Gallant, Mary J. and Harriet Hartman (2001), 'Holocaust Education for the

Millennium: Assessing our Progress', *Journal of Holocaust Education* 10/2: 1–28.

Gemünden, Gerd (2003), 'Space Out Of Joint: Ernst Lubitsch's *To Be or Not to Be*', *New German Critique* 89: 59–80.

Gilbey, Ryan (2009), 'Days of Gloury', *Sight and Sound* 19/9: 16–21.

Godwin, Mike (n.d.) 'Meme, Counter-meme', <http://www.wired.com/wired/archive/2.10/godwin.if_pr.html> (last accessed 30 June 2012).

Goldberg, Amos (2009), 'The Victim's Voice and Melodramatic Aesthetics in History', *History and Theory* 48/3: 220–37.

Goldman, William ([1974] 1975), *Marathon Man*, New York: Dell.

Goldstein, Jeffrey (ed.) (1998), *Why We Watch: The Attractions of Violent Entertainment*, Cary, NC: Oxford University Press.

Golsan, Richard J. (2010), 'The American Reception of Max Aue', *Substance 121* 39/1: 174–83.

Goñi, Uki (2003), *The Real Odessa*, London: Granta.

Gordon, Joan (2002), 'Utopia, Genocide, and the Other', in Veronica Hollinger and Joan Gordon (eds), *Edging into the Future: Science Fiction and Contemporary Cultural Transformation*, Philadelphia: University of Pennsylvania Press, pp. 204–17.

Greene, Graham ([1936] 2009), *A Gun for Sale*, London: Vintage.

—([1938] 1970), *Brighton Rock,* London: Penguin.

—([1980] 1999), *Ways of Escape*, London: Vintage.

Groot, Jerome de (2010), *The Historical Novel*, London: Routledge.

Gubar, Susan (2006), 'Racial Camp in *The Producers* and *Bamboozled*', *Film Quarterly* 60/2: 26–37.

Hadley Chase, James ([1939] 2010), *No Orchids for Miss Blandish*, Breinigsville, PA: Disruptive Publishing.

Hake, Sabine (2002), *German National Cinema*, London: Routledge.

Handelzalts, Michael (2011),'When we talk about the Holocaust', *Haaretz*, 4 February, http://www.haaretz.com/weekend/magazine/when-we-talk-about-the-holocaust-1.341245> (last accessed 13 October 2012).

Harper, Sue (1997), 'Popular Film, Popular Memory: The Case of the Second World War', in Martin Evans and Ken Lunn (eds), *War and Memory in the Twentieth Century*, Oxford: Berg, pp. 163–77.

Harris, Jonathan (2010), 'Inside the Death Drive: A Conversation Between Jake Chapman and Jonathan Harris', in Jonathan Harris (ed.), *Inside the Death Drive: Excess and Apocalypse in the World of the Chapman Brothers*, Liverpool: Liverpool University Press, pp. 173–213.

Harris, Robert ([1986] 1991), *Selling Hitler*, London: Faber & Faber.

—(1993), *Fatherland*, London: Arrow.

—(2012), 'Robert Harris on writing *Fatherland*', *Guardian*, 14 April, Review section, p. 6.

Hawkes, John ([1949] 1962), *The Cannibal*, New York: New Directions.

Herzog, Dagmar (2004), *Sexuality and German Fascism*, Oxford: Berghahn.

Hilberg, Raul (1993), *Perpetrators, Victims, Bystanders*, New York: Harper Perennial.

—(2003), *The Destruction of the European Jews*, 3 vols, 3rd edn, New Haven: Yale University Press.

Hilsenrath, Edgar ([1977] 2007), *Der Nazi und der Friseur*, Munich: dtv.

Hirschhorn, Clive (1975), *The Films of James Mason*, London: LSP Books.

Hitler – ein Film aus Deutschland (1977), dir. Hans-Jürgen Syberberg, West Germany/France/UK: TMS Film GmbH, Solaris Film, WDR, INA, BBC.

Hoffmann, Peter (1996), *The History of the German Resistance, 1933–1945*, trans. Richard Barry, 3rd English edn, Montreal and Kingston: McGill-Queen's University Press.

Hopkins, Chris (2003), 'Leftists and Thrillers: The Politics of a Thirties Sub-Genre', in Antony Shuttleworth (ed.), *And in Our Time: Vision, Revision, and British Writing of the 1930s*, Lewisburg: Bucknell University Press, pp. 147–63.

Hörisch, Jochen (2010), 'Nazis, Sex und Religion: Unkorrekte Konstellationen in Bernhard Schlinks *Der Vorleser* und Jonathan Littells *Die Wohlgesinnten*', *Merkur* 734: 593–602.

Horsley, Lee (2001), *The Noir Thriller*, Basingstoke: Palgrave.

Höß, Rudolf (1964), *Kommandant in Auschwitz: Autobiographische Aufzeichnungen des Rudolf Höß*, ed. Martin Broszat, Munich: dtv.

Hôtel Terminus (1988), dir. Macel Ophüls, France/West Germany/USA: Samuel Goldwyn Co., Memory Pict. Co.

Housden, Martyn (1997), *Resistance and Conformity in the Third Reich*, London: Routledge.

Huyssen, Andreas (1995), *Twilight Memories: Marking Time in a Culture of Amnesia*, New York: Routledge.

I Confess (1953), dir. Alfred Hitchcock, USA: Warner Brothers.

Ice Cold in Alex (1958), dir. J. Lee Thompson, UK: ABPC.

Ilsa, She-Wolf of the SS (1975), dir. Don Edmonds, USA/West Germany: Aeteas.

Indiana Jones and the Last Crusade (1989), dir. Steven Spielberg, USA: Paramount, Lucasfilm.

Inglorious Bastards (1978), dir. Enzio Castellari, Italy/USA: Film Concorde.

Inglourious Basterds (2009), dir. Quentin Tarantino, USA/Germany: Universal Pictures, The Weinstein Co., A Band Apart, Zehnte Babelsberg, Visiona Romantica.

Jaggi, Maya (2010), 'A life in writing: Gunter Grass', *Guardian*, 30 October, Review section, p. 12–13.

Jameson, Fredric (1983), 'Postmodernism and Consumer Society', in Hal Foster (ed.), *The Anti-Aesthetic*, Port Townsend: Bay Press, pp. 111–25.

Janes, Robert, J. (1992), *Mayhem*, London: Orion.

Jones, Sydney (2010), 'Philip Kerr's Berlin', *Scene of the Crime*, 12 February, <http://jsydneyjones.wordpress.com/2010/02/12/philp-kerrs-berlin> (last accessed 14 August 2010).

Judgment at Nuremberg (1961), dir. Stanley Kramer, USA: Roxlom Films.

Kandel, Liliane (1997), 'La lettre volée de Daniel J. Goldhagen', *Les Temps modernes* 592: 38–55.

Kanfer, Stefan (2008), *Somebody: The Reckless Life and Remarkable Career of Marlon Brando*, London: Faber & Faber.

Kanon, Alfred (2001), *The Good German*, London: Sphere.

Kapczynski, Jennifer M. (2007), 'The Treatment of the Past: Geza Radvanyi's *Der Arzt von Stalingrad* and the West German War Film', in Sabine Hake and John Davidson (eds), *Framing the Fifties: Cinema in A Divided Germany*, Oxford: Berghahn, pp. 137–51.

Kelly's Heroes (1970), dir. Brian G. Hutton, Yugoslavia/USA: Avala, Katzka-Loeb, MGM.

Kerr, Philip (1992), *Berlin Noir*, Harmondsworth: Penguin.

— (2004), *The One from the Other*, London: Quercus.

— (2008), *A Quiet Flame*, London: Quercus.

— (2009), *If the Dead Rise Not*, London: Quercus.

— (2010), *Field Grey*, London: Quercus.

Kershaw, Ian (1983), *Popular Opinion and Political Dissent: Bavaria 1933–1945*, Oxford: Oxford University Press.

— (2001), *The 'Hitler Myth': Image and Reality in the Third Reich*, Oxford: Oxford University Press.

Kim, Julie H. (ed.) (2005), *Race and Religion in the Postcolonial British Detective Story*, Jefferson: McFarland.

Kinder, Marsha (2001), 'Violence American Style: The Narrative Orchestration of Violent Attractions', in J. David Slocum (ed.), *Violence and American Cinema*, New York: Routledge, pp. 63–103.

King, Stephen ([1982] 2003), 'Apt Pupil', in Stephen King, *Different Seasons*, London: Time Warner, pp. 115–319.

Klee, Ernst and Willi Dreßen (eds) (1989), *'Gott mit uns': Der deutsche Vernichtungskrieg im Osten, 1939–1945*, Frankfurt am Main: Fischer.

Klee, Ernst, Willi Dreßen and Volker Riess (eds) (2000), '"Once again I've got to play general to the Jews": From the War Diary of Blutordensträger Felix Landau', in Omer Bartov (ed.), *Holocaust: Origins, Implementation, Aftermath*, London: Routledge, pp. 185–203.

Kleeblatt, Norman L. (2002), *Mirroring Evil: Nazi Imagery: Recent Art*, exhibition catalogue, New York: Jewish Museum, New Brunswick, NJ: Rutgers University Press.

Klemperer,Victor (1970), *LTI: Notizbuch eines Philologen*, Leipzig: Reclam.

Klüger, Ruth (1992). *Landscapes Of Memory: A Holocaust Girlhood Remembered*, London: Bloomsbury.

Knight, Stephen (1980), *Form and Ideology in Crime Fiction*, Basingstoke: Macmillan.

Kodalle, Klaus (ed.) (1981), *Tradition als Last? Legitimationsprobleme der Bundeswehr*, Köln: Verlag Wissenschaft und Politik.

Koepnik, Lutz (2002a), *The Dark Mirror: German Cinema Between Hitler and Hollywood*, Berkeley: University of California Press.

— (2002b), 'Reframing the Past: Heritage Cinema and Holocaust in the 1990s', *New German Critique* 87: 47–82.

Kolberg (1945), dir. Veit Harlan, Germany: UFA.

Koppenfels, Martin von (2010), 'Kommissbrot: Jonathan Littell's Glossary', *Modern Language Notes* 125/4: 927–40.

Kreimener, Klaus (1973), *Kino und Filmindustrie in der BRD. Ideologieproduktion und Klassenwirklichkeit nach 1945*, Kronberg: Scriptor, 1973.

Kristeva, Julia (1984), *The Powers of Horror*, trans. Leon S. Roudiez, New York: Columbia University Press.

— (2007), 'De l'abjection à la banalité du mal'. Lecture given at the Centre Roland Barthes Université Paris-VII, 24 April 2007, <http://www.kristeva.fr/abjection.html> (last accessed 12 August 2012).

Kuhlbrodt, Dietrich (2006), *Deutsches Filmwunder: Nazis immer besser*, Frankfurt am Main: Konkret.

LaCapra, Dominick (2004), *History in Transit: Experience, Identity, Critical Theory*, Ithaca: Cornell University Press.

—(2011), 'Historical and Literary Approaches to the "Final Solution": Saul Friedländer and Jonathan Littell', *History and Theory* 50/1: 71–97.

Lacombe Lucien (1974), dir. Louis Malle, France/West Germany/Italy: NEF, UPF, Vides Cinematografica.

Landkammer, Joachim (2006), '"Wir spüren nichts": Anstößige Thesen zum zukünftigen Umgang mit der NS-Vergangenheit', in Joachim Landkammer, Thomas Noetzel and Walter Ch. Zimmerli (eds), *Erinnerungsmanagement*, Munich: Fink, pp. 51–82.

Landsberg, Alison (2004), *Prosthetic Memory: The Transformation of American Remembrance in the Age of Mass Culture*, New York: Columbia University Press.

Landy, Marcia (1996), '"Which Way is America?": Americanism and the Italian Western', *boundary 2* 23/1: 35–59.

Large, David Clay (ed.) (1991), *Contending with Hitler: Varieties of German Resistance in the Third Reich*, Cambridge and Washington, DC: Cambridge University Press and German Historical Institute.

Lawrence, Amy (2010), *The Passion of Montgomery Clift*, Berkeley: University of California Press.

Lawson, Dominic (1990), 'Saying the unsayable about the Germans', *Spectator*, 14 July, pp. 8–10.

Lebow, Richard Ned, Wulf Kansteiner and Claudio Fogu (eds) (2006), *The Politics of Memory in Postwar Europe*, Durham, NC: Duke University Press.

Lee, Alison (1990), *Realism and Power: Postmodern British Fiction*, London: Routledge.

Lemonier, Marc (2007), *Les Bienveillantes décryptées*, Paris: Le Pré aux clercs.

Lennon, John and Malcolm Foley (2007), *Dark Tourism*, London: Thomson.

Levin, Ira ([1976] 1991), *The Boys from Brazil*, London: Bloomsbury.

Light, Alison (1991), *Forever England: Femininity, Literature and Conservatism Between the Wars*, London: Routledge.

Lili Marleen (1981), dir. Rainer Werner Fassbinder, West Germany: BR, CIP, Rialto.

Littell, Jonathan (2006a), *Les Bienveillantes*, Édition revue par l'auteur, Paris: Gallimard.

—(2006b), 'Lettre à mes traducteurs I', Barcelona, 3 November, www.lyonel.baum.pagesperso-orange.fr/traduct.html (last accessed 12 August 2012).

—(2008), *Die Wohlgesinnten. Marginalienband*, Berlin: Aufbau Verlag.

—(2009a), *Das Trockene und das Feuchte: Ein kurzer Einfall in faschistisches Gelände*, trans. Hainer Kober, with a postscript by Klaus Theweleit, Berlin: Berlin Verlag.

—(2009b), *The Kindly Ones*, trans. Charlotte Mendell, London: Chatto & Windus.

Littell, Jonathan and Pierre Nora (2007), 'Conversation sur l'histoire et le roman', *Le Débat* 144 (March/April): 25–44.

Lovitt, Carl R. (1992), 'The Rhetoric of Murderers' Confessional Narratives:

The Model of Pierre Rivière's Memoir', *Journal of Narrative Technique* 22/1: 23–34.

Lukács, Georg ([1936] 1969), *The Historical Novel*, trans. Hannah and Stanley Mitchell, Harmondsworth: Penguin.

Lumsden, Robin (2001), *A Collector's Guide to the Allgemeine-SS*, London: Ian Allen.

MacDonogh, Giles (1989), *A Good German: Adam von Trott zu Solz*, London: Quartet.

McEwan, Ian (1992), *Black Dogs*, London: Vintage.

McGlothlin, Erin (2007), 'Narrative Transgression in Edgar Hilsenrath's *Der Nazi und der Friseur* and the Rhetoric of the Sacred in Holocaust Discourse', *The German Quarterly* 80/2: 220–39.

McGovern, James ([1957] 1959), *Fräulein*, London: Ace.

MacInnes, Colin ([1950] 1966), *To the Victor the Spoils*, Harmondsworth: Penguin.

Maior, Patrick (2008), '"Our Friend Rommel": The *Wehrmacht* as "Worthy Enemy" in Postwar British Popular Culture', *German History* 26/4: 520–35.

Malaparte, Curzio ([1944] 2005), *Kaputt*, trans. Cesare Foligno, New York: NYRB.

Malet, Léo (1991), *Mission to Marseilles*, London: Pan.

Mallmann, Klaus-Michael (2002), '"Mensch, ich feiere heut' den tausendsten Genickschuss": Die Sicherheitspolizei und die Shoah in Westgalizien', in Gerhard Paul (ed.), *Die Täter der Shoah: Fanatische Nationalsozialisten oder ganz normale Deutsche?*, Göttingen: Wallstein, pp. 109–37.

Marathon Man (1976), dir. John Schlesinger, USA: Paramount.

Markovits, Andrei S. and Simon Reich (1997), *The German Predicament: Memory and Power in the New Europe*, Ithaca: Cornell University Press.

Marlowe, Stephen (1978), *The Valkyrie Encounter*, London: NEL.

Mast, Gerald (1979), *The Comic Mind: Comedy and the Movies*, 2nd edn, Chicago: University of Chicago Press.

Mein Führer: Die wirklich wahrste Wahrheit über Adolf Hitler (2007), dir. Daniel Levy, Germany: ARTE, BR, WDR.

Merivale, Patricia and Susan Elizabeth Sweeney (eds) (1998), *Detecting Texts: The Metaphysical Detective Story*, Philadelphia: University of Pennsylvania Press.

Merle, Robert ([1952] 2011), *Der Tod ist mein Beruf*, trans. Curt Noch, Berlin: Aufbau.

Mommsen, Hans (2003), *Alternatives to Hitler: German Resistance Under the Third Reich*, trans. Angus McGeoch, London: I.B. Tauris.

Morituri (1965), dir. Bernhard Wicki, USA: Arcola, Colony Prod., Twentieth Century Fox.

Morley, Sheridan (1989), *James Mason: Odd Man Out*, New York: Harper & Row.

Mosse, George (1996), *The Image of Man: The Creation of Modern Masculinity*, Oxford: Oxford University Press.

Moyle, Lachlan R. (1994), 'The Ridley–Chequers Affair and German Character: A Journalistic Main Event', in Harald Husemann (ed.), *As Others See Us: Anglo-German Perceptions*, Frankfurt am Main: Peter Lang, pp. 107–22.

—(1997), 'Once a German – Always a German! Germans and Germany in

Contemporary British Press Cartoons', in C.C. Barfoot (ed.), *Beyond Pug's Tour: National and Ethnic Stereotyping in Theory and Literary Practice*, Amsterdam: Rodopi, pp. 422–43.

Moyn, Samuel (2009), 'A Nazi Zelig: Jonathan Littell's *The Kindly Ones*', 4 March 2009, *The Nation*, <http://www.thenation.com/print/article/nazi-zelig-jonathan-littells-kindly-ones> (last accessed 12 May 2012).

Muir, Robin (2005), *The World's Most Photographed*, London: National Portrait Gallery.

Murphy, Robert (2000), *British Cinema and the Second World War*, London: Continuum.

Naremore, James (2008), *More Than Night: Film Noir and its Contexts*, Berkeley: University of California Press.

Natioli, Joseph (2009), 'The Deep Morals of *Inglourious Basterds*', *senses of cinema* 52, <http://www.sensesofcinema.com/2009/52/the-deep-morals-of-inglourious-basterds/> (last accessed 22 October 2010).

Nietzsche, Friedrich ([1874] 1997), 'On the Uses and Disadvantages of History for Life', in Friedrich Nietzsche, *Untimely Meditations*, ed. Daniel Breazeale, trans. R.J. Hollingdale, Cambridge: Cambridge University Press, pp. 57–125.

Noakes, Lucy (1997), 'Making Histories: Experiencing the Blitz in London's Museums in the 1990s', in Martin Evans and Ken Lunn (eds), *War and Memory in the Twentieth Century*, Oxford: Berg, pp. 89–105.

Norris, Margot (2000), *Writing War in the Twentieth Century*, Charlottesville: University Press of Virginia.

O'Brien, Geoffrey (1997), *Hardboiled America: Lurid Paperbacks and the Masters of Noir*, 2nd edn, New York: DaCapo Press.

Ogdon, Bethany (1992), 'Hardboiled Ideology', *Critical Quarterly* 34/1: 71–88.

Olympia (1938), dir. Leni Riefenstahl, Germany: Olympia Film, International Olympic Committee, Tobis Film.

Once Upon a Time in the West (1968), dir. Sergio Leone, Italy/USA: Finanzia San Marco, Rafran Cinematografica, Paramount.

Operation Valkyrie: The Stauffenberg Plot to Kill Hitler (2008), dir. Jean-Pierre Isbouts, USA: Pantheon, Schwartz & Co.

Orwell, George ([1939] 1990), *Coming Up for Air*, London: Penguin.

—([1944] 1975), 'Raffles and Miss Blandish', in *Decline of the English Murder and Other Essays*, Harmondsworth: Penguin, pp. 63–80.

Overy, Richard (2012), 'Bombing and the just war', *Guardian*, 23 June, p. 38.

Paris, Erna (2000), *Long Shadows: Truth, Lies and History*, London: Bloomsbury.

Paul, Gerhard (ed.) (2002), *Die Täter der Shoah: Fanatische Nationalsozialisten oder ganz normale Deutsche*, Göttingen: Wallstein.

Pearson, Nels and Marc Singer (eds) (2009), *Detective Fiction in a Postcolonial and Transnational World*, Farnham: Aldershot.

Peukert, Detlev (1989), *Inside Nazi Germany: Conformity, Opposition and Racism in Everyday Life*, trans. Richard Deveson, London: Penguin.

Pia, Jack (1974), *SS Regalia*, New York: Ballantine.

Piette, Adam (1995), *Imagination at War: British Fiction and Poetry 1939–1945*, London: Papermac.

Plain, Gill (2001), *Twentieth-Century Crime Fiction*, Edinburgh: Edinburgh University Press.

Porter, Dennis (1981), *The Pursuit of Crime: Art and Ideology in Detective Fiction*, New Haven: Yale University Press.

Priestley, J.B. (1940), *Midnight on the Desert*, London: Readers' Union & Heinemann.

Prince, Stephen (1998), *Savage Cinema: Sam Peckinpah and the Rise of Ultraviolent Movies*, London: Athlone.

—(2004), 'Genre and Violence in the work of Kurosawa and Peckinpah', in Yvonne Tasker (ed.), *Action and Adventure Cinema*, London: Routledge, pp. 331–45.

Puzo, Mario ([1955] 1971), *The Dark Arena*, London: Pan.

Quinn, Daniel (2001), *After Dachau*, New York: Context.

Rabinowitz, Paula (2002), *Black & White & Noir: America's Pulp Modernism*, New York: Columbia University Press.

Radisch, Iris (2008), 'Am Anfang steht ein Missverständnis', *Die Zeit*, 18 February, <http://www.zeit.de/2008/08/L-Littell-Radisch/komplettansicht> (last accessed 12 May 2012).

Raiders of the Lost Ark (1981), dir. Steven Spielberg, USA: Lucasfilm, Paramount.

Ramsden, John (1998); 'Refocusing "The People's War": British War Films of the 1950s', *Journal of Contemporary History* 33: 35–64.

Rättig, Ralf (2010), 'Stefan George und Claus von Stauffenberg: Ein Gespräch mit dem Historiker Peter Hoffmann', *George Jahrbuch* 8: 129–41.

Rau, Petra (2009a), *English Modernism, National Identity and the Germans, 1890–1950*, Farnham: Ashgate.

—(2009b), 'The War in Contemporary Fiction', in Marina Mackay (ed.), *The Cambridge Companion to the Literature of the Second World War*, Cambridge: Cambridge University Press, pp. 207–20.

Rayner, Jonathan (2007), *The Naval War Film: Genre, History, National Cinema*, Manchester: Manchester University Press.

Razinsky, Liran (2010), 'Not the Witness We Wished For: Testimony in Jonathan Littell's *The Kindly Ones*', *Modern Language Quarterly* 71/2: 175–97.

Reik, Theodor (1959), *The Compulsion to Confess: On the Psychoanalysis of Crime and Punishment*, New York: Farrar, Strauss and Cudahy.

Reiner, Robert C. (2009), 'Does Laughter Make the Crime Disappear? An Analysis of Cinematic Images of Hitler and the Nazis, 1940–2007', *senses of cinema* 52, <http://www.sensesofcinema.com> (last accessed 11 May 2011).

Riera, Monica and Gavin Schaffer (eds) (2008), *The Lasting War: Society and Identity in Britain, France and Germany After 1945*, Basingstoke: Palgrave.

Rome, Open City (1945), dir. Frederico Fellini, Italy: Excelsa.

Rose, Gillian (1996), *Mourning Becomes the Law: Philosophy and Representation*, Cambridge: Cambridge University Press.

Rose, Sonya O. (2004), *Which People's War? National Identity and Citizenship in Wartime Britain, 1939–1945*, Oxford: Oxford University Press.

Rosenbaum, Ron (2009), 'Don't give an Oscar to *The Reader*', *Slate*, 9 February, <http://www.slate.com/id/2210804/pagenum/2> (last accessed 20 March 2011).

Rosenfeld, Alvin (1985), *Imagining Hitler*, Bloomington: Indiana University Press.

Rosenfeld, Gavriel D. (2005a), 'Alternate Holocausts and the Mistrust of Memory', in Jonathan Petropoulos and John K. Roth (eds), *Gray Zones: Ambiguity and Compromise in the Holocaust and Its Aftermath*, New York: Berghahn, pp. 240–52.

—(2005b), *The World Hitler Never Made: Alternate History and the Memory of Nazism*, Oxford: Oxford University Press.

Rosenstraße (2003), dir. Margarete von Trotta, Germany/Netherlands: Studio Hamburg, Letterbox, TMG, Get Reel.

Roth, Joseph ([1938] 2004), 'The Myth of the German Soul', in Joseph Roth, *The White Cities: Reports from France, 1925–39*, trans. Michael Hofmann, London: Granta, pp. 233–7.

Salò, or the 120 Days of Sodom (1975), dir. Pier Paolo Pasolini, Italy/France: PEA, Les Procuctions Artistes Associés.

Salon Kitty (1976), dir. Tinto Brass, Italy/West Germany/France: Coralta Cinematografica, Cinema Seven, Les Productions Fox Europa.

Samek, Tomasz (2001), *In the Middle of Europe: Konzentrationslager Majdanek*, exhibition catalogue, Münster and Lublin: Stadtmuseum Münster/ Państwowe Muzeum na Majdanku.

Santner, Eric L. (1992), 'The Trouble with Hitler: Postwar German Aesthetics and the Legacy of Fascism', *New German Critique* 57: 5–24.

Sanyal, Debarati (2010), 'Reading Nazi Memory in Jonathan Littell's *Les Bienveillantes*', *L'Esprit createur* 50/4: 47–66.

Sartre, Jean-Paul ([1947] 1966), *What is Literature?*, trans. Bernard Frechtman, New York: Washington Square Press.

Saupe, Achim (2009), *Der Historiker als Detektiv – der Detektiv als Historiker: Historik, Kriminalistik und der Nazionalsozialismus als Kriminalroman*, Bielefeld: Transcript.

Sauvage, Pierre (1976/7), 'Aldrich interview', *Movie* 23: 59.

Schindler's List (1993), dir. Steven Spielberg, USA: Universal Pic., Amblin.

Schlink, Bernhard (1995), *Der Vorleser*, Zurich: Diogenes.

Schtonk! (1992), dir. Helmut Dietl, Germany: WDR.

Schwindt, Barbara (2005), *Das Konzentrations- und Vernichtungslager Majdanek: Funktionswandel im Kontext der 'Endlösung'*, Würzburg: Königshausen & Naumann.

Seeßlen, Georg (1994), *Tanz den Adolf Hitler: Faschismus in der populären Kultur*, Berlin: Edition Tiamat.

—(2009), *Quentin Tarantino gegen die Nazis: Alles über Inglourious Basterds*, Berlin: Bertz & Fischer.

Seltzer, Mark (1998), *Serial Killers: Death and Life in America's Wound Culture*, New York: Routledge.

Semelin, Jacques (2005), *Purify and Destroy: The Political Uses of Genocide*, trans. Cynthia Schoch, London: Hurst.

Sereny, Gitta (1995), *Into That Darkness: From Mercy Killing to Mass Murder*, London: Pimlico.

Shane (1953), dir. George Stevens, USA: Paramount.

Shirer, William (1962), *The Rise and Fall of the Third Reich*, Greenwich: Crest.

Short, Geoffrey and Carol Ann Reed (2004), *Issues in Holocaust Education*, Aldershot: Ashgate.

Snyder, Robert Lance (2009), 'Eric Ambler's Revisionist Thrillers: Epitaph for a Spy, A Coffin for Dimitros, and The Intercom Conspiracy', *Papers in Language and Literature* 45/3: 227–61.

Sobchack, Vivian C. (2000), 'The Violent Dance: a Personal Memoir of Death in the Movies', in Stephen Prince (ed.), *Screening Violence*, London: Continuum.

Sontag, Susan ([1964] 1994), 'Notes on Camp', in Sontag, *Against Interpretation*, London: Vintage, pp. 275–93.

—([1975] 1996), 'Fascinating Fascism', in Sontag, *Under the Sign of Saturn*, London: Vintage, pp. 73–109.

—([1980] 1996), 'Syberberg's Hitler', in Sontag, *Under the Sign of Saturn*, London: Vintage, pp. 137–69.

—(2003), *Regarding the Pain of Others*, London: Hamish Hamilton.

—(2007), 'Regarding the Torture of Others', in Sontag, *At the Same Time: Essays and Speeches*, ed. Paolo Dilonardo and Anne Jump, London: Hamish Hamilton, pp. 128–45.

Sophie Scholl: die letzten Tage (2005), dir. Marc Rothemund, Germany: Broth, Goldkind.

Spiegelman, Art (2011), *Metamaus*, London: Vintage.

Spotts, Frederic (2003), *Hitler and the Power of Aesthetics*, London: Pimlico.

SS Experiment Love Camp (1976), dir. Sergio Garrone, Italy: SEFI.

Stahl, Roger (2010), *Militainment, Inc.: War, Media and Popular Culture*, New York: Routledge.

Stauffenberg: Der 20. Juli 1944 (2004), dir. Jo Baier, Germany: teamWorx, ARD Degeto, EOS Entertainment, RAI, RBB, SWR, WDR, ORF.

Steiner, George ([1979] 1981), *The Portage to San Christobal of A. H.*, New York: Simon & Schuster.

Suleiman, Susan Rubin (2009), 'When the Perpetrator Becomes a Reliable Witness of the Holocaust: On Jonathan Littell's *Les Bienveillantes*', *New German Critique* 106 36/1: 1–19.

Sutherland, John (1981), *Bestsellers: Popular Fiction of the 1970s*, London: Routledge.

Symonds, Alex (2006), 'An Audience for Mel Brooks's *The Producers*: the Avant-garde of the Masses', *Journal of Popular Film and Television* 34/1: 24–32.

Takaki, Ronald (2000), *Double Victory: A Multicultural History of America in World War II*, New York: Little Brown.

Tarantino, Quentin (2009), *Inglourious Basterds: A Screenplay*, London: Bloomsbury.

Tate, Trudi (1998), *Modernism, History and the First World War*, Manchester: Manchester University Press.

The Big Gundown (1966), dir. Sergio Sollima, Spain/Italy: PEA, Rome Produizone Cinematografica, Tulio Demicheli.

The Bloodrayne: The Third Reich (2010), dir. Uwe Boll, USA/Canada/Germany: Boll Kino, Brightlight Pic., Herold Pro.

The Boys from Brazil (1978), dir. Franklin J. Schaffer, UK/USA: Lew Grade, Producers Circle, ITC.

The Damned (1969), dir. Luigi Visconti, Italy/West Germany: Ital-Noleggio Cinematografico, Praesidens, Pegaso.

The Desert Fox (1951), dir. Henry Hathaway, USA: Twentieth Century Fox.

The Desert Rats (1953), dir. Robert Wise, USA: Twentieth Century Fox.

The Dirty Dozen (1967), dir. Robert Aldrich, UK/USA: MGM, MKH, Seven Arts.

The Great Dictator (1940), dir. Charles Chaplin, USA: Charles Chaplin Pro.

The Journey to Valkyrie (2008), dir. Bryan Singer, on *Valkyrie*, DVD, USA: MGM.

The Night of the Generals (1967), dir. Anatole Litvak, UK/France: Columbia Pic., Horizon Pic., Filmsonor.

The Night Porter (1974), dir. Liliana Cavani, Italy: Ital-Noleggio Cinematografico, Lotar Film.

The Passage (1979), dir. J. Lee Thompson, UK: Hemdale, Passage Films, Monday Films.

The Pianist (2002), dir. Roman Polanski, France/Poland/Germany/UK: R.P. Productions, Heritage Films, Studio Babelsberg.

The Plot to Kill Hitler (1990), dir. Lawrence Schiller, Yugoslavia/USA: Jadran Film, Warner Bros.

The Producers (1968), dir. Mel Brooks, USA: Embassy Pic., Springtime Prod., U-M Prod.

The Reader (2008), dir. Stephen Daldry, USA/Germany: Weinstein, Mirage, Neunte Babelsberg.

The Restless Conscience (1992), dir. Hava Kohav Beller, USA: docurama.

The Searchers (1956), dir. John Ford, USA: Warner Bros.

The Serpent's Egg (1977), dir. Ingmar Bergman, West Germany/USA: Bavaria, De Laurentiis, Rialto.

The Tramp and The Dictator (2002), dir. Kevin Brownlow and Michael Kloft, UK: BBC, Photoplay, Spiegel TV.

The Wild Bunch (1969), dir. Sam Peckinpah, USA: Warner Bros, Seven Arts.

The Young Lions (1958), dir. Edward Dmytryk, USA: Twentieth Century Fox.

Theweleit, Klaus (1977), *Männerphantasien*, vol. 1: *Frauen, Fluten, Körper, Geschichte*, Frankfurt am Main: Verlag Roter Stern.

—([1978] 1985), *Männerphantasien*, vol. 2: *Männerkörper: Zur Psychoanalyse des weißen Terrors*, Frankfurt am Main: Verlag Roter Stern.

—(2009), 'On the German Reaction to Jonathan Littell's *Les bienveillantes*', *New German Critique* 36/1: 21–34.

Timm, Elizabeth (n.d.), *Hugo Ferdinand Boss (1885–1948) und die Firma Hugo Boss: Eine Dokumentation*, <http://www.metzingen-zwangsarbeit.de/hugo_boss.pdf> (last accessed 31 March 2011).

To Be or Not To Be (1942), dir. Ernst Lubitsch, USA.

To Hell and Back (1955), dir. Jesse Hibbs, USA: UI.

Todorov, Tzvetan (1999), *Facing the Extreme: Moral Life in the Concentration Camps*, trans. Arthur Denner and Abigail Pollack, London: Weidenfeld & Nicholson.

—(2003), *Hope and Memory: Reflections on the Twentieth Century*, trans. David Bellos, London: Atlantic.

Torgovnik, Marianna (2005), *The War Complex: World War II in Our Time*, Chicago: University of Chicago Press.

Tournier, Michel ([1970] 2000), *The Ogre*, trans. Barbara Bray, London: Penguin.

Triumph des Willens (1935), dir. Leni Riefenstahl, Germany: Leni Riefenstahl Pro., Reichspropagandaleitung der NSdAP.

Unforgiven (1992), dir. Clint Eastwood, USA: Warner Bros, Palpaso.

Uklański, Piotr (1998), *The Nazis. Exhibition catalogue*, London: Scalo.

Uni, Assaf (2008), 'The Executioner's Song', interview with Jonathan Littell, *Haaretz*, 30 May, <http://www.webarchive.org/web/20080601025801/http://www.haaretz.com/hasen/spages/988410.html> (last accessed 12 May 2012).

Valkyrie (2008), dir. Bryan Singer, USA/Germany: MGM, United Artists, Bad Hat Harry Prod.

Vice, Sue (2000), *Holocaust Fiction: From William Styron to Binjamin Wilkomirski*, London: Routledge.

Von Ryan's Express (1965), dir. Mark Robson, USA: Twentieth Century Fox.

Walters, Guy (2010), *Hunting Evil*, New York: Bantam.

Warshow, Robert ([1954] 2004), 'Movie Chronicle: The Westerner', in Leo Braudy and Marshall Cohen (eds), *Film Theory and Criticism*, 6th edn, Oxford: Oxford University Press, pp. 703–16.

West, Paul (1989), *The Very Rich Hours of Count von Stauffenberg*, New York: Overlook.

Westermann, Bärbel (1990), *Nationale Identität im Spielfilm der fünfziger Jahre*, Frankfurt am Main: Peter Lang.

Westervelt, Eric (2009), 'Prewar Berlin inspires crime novelist's dark side', 13 August, NPR series 'Crime in the City', <http://www.philipkerr.org/> (last accessed 13 October 2012).

Where Eagles Dare (1968), dir. Brian G. Hutton, USA/UK: MGM, Jerry Gershwin Pro., Elliott kastner Pro.

White, Hayden (1985), 'The Historical Text as Literary Artifact', in Hayden White, *Tropics of Discourse: Essays in Cultural Criticism*, Baltimore: Johns Hopkins University Press, pp. 81–100.

Williams, Melanie (2006), '"The Most Explosive Object to Hit Britain since the V2!": The British Films of Hardy Krüger and Anglo-German Relations during the 1950s', *Cinema Journal* 46/1: 85–107.

Williams, Tony (2004), '*The Dirty Dozen*: The Contradictory Nature of Screen Violence', in Yvonne Tasker (ed.), *Action and Adventure Cinema*, London: Routledge, pp. 345–58.

Wilson, Robert (2000), *A Small Death in Lisbon*, London: Harper Collins.

Wood, Nancy (1999), *Vectors of Memory: Legacies of Trauma in Postwar Europe*, Oxford: Berg.

Young, James E. (1993), *The Texture of Memory: Holocaust Memorials and Meaning*, New Haven: Yale University Press.

—(1998), *Writing and Rewriting the Holocaust: Narrative and the Consequences of Interpretation*, Bloomington: Indiana University Press.

Zelig (1983), dir. Woody Allen, USA: Orion Pic.

Zombie Lake (1981), dir. Jean Rolin, France/Spain: Eurociné, J.E. Films.

Index